YOU SOUND TALLER ON THE TELEPHONE

A
Practitioner's
View
of
the
Principalship

Dennis R. Dunklee

CORWIN PRESS, INC.
A Sage Publications Company
Thousand Oaks, California

For information:

Corwin Press, Inc.
A Sage Publications Company
2455 Teller Road
Thousand Oaks, California 91320
E-mail: order@corwinpress.com

SAGE Publications Ltd.
6 Bonhill Street
London EC2A 4PU
United Kingdom

SAGE Publications India Pvt. Ltd.
M-32 Market
Greater Kailash I
New Delhi 110 048 India

Printed in the United States of America

Library of Congress Cataloging-in-Publication Data

Dunklee, Dennis R.
    You sound taller on the telephone: A practitioner's view of the principalship / by Dennis R. Dunklee.
        p. cm.
    ISBN 0-8039-6849-3 (cloth: acid-free paper)
    ISBN 0-8039-6850-7 (pbk.: acid-free paper)
    1. School principals.   2. School management and organization.
I. Title.
    LB2831.9 .D85   1999
    371.2'012—dc21   98-51238

This book is printed on acid-free paper.

99   00   01   02   03   04   05   7   6   5   4   3   2   1

Corwin Editorial Assistant:	Kristen L. Gibson
Production Editor:	Wendy Westgate
Editorial Assistant:	Nevair Kabakian
Typesetter/Designer:	Lynn Miyata
Cover Designer:	Michelle Lee

Contents

Preface

This comprehensive case study is designed for anyone interested in viewing the professional life of a school principal from the inside out. It invites readers to involve themselves in an examination of school leadership and management. For the most part, theory takes a backseat when the main character, school administrator Grant Sterling, tackles a problem. Sterling builds his solutions with tools and materials he finds in his community, his district, his school, and the personal strengths and weaknesses of the people with whom he works. He employs common sense, sensitive intuition, and a passion for the welfare of his students.

The case study examines Sterling's professional life through a series of episodic encounters. It invites readers to observe Sterling's approaches and examine the practice of effective leadership.

Those familiar with traditional leadership books may find this case study methodology somewhat disjointed. But there is a purpose here. School leadership itself can be somewhat disjointed, because leadership and management problems are not well adapted to the academic constraints of time or space.

Solving real-world problems on the scene while fitting those solutions into a short- or long-range plan often requires both innovation and a strong will. When Sterling solves his problems, he looks at the details of the case, seeking elements he can use to his students' advantage. Those solutions may not satisfy all his constituents. Life rarely does. But when Sterling locks his office and goes home at the end of his workday, he does so with the understanding that he has left the school better than he found it. Perhaps this is the most telling characteristic of an effective school leader.

About the Case Study Method

This book was developed entirely on case study methodology and represents a real-life education leadership experience systematically presented through episodic progression.

All incidents in this case study depict actual events in everyday education leadership practice. In one way or another, prepractitioners will encounter some part of each episode if and when they enter school administration. Practitioners will immediately identify with most of the dilemmas portrayed. This integrated study, with its framework paradigms "How Leaders Lead" and "Behaviors That Define an Education Manager," is designed to bring reality-based problem solving into education leadership coursework. The framework paradigms, or the Sterling Paradigm, can be accessed on-line at http://www.corwinpress.com/dunklee.htm, and also include "Interstate School Leaders Licensure Consortium: Standards for School Leaders," "Putting the Standards Into an Evaluation Format," and Matrix of Primary Competencies, Behaviors and Continuing Education Applicability Illustrated by Episode."

Because in real practice school leadership problems seldom have a definitive "right answer," the episodes presented for study and analysis are designed to evoke not a clear right answer but rather a perceived effective answer for the problem at hand. Education leaders often act in the face of disparate dilemmas, ambivalence, and paradoxes. Dilemmas of practice are rarely solved; rather, they are carefully managed. Managing in the complex, ever-changing education environment requires both a recognition of and an ability to analyze each situation based on multiple and often conflicting influences. Sterling looks for the best answers to resolve situations, rather than seeking the often elusive definitive right answers.

To that end, each episode within the framework of the appended paradigms (http://www.corwinpress.com/dunklee.htm) invites interpretation and debate. The discussion questions for each episode encourage multiple perspectives and levels of analysis. Individual readers, based on their background, personal beliefs, and individual skills, will most certainly analyze the same episode in very diverse ways. Perspectives will differ, multiple interpretations will evolve, and debate is inevitable. Although the questions are clearly designed for prepractitioners, practitioners and others should find them equally challenging.

The high-energy interaction that develops when preservice and inservice practitioners engage in the same task of analysis, action planning, and evaluation provides those interested in education leadership the opportunity to engage directly in their own continuing education, as well as the opportunity to develop important group process and teamwork skills. Readers enhance their abilities to present and defend their viewpoints, to persuade and convince others, to collaborate and build on the ideas and knowledge of others, and to listen carefully.

Innovative designers of education leadership curricula recognize that successful pre- and inservice programs must embody approaches and materials that constantly, purposefully, and explicitly connect the worlds of theory and practice. In today's formidable and complex school leadership environment, a sound understanding of both knowledge and action is fundamental to effective education leaders.

Education leaders are continuously confronted with situations requiring decisions and actions that depend on careful analysis of the context and the development of comprehensive strategies. To survive in this environment, effective leaders must rely on fundamental knowledge; disciplined techniques of analysis; the ability to generate multiple and creative action plans and connect such plans to probable outcomes; and the capacity to evaluate the effectiveness of outcomes critically. The comprehensive case presented in this book is designed to promote the development of the skills, integrity, and courage to select appropriate actions.

The book also provides an invaluable platform for readers to examine their own core set of beliefs or values, perhaps never personally explored in a leadership paradigm. Explicitly articulating personal beliefs assists pre- and inservice leaders as they face the recurring tensions and dilemmas of practice.

For instructors using this book as a text, Richard Elmore provides a simple but powerful rationale for case study methodology analogous to the book:

> I stood in front of the class doing what I imagined university professors were supposed to do: lecturing, brilliantly (I thought) weaving the theoretical literature of the field together with practical anecdotes, and the occasional joke. The students sat, in rapt attention, diplomatically jotting the occasional note, laughing at the appropriate moments, dutifully raising the occasional question about some obscure point in my lecture. I had a modest reputation for being an engaging lecturer, and my students were doing what dutiful students do in the presence of a modestly talented lecturer: They were giving me the periodic reinforcement I needed to plow through the 2-hour session, and I was reciprocating by giving them the occasional stimulating remark that would stave off their drowsiness. About 50 minutes into this particular lecture, I had an epiphany. I suddenly heard my voice bouncing off the back wall of the classroom, a disembodied echo. It occurred to me that I was talking largely to myself. It occurred to me that I had no idea—none whatsoever—what my students were actually thinking, what knowledge they were accumulating, or what their understanding was of what I was actually teaching, if teaching was defined as creating an occasion for student learning. I stopped in midsentence. I posed a hypothetical problem, and I asked a succession of students what they would do if they were confronted with that problem. Something miraculous, and mysterious happened. I began to hear what students were, or were not, learning, rather than listening to my own disembodied voice. (1997, p. xi)

Notes for the Instructor and the Student

To facilitate understanding of the theories and concepts presented in this book and the ability to put these theories into practice, students should be able to discuss their answers, orally and in writing, to all the questions included in chapters and episodes. Specifically:

1. Students should consider the questions presented in the Introduction to this book as they read each chapter and episode.

2. There are general questions presented throughout the case study. Students should apply these questions to each episode.

3. Many episodes pose specific questions that apply only to a particular episode. Again, students should consider these.

4. Many episodes also have one or more questions under the heading of "What if . . ." Students should give free rein to their imaginations as they consider these hypothetical questions and are encouraged to develop additional what ifs.

This book is dedicated to Dr. Marvin F. Westfall, truly a Renaissance man. Perhaps this book will advance his attempts to solve the theory he calls the *RA Theory of In-Between Times*. I also wish to thank Richard F. Dunklee, who continues to inspire and amuse his son.

Reference

Elmore, R. F. (1997). Foreword. In K. K. Merseth, *Case studies in educational administration*. New York: Longman.

About the Author

Dennis R. Dunklee received his PhD in school administration and foundations from Kansas State University. His major area of research was in the field of education law, and his dissertation was on tort liability for negligence. He holds a bachelor's degree in elementary and secondary vocal and instrumental music education from Wichita State University and a master's degree in elementary and secondary school administration from Washburn University. During his 25 years in public schools, he served as a teacher, elementary school principal, junior high/middle school principal, high school principal, and central office administrator. He has been at George Mason University since 1986 and is an Associate Professor in the Education Leadership Department in the Graduate School of Education. He teaches courses in education law and school administration and serves as an adviser/chair for master's and doctoral candidates in school leadership, as well as in community college leadership. Because of his expertise and practical experience, he is frequently called on as a consultant in the areas of effective schools, school law, administrator evaluation, instructional supervision, school community relations, problem solving, and conflict resolution. In addition, he has been involved as a consultant and expert witness in numerous school-related lawsuits nationwide. As a university scholar, he has published three textbooks, two monographs, and more than 75 articles on issues in the fields of school law, business management, administrative practice, and leadership theory. He is active in a number of professional organizations; has presented papers at national, regional, state, and local conferences; and is a widely sought-after clinician for inservice workshops.

Introduction

In an almost literal sense, the principalship is a moving, dynamic occupation. From the start to the finish of each school day, the rhythm of the job is typified by frequent and abrupt shifts from one concern to another and by the natural excitement that pervades any organization that deals primarily with young people. The principal's job is different from other managerial positions because it is essentially an oral occupation, a job of talking. The principal runs the school mostly by talking with other people, usually one at a time, throughout the day.

Effective principals cover a great deal of ground as they manage their schools. From office to corridor, to classroom, to gymnasium, to boiler room, to playground, to teachers' lounge, and back they carry their offices around with them most of the school day. Unlike managers in many other organizations, principals spend most of their time at other people's desks. It is the principal who investigates areas of risk or potential problem, who facilitates the stream of messages from one area of the building to another, and who is always on call for those needing help.

Managing the daily operation of a school while providing the leadership necessary to guide the school to educational excellence is an extremely complex task in an extremely complex organizational environment. To meet the challenges of their work, effective school leaders fully understand and appreciate management and leadership theory, but depend less on what they've learned about theory than what they learn through practice. A key characteristic of effective education leaders is the ability to reflect continuously on their practice of leadership and management, completely apart from the normal concerns about curricular and instructional matters.

Because of the diversity of students, teachers, and others, and because of the types of services schools provide, on a typical day in a typical school, events occur in a nonlinear pattern, that is, with skips and bounds, jumps and starts. An effective leader consciously maintains decorum and exhibits linear behavior. In other words, the effective leader handles the inherent daily nonlinear conditions by operating in a "cruise-control mode" to routinize the skips, bounds, jumps, and starts and to reduce apparent crisis situations to relatively routine management operations and inter-actions. This behavior allows the effective leader the time and energy to consider quickly—"What will the broad and narrow consequences of my act be?"—and then act decisively. This behavior also allows the effective leader the time and energy necessary to reflect critically about an action taken—"Should I have done something differently? Do I need to implement some form of crisis control?"

This is the world in which Grant Sterling practices his profession. Grant Sterling, the primary actor in this case study, is a school principal. By observing Sterling's actions in a variety of commonplace situations and circumstances, this case study invites the reader to examine the practice of school-based leadership and management. The review and discussion of the leadership and management practices illustrated in the study's episodes naturally lead back to review and better understanding of underlying theory. Because school leadership is equally shared by men and women, and because, by default, Sterling has to be one gender or the other, questions specifically invite and encourage all readers to consider how gender roles may affect the approach to each situation described.

This case study has three goals: to prepare effective education leaders, to assure practitioners that they are not alone, and to provide readers with insight into the leadership challenges faced by school principals. To these ends, the book addresses seven key objectives:

1. To place those interested in school leadership in a hypothetical principalship by drawing them, in a very personal way, into a leadership and management role, the same way one is drawn into a good novel.

The book invites readers to become hypothetical principal Grant Sterling, and feel what it's like—really like—to be a leader. The book provides readers the opportunity to experience, through Sterling's actions, interactions, and nonactions, his success, pain, worry, humor, power, and loneliness.

Most readers have probably never been invited to discuss freely the problems of school leadership or management with a principal. If they had, they might come to recognize that the principalship can be a very lonely job—even in one's own school.

This book intends to help readers experience the loneliness of leadership and decision making so that they will not be disabled by it when in a leadership role.

2. To provide a way for readers to avoid the inclination to think about school management issues solely in terms of their own situations and experiences.

Although almost every reader has come in contact with a school principal, few have been in a position to appreciate the art of effective school leadership behavior. Even when they were K-12 students themselves, they probably were aware of the principal only as the person who ran the school or who made the rules and scolded them with more intensity than their teachers did. As a group, education leadership students who are teachers tend to see the world of schooling as what goes on in their own individual classrooms, and see all principals in terms of their school's principal. Those readers already working as practitioners will recognize the case study situations as typical of those school principals face every day, so will be particularly interested in how Grant Sterling responds in attempting to demonstrate effective leadership.

Further, in my experience, people often view the principal as a former teacher who now has administrative responsibilities—but not necessarily as a leader. From teachers' perspectives, the principal has a kind of authority and a multitude of responsibilities for which they often feel no direct concern. They often have no real clue why principals do what they do. They frequently see the principal as a person who has more allegiance to the job or to "the bosses" than to the needs of students and teachers. Students of education leadership need to be able to see a much larger picture of the education enterprise before they can truly understand theory, much less apply it to practice! Although education theory, history, and philosophy are extremely important in the development of effective school-based leaders, these disciplines present difficult concepts for readers to understand unless they've experienced some form of lifelike practice.

3. To examine, through Sterling's behavior, how effective management enhances school leadership, and vice versa. In this regard, the book focuses on the practices of time management; choosing what to contribute to the everyday operations of an effective school; knowing where and how to marshal energy for best outcome(s); determining the right priorities; integrating these for effective decision making, and ultimately survival and success in the world of school-based management and leadership.

4. To demonstrate that effective school leaders manage the meaning of schooling. This means that they, as leaders, must have a clear understanding of the purpose of schools and manage the organization toward fulfilling that purpose, the primary theme about which all activity must be organized.

5. To demonstrate that effective school leaders manage attention and trust. Management of attention means leaders' ability to get faculty, staff, students, and patrons to focus on and expend their energies toward fulfilling the purpose of school: the teaching of children and young adults. Management of trust means leaders' ability to behave in such a way that others believe in them, and their style of leadership is never an issue.

6. To illustrate behaviors that will help future readers understand how important it is for principals and leaders to be good actors in a difficult role. Among the more important are self-management; knowing who you are and what your

strengths and weaknesses are; effective calculated risk taking; and recognition that there are no such events as crises if you use available tools.

7. To introduce, and define through episodic development, a new and intriguing theory of leadership—a theory that I call *aggregate impression leadership.* This book is designed to enable the reader to develop, over time, and episode by episode, an understanding of Sterling's leadership style—thus, the reader's aggregate impression of Sterling.

Sterling's leadership and management behaviors, actions or inactions, are based on a paradigm that encompasses a wide variety of behaviors that define effective education leaders and managers. In addition, Sterling's problem-solving methodology can be explored even deeper by examining the standards for school leaders and evaluation criteria that have been identified by leading researchers and organizations in the field of education leadership. The frameworks are located on-line at http://www.corwinpress.com/dunklee.htm.

Questions provide readers with the opportunity to discuss issues and motives inherent in each episode candidly.

Welcome to the professional world of Grant Sterling. A world, for the purpose of this case study, that is limited to kids, parents, teachers, and the administration of schools. A world that demands that effective leaders practice the elusive art of common sense coupled with dynamic passion, the definitive art of situational problem solving, and the astute art of smart guessing. A world in which Grant Sterling attempts to follow the "other alternative," identified as "transformation" by philosopher and educator John Dewey.

Is it the social function of the school to perpetuate existing conditions or to take part in their transformation? One decision will make the administrator a time server. He will make it his business to conform to the pressures exercised by school boards, by politicians allied with heavy taxpayers, and by parents. If he decides for the other alternative, many of his tasks will be harder, but in that way alone can he serve the cause of education. For this cause is one of development, focusing indeed in the growth of students, but to be conceived even in this connection as a part of the larger development of society. (1946, p. 69)

Are the episodes in this case study fact or fiction? The format of the book is fiction. According to Sterling, however, "Most of the episodes presented in this book portray actual events. I tell it like it is. Of course, all the names of people and places are totally fictitious (although some of them have a notable resonance for me)." Our interest in relating these events is not in who the actors are, but in what we can learn by observing their actions and interactions.

For Discussion

1. Discuss this statement: "Sterling builds his solutions with tools and materials he finds in his community, his district, his school, and the personal strengths and weaknesses of the people with whom he works."

2. Discuss this statement and its relationship to questions 4 and 5 below: "School leadership itself can be somewhat disjointed, because leadership and management problems refuse to fit neatly into academic constraints of time and space."

3. How would you relate the statement "they [principals] carry their offices with them" to school climate?

4. Assuming that even the most effective schools function normally in nonlinear ways, how do effective principals prepare themselves to act in a linear manner?

5. When events are occurring in a nonlinear pattern, how does an effective principal focus on key priorities and appropriate actions? How does an effective principal find the linear thread?

6. What influence does a principal's skill with time management have on school climate?

7. Is there any relationship between management of trust and style of leadership?

8. How important is it for an effective principal to know "who he or she is?"

9. How would you define *calculated risk taking*? What role, if any, does it play in effective leadership?

10. How would you define *smart guessing*? What role, if any, does it have in the control of nonlinear situations?

Reference

Dewey, J. (1946). *Problems of men.* New York Philosophical Library.

1

The Contemporary Years

Sterling shook her hand. "I'm delighted about your new responsibilities, Katherine, and I'm really happy for you. Just remember . . ."

"Wait, Dr. Sterling," Katherine interrupted him and whispered, "I know. Stay focused, take names and kick, uhh." She was too much of a lady to finish her remark. Sterling laughed. He knew that she was perfectly capable of doing whatever was necessary to manage a school successfully.

"Thank you for all your help and counsel, Dr. Sterling. You are the best! I hope I can make you proud of me. I'm really happy and excited about my first principalship!"

Sterling gave her a hug before she left, then turned and looked out his third-floor office window at the university commons below. Spring was arriving and students were taking claim to the sun and warmth. He could usually judge the temperature outside by the cadence of students moving to and from classes. They were in no hurry today. He watched Katherine walking toward the west student parking lots. She, unlike other students, hurried like a person with a mission.

"I remember that feeling!" he thought as he turned and closed his office door.

A colorful mobile suspended from the ceiling rotated slowly in the gentle breeze. The mobile was a collection of icons that graphically depicted many of the academic and extracurricular courses typical of a public school—a treble clef for music, a hammer for industrial arts, a globe for history, a book for literature, and so on. The mobile had hung proudly, been complimented on by thousands, and collected dust in every office he had occupied since his early days as principal at Center Junior High School. June Hazel, an art teacher at Center, had made that for him just after he helped her avoid a nervous breakdown and take an early retirement. "Thanks again, June!" Sterling thought.

One wall of his office was lined with a bank of file cabinets. Some drawers contained curricular materials for the graduate courses he taught to prospective principals and superintendents. Other drawers held university and department business, master's and doctoral student files, student placement information, and general correspondence. One out-of-the-way drawer was marked "Personal." He rolled his desk chair toward it and pulled it open.

"Twenty-five years of public school teaching and administration, all in one drawer!" he mused.

Way in the back, obscured by files of thank-you notes, award certificates, newspaper articles, and other memorabilia, he found a couple of hand puppets he used to keep in his desk to cheer up unhappy kids. Sterling could always make kids, and at times adults, laugh with some of the toys he kept in his office. Reaching past the motionless puppets, he lifted a shoebox to his lap. He'd had a huge box of yo-yos and squirt guns a number of years ago, but gave those away to a Marine Corps toy drive. He remembered his Good Samaritan motive, recycling those "instruments of educational distraction."

"Let all those who follow me have the opportunity to build such a wonderful and voluminous collection," Sterling thought.

"Now," he smiled, "Katherine will be able to start her own collection this fall!"

Removing the cover of the shoebox, he winced at the rediscovery of some of the contraband he had taken from kids of all ages—a duck call, a 12-inch switchblade with a scrimshaw handle, a rusty starter's pistol, brass knuckles (two pairs), an antique dental pick, a set of numchucks, assorted pocket knives, a table knife . . .

"I wonder how many guns, knives, and other assorted weapons I destroyed or turned over to the police during my years as a principal?"

He closed the shoebox, gently returned it to the drawer, and rolled his chair to the window to enjoy vicariously the activities of the students on the spring-green commons.

Sterling had been a university professor for 9 years. When he completed his PhD, his doctoral advisers vigorously urged him to consider retiring from public school administration and think seriously about entering higher education. They felt he should provide prospective school administrators the benefit of his experience. He had followed their advice, settled into university life, and within a short time attained a record of achievement in the mandatory teaching, research, and publishing. He was now chair of the education leadership department.

"I hope my graduates will have as much fun as I did. I hope they can see the humor in their work. I would do it again."

He realized, as he looked back over the years of success, failure, and survival, that he had difficulty connecting his own methods of school management with much of the assumed gospel of school administration.

He knew there wasn't a type of management or leadership theory that he hadn't attempted to practice. Most of the time, he found, theory alone didn't relate to real situations.

He practiced what he now recognized as some form of intuitive problem solving. He used to call this method "flying by the seat of his pants." He responded to situations with whatever he perceived, at the moment, to be the best solution to the immediate problem—a technique management theorists now define as a form of *situational leadership*. Looking back now, he called it self-confidence and educated guesswork. He seldom had definitive answers, just decisive actions and good intuition based on available information.

Effective leadership requires a person to be an effective actor. There wasn't a role he hadn't played. There wasn't a facade he hadn't assumed. If someone asked him to describe what type of leadership he practiced, he would tell them that in his perception, the role of leader is simply a collection of ways that others see you when you're role-playing. He called that aggregate impression "leadership."

He knew he would go back. He would do it again, probably just the same way.

For Discussion

Be prepared to discuss the following statement:

> He realized, as he looked back over the years of success, failure, and survival, that he had difficulty connecting his own methods of school management with much of the assumed gospel of school administration.
>
> He knew there wasn't a type of leadership theory that he hadn't attempted to practice. Most of the time, he found, theory alone didn't quite relate to real situations.
>
> He practiced what he now recognized as some form of intuitive problem solving. He used to call this method "flying by the seat of his pants." He responded to situations with whatever he perceived, at the moment, to be the best solution to the immediate problem—a technique management theorists now define as a form of *situational leadership*. Looking back now, he called it self-confidence and educated guesswork. "I seldom had definitive answers, just decisive actions and good, I think, intuition based on available information."

2

The Center Years

The Summons

"I can't believe I'm doing this. I can't believe I said yes," Sterling thought as he approached the massive front door leading into Center Junior High School. Constructed as a WPA project during the Depression years of the 1930s, the school looked like a massive gothic cathedral encased in dirty granite. "I wonder where the gargoyles are," he thought, "And are they friendly or not?"

As he reached for the door handle, his question was at least partly answered by the phrases "Burn Baby Burn" and "Fuck Plantation Wilson" angrily carved in the door. A blaze orange sticker announced "VISITORS MUST REPORT TO THE MAIN OFFICE. VIOLATORS WILL BE PROSECUTED."

Just 24 hours earlier, Sterling had been water skiing behind his brother's boat when a lake patrol boat pulled alongside. He had guessed that their towing and skiing escapade would probably attract the patrol. Sterling's brother had a tendency to try to propel Sterling off his ski by driving too fast and cutting figure eights across the lake. As the patrol boat approached, Sterling recognized Bill Kennedy. Kennedy had worked these waters for as long as Sterling could remember. They often swapped tales over a beer or two at Sterling's father's dock.

"Grant Sterling!" Kennedy barked, "You've got a long-distance phone call at your dad's house! School business or somethin'. Your dad asked me to find you."

By the time he reached the dock and walked up the steep hill leading to the house, he was starting to feel the effects of beer in the hot sun, water up his nose, and the stiffness of muscle that attacks a 27-year-old who acts like a 16-year-old. He recognized the phone number as the switchboard at his school district's central office. A flood of thoughts washed through his mind, all leading to the question, "What did I do wrong now?" Actually, the superintendent sounded friendly on the phone—even apologetic for interrupting Sterling's vacation. But the urgency in his voice was clear. He had to talk to Sterling face to face, ASAP.

He had plenty of time to think about the superintendent's summons as he drove 300 miles through small town after small town. Sterling liked the ambiance of towns in which the tallest buildings were water towers with high school mascots painted on them. Towns where the vehicles of choice seemed to be faded red or blue Ford pickups and 10- to 15-year-old Oldsmobiles or Buicks whose power windows had been rendered inoperable by the rain and dust of country roads.

After stopping for a quick shower at home, Sterling waited anxiously in Superintendent Boughton's outer office. He had tremendous respect for this man, who had guided the school district through a year of violent turmoil only to be rewarded with 2 weeks of hospitalization for exhaustion.

"Grant! Thank you for coming in on such short notice," Boughton smiled as he ushered Sterling into his office. The superintendent got right to the point: "Grant, I want you to take over as the principal at Center Junior High starting today."

Permanent Principal—A Contradiction?

An hour later, as Sterling approached Center, he could still hear the superintendent's challenge: "If you pull this off, Sterling, great things could happen with your career! If you fail, no loss. You asked to return to the classroom anyway."

Sterling pulled on the door. Locked! He attempted to look through the small Plexiglas window in the door, but it was too badly scratched. He banged on the door with his fist and finally, turning around, the heel of his shoe. "Two weeks before school reconvenes and the door is locked! What about new students wanting to enroll?"

"Hold on!" a slow and muffled voice muttered as the door opened.

Sterling recognized the man propping the door ajar as one of the school's custodians. He wore the traditional dark blue work pants but evidently had left his shirt elsewhere. He was filthy, with body odor to match.

"This guy's lily-white stomach must weigh 300 pounds. What a way to greet someone at a public school," Sterling thought.

"Waddaya want?" demanded the custodian.

The custodian had seen Sterling in the building a number of times in the past. As a district curriculum supervisor, Sterling made regular visits to this school as well as the others in the district. This one, however, along with two other junior high schools and two senior high schools, had been off limits to anybody but site-assigned personnel during the race riots in the past school year.

"Who ya lookin for?"

"Bob Warner," Sterling answered.

"Up there in the office." The custodian motioned down a hall while heading off in the opposite direction.

The building smelled almost as bad as its doorman. Sterling noticed the smell of wet burned wood mixed with sawdust, plaster, and acrid latex paint. The faint smell of smoke lingered in building. Students had torched the school's auditorium and the teachers' lounge a week before school dismissed for the summer break. The once highly polished marble floors of the halls were covered with grit as far as Sterling could see. As he ascended the wide staircase, he noted how the steps were worn down toward the center. Marble timeworn by the feet of thousands of kids and adults told the history of the building.

"Archaeologists would love this place," he thought.

He opened the worn oak door marked "OFFICE." Bob Warner was standing next to a secretary's desk.

"Grant Sterling! I just got off the phone with the Supe, I couldn't be happier. Get your fanny in here! You've got work to do!"

Sterling had known Warner for 7 years. When Sterling was a first-year teacher, Warner's wife taught at the same school. He remembered her very well. Warner, although rough around the edges and usually abrasive when not playing politics, was an excellent, no-nonsense junior high principal who had retired 2 years ago under a doctor's orders. When the superintendent told Sterling about Warner "holding down the fort . . . just until we get a permanent principal," Sterling almost remarked, "Permanent principal? A rare occurrence in today's public school atmosphere. Clearly a contradiction!"

After introducing Sterling to the sole secretary, Ruth Petrie, Warner led Sterling into the principal's office.

"Where's the rest of the office folks?" Sterling asked.

"Quit. They're scared," Warner replied. "Look, Grant, we've got a lot to do before I vacate this place. The Supe called and I'm leaving at the end of the week, goin' to take out my frustrations on my fishin' gear. Before I start educatin' ya about this place, kid, did the Supe make you any promises?"

"Yeah, Bob, something like 'We'll give you anything you need to make Center whole, quiet, and a safe place for kids, parents, and teachers. Don't hesitate to ask if you need anything.' "

"Good," Warner replied. "We need to act on that promise starting today." Warner lowered his voice and partially covered his mouth with his hand. "Listen kid, you'll need to be a pushy S.O.B. to those know-it-alls downtown; they'll love you for it later. Now, here's some background info."

Warner started listing what he thought Sterling needed to know immediately. "Wilson was here for 14 years. He quit in the middle of last year. The kids and parents, especially minorities, called him 'Plantation Wilson.' You can guess why. One of the teachers, Harold Perry, filled in for him the rest of the year. He had lots of problems. They hired a black gentleman from somewhere to replace Wilson and to start at the beginning of the summer. He took one look and disappeared back to somewhere. They hired another experienced principal from somewhere. He quit last week. So the Supe called me," Warner laughed, and leaned toward Sterling with a smirk, "and begged me to fill in until they could find another sucker. You're goin' to do fine, Sterling. You've got backbone.

"Look kid, this is what you need to do. I've got the kids already scheduled in classes, teachers assigned, and a welcome-back letter ready to be mailed to parents as soon as you approve it and put your John Hancock on it. You need to concentrate on getting this building up to par and calling in some key teachers, students, parents, and probably God to try to win their advance support before school starts." Warner continued, "Do you know any good school secretaries and custodians?"

"Why?" Sterling asked.

"You need to bring in a new secretarial staff as soon as possible and consider canning that one," Warner motioned toward the main office. "You need to do the same thing with the custodial staff. Do you know Fred Rose in personnel?"

"Yes," Sterling responded.

"Here's the phone." Warner thrust the handset toward Sterling. "Call him now and demand two temps for at least 3 weeks, starting tomorrow at 8:00 a.m. If he balks, tell him to check with the Supe. Also tell him to send some prospective candidates, secretarial and custodial, for you to interview. Do you know anybody at the district shop?"

Sterling shook his head.

"Okay, call Steve Burgess at the shop and tell him I told you to call. Tell him you need five strong helpers tomorrow at 8:00 a.m. and that you need to meet with him here at the same time. Again, if he makes excuses, tell him the Supe approved it. You won't be in a position to take no for an answer for about a year. Understand? Make those calls while I take a potty break!"

In a few minutes Warner returned, peeked around the corner of the office, and offered Sterling a soda. "Did ya get 'em or did they think you were crazy?"

"I can't believe it," Sterling said, "I think the superintendent's administrative assistant called every support office in the district and told them to jump high and fast if I called. Both Fred and Steve just said, 'YES SIR!' "

"Good." Warner beamed like a parent at his kid's first recital.

"But," Warner continued, "they didn't like it. They don't like to be told how to run their little shows. Congratulations, you just made your first two enemies in the exalted realm of the high muckymucks! Now, let's continue your pep talk as we make a tour. You're goin' to love this place!"

Kiss a Frog—Make a Prince

Center Junior High was a formidable building, easily filling a city block. The architects had designed the four-story building in a traditional cube shape, with a large air shaft in the center to give every room natural light. The auditorium resembled a small opera house, with two-story cathedral windows and a balcony. The gymnasium, while small, had permanent, concrete-based, wooden bleachers to seat 800 spectators. All the class-rooms had windows, some facing the street, and some getting light and fresh air from the air shaft. The newly carpeted library/media center was well stocked and cared for.

"You know," Sterling observed, "a paint job and a good cleaning and this place would be fantastic."

"It's a great old building, isn't it?" Warner agreed. "With a little kiss-ass with the guys at the maintenance shop, you can turn this frog into a handsome prince."

Warner led Sterling to a window. "There's a large fenced field at the back of the school, tennis courts at one side, and a big concrete basketball pad on the other. Faculty and staff park their cars on the street out front. Your football team practices and plays their home games at a field about 2 blocks south of here. They're big, strong, and scary, but their record over the past few years has been pathetic."

Sterling was beginning to tire from Warner's graphic tour. He felt he really needed to get back to resolving people problems. He knew that people would make or break his efforts at Center long before Center's facilities would affect him.

"Let's find this so-called head custodian," said Sterling. "What's his name?"

"Elmer Sullivan," Warner replied, "I've been on his case since I got here; he's lazy as a dog in the midday sun. He thinks this place is clean and ready to go! I'm bettin' we'll find him sittin' on his butt down in the boiler room."

The door to the boiler room was marked with a black and yellow enameled metal sign declaring the room a nuclear shelter. The narrow stairs were cluttered with cleaning supplies and dirty chalkboard erasers patiently waiting to be cleaned. At the bottom of the stairs, a huge rust-covered, octopus-looking boiler guarded the room. In the far corner was an old desk and a torn overstuffed chair that almost accommodated the overstuffed man.

"Sure enough," Sterling thought. "It looks like Elmer has created his own little home away from home here!"

"Elmer, you know Grant Sterling don't you? He's your new principal."

"Looks like you're taking a break," Sterling remarked as he shook Elmer's hand. "Say, listen, I'd like to visit with you and your helpers tomorrow morning at 8 in my office."

"I'll be here, haven't missed a day since I've been here. Just holler when you need me," Elmer grunted.

Warner sensed that Sterling was about to lay into Elmer about the condition of the building and nudged Sterling's arm. "Let's go talk kids, Mr. Principal!"

Kids Are What It's All About

Warner walked through the main office; Sterling followed.

"Mr. Sterling and I would like to meet with you at 9 tomorrow, Mrs. Petrie. We want to go over the budget, both central and activity. Also, he's going to need all the requisitions since the new budget year for supplies, equipment, and textbooks. Oh, and a copy of the school's inventory." Warner nudged Sterling into the principal's office.

"Now listen," Warner instructed, "the meeting at 8 is all yours. I'll be there if you need help. Tonight, think about what you've seen today and what you want this place to look like in 2 weeks. I'll take the lead in the meeting with Petrie at 9. You're gonna need help on that one, okay?"

"Sounds good to me Bob, listen I . . ."

Warner interrupted, "I'll work with you until you kick my fanny out or until Friday rolls around."

"I appreciate your help, Bob—no, I NEED your experience and wisdom!"

"Yeah, you do," Warner chuckled. "Now, let's talk kids, parents, and teachers. Kids first. Kids are what it's all about."

Warner proceeded to give Sterling an overview of student demographics. Sterling was not surprised to learn that 80% of his students were black, 1% Spanish. "The rest are poor whites. Wilson once told me that the kids from this neighborhood aren't capable of learning—third-generation welfare and all that," Warner said. "That may have seemed to be true with Plantation Wilson at the helm, but you're gonna change that, Grant.

"I can't give you any info on parents," Warner apologized, "You'll need to talk to some teachers about who to trust, who to scrutinize—you know.

"I could give you poop on a few of your teachers that I know or have heard about through the grapevine, but I'd rather you form your own opinions. I don't know of any great problems, however."

With that, Warner jumped from his seat.

"Quittin' time, let's stop for a beer. You've had a busy day, young man! Get your feet firmly planted tonight, at least in your mind. If you don't do it tonight, you won't have time 'til next summer and that, Grant, will be too late!"

Stay Focused, Take Names, and Kick Butt

The phone rang, interrupting Sterling's reflection on the day's events and his meditation on Warner's caution about getting his feet planted. "Feet planted in what?" he mused. It was Steve Burgess from the district shop.

"Grant—sorry to call you at home. I was thinking about the meeting tomorrow morning and was wondering if you were thinking about replacing your head custodian? Before you answer, let me tell you that Wilson has protected Elmer for years; I don't know why. I'll support you if you want to get rid of him. I can put him in the shop until I can due process him for termination. One of the guys I'm going to bring with me tomorrow, Bob Sandinburg, is ready for a head custodial job and can help you get that place cleaned up. What's your thinking?"

"Great! Elmer will be on the way to the shop by the time you get to Center in the morning. What else can you do to help me?"

"Oh, I have a whole bag of tricks," Burgess said, "Wait 'til tomorrow."

Sterling slept well that night in spite of an acute case of nervous stomach that begged for a double dose of Kaopectate. That morning, as he prepared for the busy day ahead, he remembered asking a principal a few years ago how he managed the day-to-day hassle of the job. "Stay focused, take names, and kick butt," was the unemotional response. With that approach in mind, although he knew the principal had provided him with a questionable leadership method, Sterling was ready to go.

The main door was still locked when Sterling arrived, but Elmer was waiting just inside.

"Mr. Sterling—morning, I need to talk to you before we meet at 8."

"Fine, Elmer. We can talk here."

"Mr. Sterling, I don't like the way Warner has been bitching at me since he took over. He acts like he's the head custodian and knows what needs to be done. I know he's leaving and you're taking over. What I need to know is who's the head custodian gonna be here? You or me?"

Sterling couldn't believe the opening that Elmer had unknowingly created.

"That's easy to answer," Sterling responded. "As long as I'm responsible for this building, its contents, and the kids it serves, and as long as things aren't right and I take the blame for it, I'm the head everything, including the head custodian. I call the shots until people prove that they can handle the job. And from what I've seen so far, I don't think you're doing much to get this place ready to go. Any comment about that?"

Elmer looked at Sterling, trying to decide whether he was joking or serious.

"If you're serious about that, Mr. Sterling, then I think maybe I might request a transfer!"

"Elmer," Sterling replied nonchalantly, "I've already taken care of that for you. Get your personal belongings, drop your keys by my office, and report to Steve Burgess at the shop! Thanks for your service at Center."

Sterling proceeded up the stairs to the main office.

"You're not serious, are you, Mr. Sterling?" Elmer obviously had not heard about Sterling's reputation for cutting quickly to the bottom line.

"Elmer," Sterling said as he reached the office door, "I don't usually say things twice, but let me help you understand." Turning toward Elmer, he repeated, "I want your keys on my desk and I want you at the district shop." Elmer's face faded from flushed red to pale white as he finally realized that Sterling was dead serious.

"Good morning, Ruth," Sterling said as he closed the main office door behind him. "That's quite a pile of papers you've got on your desk." He smiled at her as he walked through the main office to his office. "Oh, by the way Ruth, I've got two temps coming in at 8. They'll be here for about 3 weeks. Put them to work. You're the boss. If any of them don't work out, let me know."

Sterling closed his door. He was trembling from head to foot. He stood and looked out the window and worked to control his shaking.

"That was one of the most difficult things I've ever had to do in my career," he thought.

"What's up, Mr. New Principal? Have a good night?" Warner startled Sterling as he thrust open the door.

"Well, I just got rid of Elmer," Sterling said. "I cut a deal with Burgess last night. I'm just takin' names and kickin' ass! What else would I be doing?"

Warner stuck out his hand, "You bastard. Congratulations! How do you feel?"

Sterling shook Warner's hand, "After a split second of irrational guilt, I feel great! How about you?"

Warner chuckled, "We're gonna burn rubber today, boy! What time is it?"

For Discussion

General Questions

Using the Sterling paradigm (http://www.corwinpress.com/dunklee.htm) as a model, and speaking from the perspective of a principal, evaluate each episode as follows:

What are the dominant behaviors exhibited by Sterling in this episode?

Is there consensus about this in the class? If not, explain the different viewpoints.

What were the primary actors' individual motives?

How effective was Sterling's behavior in this situation and why?

Can you identify other avenues or approaches that might lead to the same, or a better, conclusion?

If Sterling was a woman,

- As a female reader, can you identify methodology or behavior that you would change to bring the episode to the same, or similar, closure?

- As a male reader, what differences in methodology or behavior would you expect to see?

Specific Questions for Each Episode

The Summons

1. What advantages and/or disadvantages does a new principal have when he or she comes into a school?

2. What advantages and/or disadvantages does a new principal have when he or she comes into a "troubled" school?

Permanent Principal—A Contradiction?

3. What assistance (support) should new principals look for from central office when they take over a school?

What if . . . Sterling hadn't gotten the support he needed from others in the school district?

Kiss a Frog—Make a Prince

(No specific questions)

Kids Are What It's All About

4. Warner tells Sterling, "Get your feet firmly planted tonight, at least in your mind." What does Warner mean?
5. What public perceptions does an effective principal want to create?

Stay Focused, Take Names, and Kick Butt

6. What are the qualities of an effective custodian?
7. Does a custodian have a role in establishing educational climate? Explain.

What if . . . Elmer had refused to report to the shop?

Power Is Wonderful

The morning meetings went smoothly. At Sterling's insistence, Burgess brought in a crew of general maintenance people and painters, carpenters, plumbers, and electricians. Sterling made Bob Sandinburg the acting head custodian, with immediate orders to open every door and window to let in people and fresh air.

Ross, from personnel, promised to assist Sterling with any office and support staff he needed.

Sterling and Warner met with Mrs. Petrie and went over the school's financial situation, current orders for supplies, equipment, and teaching materials.

"Ruth, I want you to concentrate on getting all the school records in order for Mr. Sterling," Warner said. "I want you to assign one of the temps to handle the phone and the front counter and get the back-to-school letters ready for the post office. I want the other temp to clean up the supply closet and work on the filing system. Mr. Sterling is going to want you to contact a few of the teachers and parents to come in and meet with him. He'll give you those names as soon as he can."

Warner opened the office door for Mrs. Petrie and closed it behind her.

"Hope I didn't overstep my bounds with the office assignments," Warner said. "Just call it my trench experience overshadowing professional courtesy!"

"Not at all," Sterling responded.

"Good!" Warner knew that he was providing Sterling the foundation he needed to get started.

"Now, Sterling, where ya gonna take me for lunch? Let's get out of here for a while and let the folks working in the building think that we have great confidence in their ability to put this show on the road!"

During lunch, Warner gave Sterling some final advice, handed him an overcrowded ring of door, room, and closet keys, and announced in a sing-song voice that he was "goin' fishin' instead of just a-wishin'!"

"You don't need me any more, boy," Warner smiled. "I watched the way you negotiated with Burgess and Ross. I know I said I'd stay 'til the end of the week, but you need to take over and do your thing. You can call me if you need anything, and I mean that! My wife knows where I can be reached. Now, take me back to my car. You gotta get back to work—lunch hour's over!"

Power Base?

As Sterling approached Center after dropping Warner at his car, he noticed that Center's doors and windows were wide open and he could hear the sounds of hammers, electric saws, and country music from the building. One of the painters was sanding the main front door. Another crew had arrived and was washing windows. A group of junior-high-looking kids was playing basketball on one of the outside courts. Sterling meandered over.

"Any of you guys go to school here?" he asked.

"Who wants to know?" one of the kids hollered, without losing stride in the game.

"I'm Mr. Sterling, the new principal here."

His announcement appeared to fall on deaf ears as the kids rebounded a missed basket and sprinted to the other end of the court. Sterling glanced at his formidable set of school keys and thought, "Keys and title don't mean diddly to these guys!"

"When you've finished, come up to my office and I'll buy you a soda!" he hollered over his shoulder as he headed toward the main door.

As Sterling picked up the phone in his office and dialed the district's Instructional Resource Center (IRC), he looked at his watch. "Probably poor timing on my part; dragon lady Haley will have returned from lunch by now." Elma Mae Haley, the head secretary at the IRC, answered the phone in her usual sickly-sweet manner.

"Instructional Resource Center, may I . . ."

Sterling cut her short. "Elma Mae, hi. This is Grant Sterling. Is Don Dumphries in his office?"

"Mr. Sterling," Elma Mae responded. "Congratulations on your new job. We're all praying for you over here, and, uh, don't worry, we'll keep your office open for your return!"

"Thank you, Elma Mae," Sterling acknowledged in a monotone voice. "Don Dumphries?"

"He's in his office, I'll transfer your call."

"Supercilious witch!" he thought.

Don Dumphries was the supervisor of language arts for the school district and had mentored Sterling in what Dumphries labeled *the fine art of instructional supervision.* Dumphries was the only colleague that Sterling confided in when he became disillusioned with what he felt was a sedentary role. Dumphries knew that Sterling missed the interaction with kids and parents and that he had asked the superintendent to let him return to the classroom.

"Sterling! Is what I'm hearing true? Are you really? I mean, what happened? Is this really true? You at Center? Tell me, are you crazy or just plain stupid?"

Sterling was laughing. "Don, I wouldn't have taken the job if the superintendent hadn't promised me that YOU would be my new vice principal. Hasn't he called you yet?"

"NOT IN YOUR LIFETIME!" Dumphries bellowed, and added in a subdued voice, "He didn't say that, did he?"

Still laughing, Sterling let Dumphries off the hook. "No, just kiddin', Don. But listen, friend, I need to come over this afternoon and clean out my office. Could you meet me for a few minutes about 3:30 and give me some insight on your language arts folks here at Center? And if Ed, Joyce, and Marvin are around, would you ask them if we could all meet together?"

Ed, Joyce, and Marvin were also subject area supervisors who Sterling knew would give him useful information and support.

"Consider it done, Grant. I'll check with the others."

"Thanks, Don," Sterling hung up the phone.

"Mr. Sterling," Ruth peeked her head around the corner, "There's some boys out here—said you invited them in for a soda."

"Thanks, Ruth. Would you come in for a moment?" He got up from his chair and in a soft voice advised Ruth, "Not boys or girls, Ruth; from now on, please, ladies or gentlemen. Okay?"

Ruth nodded yes.

"Let's find that soda machine, gentlemen!" Sterling said as he led the streetball wizards out of the office. The soda machine had been in the teachers' lounge but now was in the hall, connected by a long orange extension cord to an electrical outlet in a classroom. Painters were putting the final touches on the badly damaged lounge.

"Let's see if any of these keys work on this machine." Sterling fingered his ring of keys looking for one of those strange-shaped ones that only soda machines and elevators recognize. With the magic words, "Ah ha!" the right key appeared, and the door opened, displaying racks of drinks.

"Go to it, men. I'll take a soda. Now, you guys know who I am, but I don't know who you are."

The kids introduced themselves, and tentative handshakes were exchanged as they all sat on the hall floor. The most outspoken student was a kid named Wart. Wart would be a ninth grader at Center.

"That's not your real name, is it?" asked Sterling.

"Naw Mr. Sterling, Stewart, but my mama an' all the kids call me Wart! How come you sittin' here with us like this? Wilson never did that."

During the next half hour, Wart and his friends offered an intriguing look at the problems at Center during the past few years. Unknowingly, they were helping Sterling develop a plan of action.

"You guys play ball here every day?" queried Sterling.

"Almost, got nothin' better to do," one of the kids acknowledged.

"Well then, I'm glad Center has some outside basketball courts. I'll probably see you guys tomorrow," he said as he got up and headed down the hall, "Gotta get back to work. Later, gentlemen!"

Sterling spent a few minutes rearranging the furniture in his office. He was always rearranging things. His friends teased him about it, equating his habit to an animal's instinct to mark territory. He straightened his desk and headed out the door.

"I'll be at the IRC for the rest of the afternoon, Ruth. Call me over there if you need me. Everything going okay?"

"Fine, Mr. Sterling. We can almost see light at the end of the tunnel!"

Sterling took a quick tour of the building before he left. Improvement was apparent as he cornered Sandinburg in the first floor hallway.

"What do you think, Bob? Looks better already to me."

Sandinburg wiped sweat from his forehead. "We're gonna make it, boss. I've got some hard workers here."

"Great, Bob. I like what you're doin'." Sterling slapped Sandinburg's shoulder and headed for the door. "Let me know if you need anything. Is the gym floor finished?"

"It's ready to go," Sandinburg said.

When Sterling arrived at the IRC, he was tickled by a sign over the front entrance depicting a caricature of Sterling wielding a paddle. In bold letters, the sign declared "CONGRATULATIONS MR. PRINCIPAL. BEHOLD THE TURTLE. HE MAKES PROGRESS ONLY WHEN HE STICKS HIS NECK OUT."

Don Dumphries saw Sterling in the parking lot and hurried out to escort him into the building.

"Great sign, Don."

"It is great, isn't it?" Dumphries craned his neck backward to admire the sign and added, "Ed finished it about an hour ago, and he and Marvin put it up. I was able to contact the folks you wanted to meet with. We'll get together in my office."

During the next hour, Sterling was able to glean good insights. Along with some current operational information, he now had the names of some of Center's stronger teachers and, most important, those he could trust for support if he could gain their confidence. Don and Ed helped him clean out his old office and load his car. Sterling fed Dragon Lady Haley an invidious piece of gossip, hoping it would come back to embarrass her, and left. On his way home, he stopped at his favorite hardware store. After some exploration, he found a gadget that would fit over his belt to hold his set of school keys. He laughed as he recalled reading somewhere that a man's power could be measured by the number of keys he carries. "Me and the custodian," he thought.

Power Is Dynamite

Sterling was up early the next morning. He was anxious to get to Center and set up some meetings with teachers, students, and parents. As he retrieved the newspaper from the front walk, a headline in the corner of the front page caught his eye. He sat on the front steps and read.

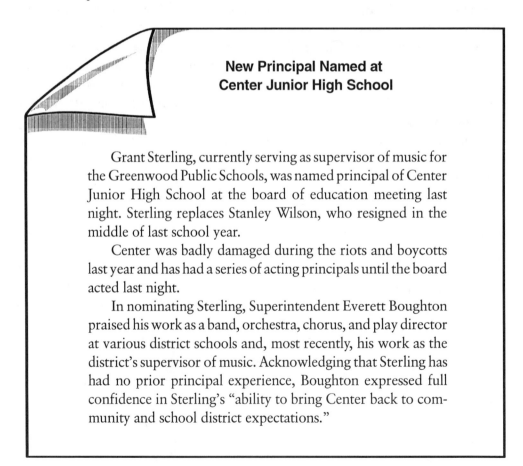

New Principal Named at Center Junior High School

Grant Sterling, currently serving as supervisor of music for the Greenwood Public Schools, was named principal of Center Junior High School at the board of education meeting last night. Sterling replaces Stanley Wilson, who resigned in the middle of last school year.

Center was badly damaged during the riots and boycotts last year and has had a series of acting principals until the board acted last night.

In nominating Sterling, Superintendent Everett Boughton praised his work as a band, orchestra, chorus, and play director at various district schools and, most recently, his work as the district's supervisor of music. Acknowledging that Sterling has had no prior principal experience, Boughton expressed full confidence in Sterling's "ability to bring Center back to community and school district expectations."

"How's the community going to look at a principal whose background is in music education?" Sterling wondered. "Most school principals are former coaches, or jocks that masqueraded as social studies teachers."

The phone was ringing as Sterling entered the house. "Someone calling to congratulate me," he hypothesized. He picked up the receiver. Before he could say hello, an intense, adult-sounding voice warned, "Honky, your white ass is dead!"

Searching for a quick reply, Sterling could only come up with a facetious "Thank you for sharing that with me" as the caller hung up.

"How many crank calls like that will I get?" he wondered out loud.

The kids were again playing basketball as he arrived at Center that morning.

"Boy, they start early," he thought. The group had grown since yesterday and as he approached the building someone hollered, "Hey, Mr. Sterling! Catch!"

A well-worn, badly bruised basketball arched toward Sterling. He dropped his notebook and barely caught the ball. Tucking the ball under his arm he walked over to the court.

"Another opportunity to let some of the neighborhood kids size me up," he thought. "And since I control the ball, I have a captive audience."

"Hey, guys," he drew them closer, "It's hot out here on the asphalt in the afternoon. I'll tell you what I'll do. I'll open the gym for you each day at 1:00 until school starts on one condition. Simply treat the gym and the building with respect. Deal?"

Suddenly Sterling was a hero. He tossed the streetball back to a party of smiling faces with accepting grins and hurried into the building.

"Power is dynamite," he chuckled to himself.

Leadership Is Lonely

In a nearby church, a group of black parents and businesspeople, supported by three local pastors, had gathered for an early morning meeting that would soon lead to Sterling's first encounter with his new school community. The men and women had two major unifying concerns. First, why did the board of education name a white principal to lead a predominately black school, and second, what, if anything, was going to change from what had existed in the immediate past? Although the parents in the group were openly anxious about the education and welfare of their kids, one of the ministers, Pastor James Lewis, was outraged.

"I think we ought to continue our boycott of that school until we get more black teachers and one of our own as principal. We have been betrayed by the board. A WASP cannot work with our community and . . ."

"Wait, Pastor," he was interrupted by a Center parent. "Don't you think we should give this man a chance? Why don't we call him and invite him over here so we can talk to him personally about our distress?"

Pastor Lewis countered abruptly. "Let's just go over to the school and confront this school board lackey now!"

Although several of the participants were apprehensive, worry about the welfare of their children led them to follow Pastor Lewis to the school.

"Good morning, Ruth. How are you today?" Sterling greeted her buoyed by the enthusiasm that he had seen on the faces of his streetball players moments before. He had replaced his concern over the menacing phone call he received early that morning with their exhilaration. Sterling always felt rejuvenated when he was around kids.

"Here's a list of teachers I'd like to meet with as soon as possible—separately . . . small groups . . . whatever. Make the appointments convenient for them, I can adjust my calendar. I'd like to start this afternoon if any of them are available."

"I'll get on it right now, Mr. Sterling," Ruth handed him a stack of mail and other papers.

"Thanks, Ruth. How about calling me Grant when we're not working with students or parents? Okay?" Sterling took the pile of papers and headed for his desk.

"All right," he thought, "time to take off the sport coat and loosen the tie." He was quickly absorbed by the stack of papers.

"Mr. Sterling! Mr. Sterling!" Stewart, a.k.a. Wart, was yelling as he propelled himself through the open door of the main office and into Sterling's office.

"That's okay, Mrs. Petrie. What's up Stewart, is somebody hurt or did you just make a three-pointer?"

"Mr. Sterling!"

Sterling could see Stewart was upset.

"You got a bunch a folks coming in to see ya . . . most parents, but that guy Lewis . . . he's a mean dude. He ain't no reverend, just says he is. Got no church, been in and out of the joint. Got no kids here . . . folks are afraid of him!"

"Thanks, Stewart," Sterling wasn't sure for what. "I'll handle it."

A quick exchange of a palm slap and Stewart disappeared out the door, brushing Pastor Lewis.

"Good morning sir. How can I help you?" Sterling's greeting seemed to fall on deaf ears as the solemn-faced pastor walked past him and went directly into his office, followed by his flock.

Sterling glanced at Ruth and could see apprehension in her eyes.

"You've seen this guy before? Is that Pastor Lewis?" He whispered.

"Many times, and yes it is," Ruth answered softly.

Sterling smiled and winked at Ruth. "Another day, another dollar!"

He joined the group in his crowded office.

"I'm Grant Sterling, the new principal here. How can I help you folks this morning?"

"We have questions that need to be answered," Pastor Lewis said in a demanding tone. "We want to know why the board put you here and why you think you belong here. We want answers. We're not leaving 'til we have them."

Sterling maintained eye contact with the pastor as he closed his office door, slowly removed his keys from his new belt hook, inserted a key in the lock, and turned it slowly until it clicked.

"You're right. None of us is leaving until you have the answers to those questions—and any others you want to ask today," Sterling said. "However, if you want straight answers from me, I would like to know who I'm talking to."

He turned away from Lewis and extended his hand to the closest member of the group. As he exchanged introductions with each person, he wondered, "What will this pompous fool who is now sitting in my desk chair do when I come to him?" He stretched his arm across the desk and offered his hand to Pastor Lewis.

"Who do you think you are?" Lewis demanded as he brushed Sterling's hand aside.

Sterling retorted and challenged, "Clearly you don't want me to know who you are, so I'll just talk to the good folks in the room who were kind enough to accept my greeting."

"All right!" Lewis quickly responded, "I'm Pastor Lewis and I'll do the talking."

"Thank you," Sterling responded, "And I'll be glad to answer any of your questions, or any questions posed by any other of the folks in the room. Fire away!"

"Why'd the board put you here? That's what we'd like to know first!"

Sterling could feel the hostility.

"Well," he said, "I can't speak for the board and I don't pretend to fully understand all their decisions, but I can tell you this . . ."

Sterling proceeded to provide the group with a brief overview of his background and his desire to make Center a good place for kids to come to school without the hassles of the past. His successes with kids had always been based on his energetic ability, although unconventional at times, to motivate and guide youngsters. This ability was now being tested by a contentious group of adults. He talked rapidly. He didn't want Lewis to interject questions to damage the positive atmosphere that he was trying to create. Lewis tried to interrupt him numerous times, but Sterling countered each time with a terse "Hold on, please, I'm not finished." He closed his remarks with a request for the time necessary, without interference, to start making things better—and to trust him, until he did something to earn their distrust."

Lewis snapped up from his seat in Sterling's chair.

"I don't think this white boy knows what he's talking about!"

"Listen Mr. Lewis, see if you can understand this?" Sterling was practically in Lewis' face. "No black, white, brown, red. No short or tall. No motivated or nonmotivated. No challenged or unchallenged. No athletic or nonathletic. It makes *no* difference at this school. Minds are what we're all about. Just minds. Is that clear enough for you?"

"Wait! hold on!" interrupted a diminutive black lady who had introduced herself to Sterling as Ida Wood.

"I like what I hear from Mr. Sterling. We can watch. We can give him the benefit of the doubt. I want to leave now. Please open the door, Mr. Sterling."

As Sterling unlocked the door, Mrs. Wood offered him her hand. The others quickly followed, each also stopping long enough to shake his hand. No words were exchanged until Lewis, now trailing his flock, walked by.

"I'll be back on the first day of school and every day after that. I don't like you, Sterling. I don't trust you!" Lewis, a tall man, well over 6 feet, glared down at 5-foot, 6-inch Sterling as he presented his ultimatum.

Sterling took a risky stance with his response.

"Tell you what, Lewis, I understand your position. I also understand that you don't have any kids here at Center. Here's my position. You will not be on these school grounds or in this building on the first day of school or any other day without my personal invitation. If you want to test me on that, feel free. Since you have no business here, however, I'll have your butt arrested in a New York minute. Is my position clear?"

Lewis strode out of the office. "I'll be back, and you can't stop me!"

Sterling sighed deeply and glanced around the outer office area. He suddenly felt a need for someone to acknowledge that he was still in one piece. But no one was in the room. He smiled and thought, "Well, power is dynamite. But this is what the pundits mean when they say leadership is lonely!"

He returned to his paperwork. Within the next few minutes, he heard Ruth and her clerical aides back at work in the main office.

He picked up his phone and dialed 1. The phone buzzed on Ruth's desk.

"Ruth, have you called any of the teachers on that list yet?"

"Not yet, Grant. I thought I'd better wait until after your visitors left," Ruth replied.

"Were you waiting to see if I came out alive?" he laughed.

"Ruth, I've changed my mind, I'd like you to invite them over to my house, Wednesday at 7:30, for an informal meeting . . . casual dress, I'll have beer and soft drinks for them. Tell them I want to pick their brains. I'd like you to come if you can."

He hung up the phone and continued with his paperwork. He heard the office crew leave for and return from lunch, and eventually looked at his watch. "1:45, and I'm still not finished with this mess," he groused. "Time to take a break."

Sterling headed for the soda machine, now back in the freshly painted lounge. He treated himself to a soda and headed out to check the work crews' progress. As he walked by the gym, he could tell by the thumping of basketballs that his streetball players had taken him up on his deal to open the gym at 1:00 each day. He opened the door and stood inside just long enough to finish his soda and be noticed by the players.

The building was beginning to look like a place that students, parents, and teachers could take pride in again. The happy sounds from the gym made him smile as he walked slowly toward his office.

"Mr. Sterling, may I talk with you for a moment?" He was greeted in the hall by Ida Wood. She evidently had decided to return after Pastor Lewis left. Ruth had shared with Sterling that Mrs. Wood was highly respected in the community. She had organized an alternate school in a local church for students to attend during the boycott of Center the previous year and had actively worked with district school administrators to reduce some of the race-related problems across the district.

"Mrs. Wood! How nice to see you again so soon!"

"Mr. Sterling, I'm really quite unhappy that you had to experience that type of forum so early in your new job. I really had hoped that the meeting would be less hostile. I'm not that kind of person."

"Mrs. Wood, I'm sorry that any of us have to look at each other with any kind of mistrust, suspicion, or whatever. But I'm not sorry that the meeting took place. I think things like that need to happen occasionally, and I welcome honest discourse even if it is uncomfortable. I'm so pleased you came back. Do you have some time, perhaps now or tomorrow, when you and I could just sit and talk about our visions for Center?"

"I'd like to do that, Mr. Sterling. How about tomorrow morning at 10? By the way, my daughter Karen will be an eighth grader at Center this year and could help us see things from a student's point of view. I'd like to bring her with me."

"Fantastic, Mrs. Wood." Sterling shook her hand. "I'm looking forward to meeting your daughter. Ten o'clock is fine!"

Sterling worked late that evening. His attention focused on how to get the school year off to a smooth start while getting the message out that he wouldn't tolerate anything less than good schooling.

"Good morning, Mr. Sterling. I'd like you to meet one of our favorite parents," Ruth said as she greeted him the next morning. "Mr. Sterling, I'd like you to meet Mr. David Berry. He has three children at Center, and his son, who is a ninth grader, is president of our student council."

"Mr. Berry, my pleasure. Please call me Grant," Sterling extended his hand. "Please sit down. Have time for a cup of coffee?"

"I do sir. Please call me David. I just stopped by to meet this gentlemen who my seventh-grade son thinks is great. He's one of the kids you let use the gym in the afternoons."

David Berry presented an imposing figure—a tall, muscular black man dressed in a freshly pressed Dickies-style work uniform.

"I understand you had a run-in with our so-called Pastor Lewis." Berry spoke with a slow whisperlike drawl. "Don't pay him no mind. He just likes to keep people riled up. My son told me he saw him, and a bunch of others, marching into Center yesterday. I talked to Lewis last night. He won't be bothering you."

Sterling wanted to say thanks, but was unsure how that might be interpreted.

Berry continued. "I also visited with Mrs. Wood last night, and she told me that she and her daughter Karen are meeting with you this morning."

"Yes," Sterling responded, "I'm looking forward to that meeting and getting to know her daughter."

Berry leaned back in his chair. "Mrs. Wood is a fine lady with a real good head on her shoulders. She is a leader in the community. Her daughter is as sharp as her mother. They can really help you get a picture of Center's problems. I can tell you this, though . . . you keep treating kids the way you've been treating my son and the others out there playing basketball, you can bet you're going to have a better time than Wilson did. You feel free to call me any time. My kids give you any problems, let me know."

With that, Berry excused himself.

The 10:00 meeting with Mrs. Wood and her eighth-grade daughter gave Sterling a chance to look inside the neighborhood. Because he had not yet finalized his agenda for grade-level orientation sessions for Center students, he asked Mrs. Wood if she would introduce him at each of the opening meetings.

"I'd be honored," she said.

For Discussion

General Questions

Using the Sterling paradigm (http://www.corwinpress.com/dunklee.htm) as a model, and speaking from the perspective of a principal, evaluate each episode as follows:

What are the dominant behaviors exhibited by Sterling in this episode?

Is there consensus about this in the class? If not, explain the different viewpoints.

What were the primary actors' individual motives?

How effective is Sterling's behavior in this situation and why?

Can you identify other avenues or approaches that might lead to the same, or a better, conclusion?

If Sterling was a woman,

- As a female reader, can you identify methodology or behavior that you would change to bring the episode to the same, or similar, closure?

- As a male reader, what differences in methodology or behavior would you expect to see?

Specific Questions for Each Episode

Power Is Wonderful

What if . . . Burgess and Ross had refused to assist Sterling?

Power Base?

1. Who are the essential people in the power base network of an effective principal?
2. What are some ways to build a power base?

Power Is Dynamite

3. What tools does a principal have available to build a positive relationship with the community?

Leadership Is Lonely

4. Who has unquestioned access to public schools? Who can be barred from entering?
5. Does a principal have an obligation to meet with special interest groups?
6. What specific actions can a new principal take to learn about his or her school and its community?
7. How can a principal learn who the power brokers are in the community?
8. Why did Sterling ask Mrs. Wood to introduce him to the students at orientation?
9. How would you explain the title of this episode?

What if . . . Sterling had refused to meet with Pastor Lewis's group? What if . . . Sterling had taken a passive, rather than an aggressive, stance toward Pastor Lewis?

Showtime

The evening get-together with the Center faculty went well. Although they were a friendly group, Sterling could sense the apprehension of many. During the next few days, teachers came and went from Center like bees gathering honey. Rooms were set up, books and equipment were unpacked, bulletin boards were decorated with welcome-back themes, and teachers popped in and out frequently to say a few words to Sterling. And, as usual, brown-nosers started making sure that he knew who they were.

He continued to meet as many students and parents as possible, often visiting homes in the neighborhood in the evenings to introduce himself. He knew that if he could get Center students and parents to support him, the faculty would have to follow. Although the faculty was the least of his concerns on the public relations front right now, he knew that he had to start the process of getting them on his side.

At a meeting with teachers new to Center, he focused mostly on policy and procedural matters, and assigned them to experienced teachers in their respective departments for mentoring. Then, before school started, he held the first formal meeting for all faculty.

"We are not to be considered by anyone to be 'blue collar' or 'union mentality' workers," he said. "We are professionals, and we will treat each other as professionals."

To reinforce this, he announced he was eliminating the teacher check-in and check-out procedures, previously controlled by a foreboding time clock bolted to the main counter in the office. He was also substantially reducing the time-consuming weekly paperwork and the practice of requiring teachers to supply the principal with their weekly lesson plans each Monday morning.

To give the faculty a feeling of empowerment, he stressed that he couldn't provide the teaching and learning environment that they deserved and needed without their help, trust, and support. At the same time, he made it clear that he was ultimately responsible for the Center program and would accept nothing less than everyone's best, including his own. He concluded with the usual welcome back, feel good, work hard, and other traditional words to the troops.

He was really trying to tell the faculty his bottom line. He wanted to succeed, he wanted them to succeed, he wanted students to succeed, and he wanted everyone to have fun doing it. Also, he would take no crap.

After he distributed the usual rules, regulations, and policy and procedures statements, the faculty began questions.

"What are you going to do if . . ."

"What are you going to do about . . ."

"Do we have to . . ."

"How are we going to . . ."

The more questions they asked, the more stressed they became. They were genuinely concerned about Sterling's ability to protect them. No one seemed to be concerned, however, about Sterling's ability to keep his own head above water. But he knew that they had real reason for concern after the past year. They didn't know that Sterling had gotten a taste of that past from Pastor Lewis, or that he had spent the short time he'd been at Center sounding out kids, parents, and others.

He knew why they were asking such questions. What they didn't know was that he didn't have definitive answers. He was, in fact, starting the school year with hunches and prayers—literally, flying by the seat of his pants.

"And if they're nervous," he thought, "they should know that I'm scared to death under this mask of confidence."

"How are you going to handle . . ."

"Why do you think . . ."

"What if . . ."

Sterling continued to respond to their concerns, faintly disguised as questions, with the best answers he could generate.

"Look," Sterling stepped forward from the table he was leaning on and interrupted the intensifying volley of questions. "The answer to all your questions is simply this. Contrary to your past experience, you will not hear me say 'I don't know' or 'We'll see.' You can expect immediate action on anything or anybody that disrupts the education process. I expect you to teach; I'll be the bad guy. Anybody who interferes with the process is to be referred to me immediately—kids, parents, whoever! I don't expect you to take any crap, and I'm not going to either.

"Now, don't we all have something better to do than sit around here and worry about ghosts? Meeting adjourned!"

The next day, Sterling stood in the hall with a group of faculty members watching the first students, seventh graders, enter the auditorium for orientation.

"This is it," he said. "Their first experience in junior high. They're probably as scared as we are at this point," he laughed. "But don't tell anybody!"

When Ida Wood introduced him at the assemblies that day, she went further than just simple introduction—she set the tone for the school year. She implored seventh graders not to be followers, but to learn to be independent thinkers. She appealed to eighth graders to study hard and start assuming the mantle of leadership that they would inherit next year. She challenged ninth graders to support Sterling in his efforts to make Center the best school in the district by providing him with the student leadership he was going to expect.

"Wow," he thought as he sat on stage, "she's a better showperson than I am!"

Wood was so effective that all Sterling had to do was to build on her admonitions. He concluded his now-abbreviated remarks to each group with a promise and a warning. He promised students to make their school year fun if they, in turn, studied hard and treated teachers with respect. He warned students: "There are two principals in my office. One is a good guy. The other? You don't want to meet him! School officially starts tomorrow. The bell rings at 8:15 sharp. See you in classes tomorrow!"

He spent the rest of the day struggling to teach seventh graders how to lock and unlock their lockers. "Combination locks are to seventh graders what federal income tax forms are to their parents," he thought as he moved from one frustrated kid to another. He knew from experience that this single event, the lock experience, could easily be the most horrifying experience that many junior high kids experience. He was pleased to see that ninth graders were stopping to help. He overheard one seventh grader proclaim to his ninth grade mentor that he was going "to write the combination to my lock inside of my locker—just in case I forget my combination!" The older student just scowled at him and said, "Right, kid! Think about that!"

And They're Off!

The bell rang, signaling the start of the new school year. The main office was suddenly crowded with students and parents needing help. As secretaries and counselors resolved those problems, Sterling left to patrol the halls.

"Come on, get to class, the tardy bell is about to ring!"

"Room 303—third floor, you're on the second floor!"

"Let me help you with your lock. What's your combination?"

"We don't run in the halls!"

"Nice shoes!"

8:30 a.m.—a bell echoed through the halls. After a minute or so of bedlam, silence. School had started.

"One hundred eighty days from now, at 3:30 p.m., that same bell will tell us whether we've survived the school year," Sterling mused as he looked at his watch.

"One hundred eighty one days from now, the powers that be will be deciding whether to praise or bury Caesar—a.k.a. Grant Sterling," he thought as he looked down the now-vacant hall.

A Sterling Moment (Good Morning, Principal)

"FUCK YOU STIRLIN."

"Someone is clearly expressing hostility, First Amendment rights, or a definite inability to spell my name correctly," Sterling laughed at his interpretation as he viewed the graffiti.

About a week into the school year, as he pulled into his usual parking space each day, he had noticed Bob Sandinburg, the head custodian, laboriously cleaning the bold epistle from the building. The graffiti, which reappeared each morning, had obviously been deliberately placed where Sterling could not miss it as he parked.

"I could probably find the guilty party," he thought, "but that would make the act a 'big deal.' It's really not worth the effort. Whoever it is will eventually get tired and stop."

Three weeks later, he noticed something different about the persistent message. His name was now being spelled correctly.

He knew that he had finally gained the mystery writer's grudging respect when, eventually, the message read "FUCK YOU MR. STERLING."

With that proclamation, the daily graffiti stopped.

"I have finally arrived!" was the subliminal message that Sterling read in the now unblemished wall. "But," he chuckled, "I may never know what I did right."

From Setback to Serendipity ▨

Ruth Petrie, Sterling's secretary, continued to make improvements in the main office. He recalled that he had been advised by Warner to replace her as soon as possible, but Ruth seemed to be working out fine.

Two weeks after school started, while he was away from the building for a late-afternoon meeting, Ruth fell down the back stairs as she left the building for the day and broke her hip. Sterling rushed to the hospital to check on her condition and found that she was scheduled for surgery the next morning.

All Sterling could think about as he walked to her room was how he was going to keep the main office functioning until she was able to return.

"Grant, I'm fine," she said, "My doctor says I'll be up and walking in a few days—just a hair-line fracture."

"Thank goodness," he said with a sigh of relief.

"But," she continued, "I won't be coming back to work. I've been thinking about resigning for quite a while now—nothing to do with you, I just want to spend more time with my daughter, who is expecting a baby. So, even if I came back to work, it might be weeks from now."

Sterling's mind raced to find the right words to convince her to come back, at least for a while—at least long enough to train a replacement. He didn't know anything about the day-to-day operation of the main office—reports, budgets, all the details.

Ruth interrupted his silent, but frantic, contemplation of catastrophe and jerked him quickly back to reality. "I'll have my husband bring you my letter of resignation, effective when my sick leave runs out. Would you look in the third file from the left, second drawer from the top, under medical forms and give him an application for me to fill out for workers' compensation? And I'll also need an accident form. I think the form number is . . ."

He interrupted her. "Ruth, are you sure? You've really been a big help . . ."

"Yes, Grant, I'm sure. The aides you hired for me can keep the office running until you find a replacement."

Sterling called personnel first thing the next morning to notify them of the impending resignation. A lady named Marguerite took the call. "We'll start advertising as soon as we get her formal resignation," she replied in a matter-of-fact fashion that did nothing to alleviate his anxiety.

Later that day, Sterling got a call from the assistant superintendent for personnel. "Grant, Bob Wainwright here . . . understand you need a new head secretary at Center, and I'd like to ask you for a favor. My wife and I have good friends, Jeanne and Stu Smith, who have recently transferred here. Jeanne was my secretary at Green Valley High before I came here, and she's excellent. Would you talk to her and see if you can work together? I think you'll be pleased."

Wainwright's prediction was right on target. Sterling and Jeanne hit it off imme-diately and, with Wainwright's blessing, she reported to work the next day. Sterling gave her the green light to manage the office, and within a short time, she transformed it into a place of business, as well as a place that was kid, parent, and teacher friendly. She had a natural feel for schools and how they operate, and was soon making the kinds of decisions that allowed Sterling the opportunity to get away from his desk more often.

He was relieved that the problem was resolved so well and elated that he could now really devote his time to leadership. He firmly believed that school principals use their time best by walking around conducting business where the front-line action takes place.

Jeanne agreed with him, "You shouldn't have to worry about the day-to-day operations of the main office." Her experience and talent allowed him the freedom to practice "management by walking around."

"Oh, and Jeannie—please teach me about how the office works, will you?"

For Discussion

General Questions

Using the Sterling paradigm (http://www.corwinpress.com/dunklee.htm) as a model, and speaking from the perspective of a principal, evaluate each episode as follows:

What are the dominant behaviors exhibited by Sterling in this episode?

Is there consensus about this in the class? If not, explain the different viewpoints.

What were the primary actors' individual motives?

How effective was Sterling's behavior in this situation and why?

Can you identify other avenues or approaches that might lead to the same, or a better, conclusion?

If Sterling was a woman,

- As a female reader, can you identify methodology or behavior that you would change to bring the episode to the same, or similar, closure?

- As a male reader, what differences in methodology or behavior would you expect to see?

Specific Questions for Each Episode

Showtime

1. What are the primary messages Sterling wants to communicate to his faculty?

2. Where is an effective principal's first allegiance?

What if . . . Sterling had said to the faculty, "This is my first principalship and, of course, I'm new to this school. I plan to study the situation here, after school gets under way, and determine what changes need to be made for next year"?

And They're Off!

3. At the end of your first year as a principal, what would you want your faculty, the parent community, and the student body to say about you?

A Sterling Moment (Good Morning, Principal)

(No specific questions)

From Setback to Serendipity

4. What qualities would you look for in a secretary?
5. What role would you expect your secretary to fill?
6. What was Sterling's rationale when he told Jeannie to "teach me how the office works"?

What if . . . Sterling, as a first-year principal, had to train a new, inexperienced secretary?

Make Sure the Toilet Seat Is Down

Sterling liked to be in his office at Center at least 2 hours before teachers arrived. He used this time to tackle the paperwork that had accumulated during the previous day and mysteriously multiplied overnight. He felt sure that a troll under his desk produced additional paperwork as a toll that Sterling had to pay to cross the bridge to chaos-land each day.

In addition to the troll, June Hazel, the school's art teacher, would slip into his office, move a chair to the edge of his desk, and plop herself down to present a list of problems she wanted him to resolve immediately. At first, Sterling thought she was just weird. After a few days, he theorized it was her way of brown-nosing. He finally realized that she simply needed some positive strokes from the boss each day.

June had been the art teacher at Center for 37 years. She was an excellent artist and teacher, and had been adored by her students. During the past few years, however, she had not been as effective as she used to be, and enrollment in her classes was declining. Sterling and the district's art supervisor had talked about the possibility of suggesting that she retire. They knew that Center was the only school at which she had ever taught, and that she had been deeply affected, if not traumatized, by the change in the community, especially the riots of the past year. They decided to give her another year before they broached a retirement option. For now, she simply needed someone to reassure her that everything was all right and that she was doing a good job.

Sterling, on the other hand, needed to get his paperwork done. At first, he put aside his work and carefully listened to June. Each morning, he ushered her from his office, gently at first, then with growing abruptness: "June, get out please, I've got to get my work done!" She would return, smiling, the next morning.

He started arriving at his office a half hour earlier—June would be waiting. An hour earlier—June would be waiting. In desperation, he tried a new tactic. June usually stood at the faculty mailboxes and shuffled through her mail for about 3 minutes after Sterling unlocked his office door. One day, he rushed into his office, grabbed papers, pencils, and a notepad, and locked himself in the private bathroom that had been graciously provided in the principal's office by architects long departed but, today especially, not forgotten. He sat, pants up, on the john and slowly worked his way through his paperwork. When he emerged 45 minutes later, June Hazel was nowhere in sight.

"Good," he thought, "I'll just do this for a few days and maybe we'll break June's need for a 'fix!' Practicing sensitivity is sometimes tougher on the boss than it is on the employee."

On the third day, Sterling replaced the standard length cord on his phone with a longer one that he could snake under the bathroom door before he left at the end of each day.

"Now," he laughed, "this temporary 'throne of power' has communications!" He chuckled at the image of himself sitting on the john, surrounded by papers while he talked on the phone. If they could see him, the office staff would surely think he'd lost his mind.

When he arrived for work one morning about 2 weeks after he had initiated the infamous "bathroom escape method," June was noticeably absent from the office.

"This seems to be working," he thought. "I'll try the desk routine again and see what happens." Ten minutes later, as he was about to pat himself on the back for being so ingenious, June appeared, pulled up a chair, and sat down.

"I'm glad you're feeling better, Grant. The flu must have really gotten you bad!"

He rested his head against his hand and arm. "Damn," he thought, "What now? Another 2 weeks on the john?"

"June, why do you come in here each morning? You can see that I have a mountain of paperwork to do. Some of it even includes supply and equipment orders for you. I come in early so that I can get some of this done before teachers and kids arrive. What . . . what is it that you really want?"

June's eyes welled up in tears. "I'm scared, Grant. I just need to know that last year isn't going to repeat itself. You are so confident that everything is going to be all right. I wish I had some of your courage! Maybe I need to retire—I'm eligible, you know—I just would miss the kids so much. I don't know what to do. I'm a nervous wreck! I'm sorry."

"June, I would hate to lose you, but you can't go on like this." Sterling thought he heard the troll under his desk say something like, "Yes! Yes! I want my bathroom back!" He felt that this might be an opportunity to cultivate the idea of retirement, especially because June brought it up.

"Maybe you ought to consider a retirement option before your health is affected," he said. "You need to take care of yourself first. The kids will survive. Why don't you talk with your husband about this tonight, and I'll make an appointment for you to visit with someone from personnel later this week."

He called the personnel office later that day and made an appointment for June. He also talked to the assistant superintendent for personnel and convinced him that he needed to allow Sterling to hire a replacement for June as soon as possible to give June time to train a new teacher. He rationalized that this would help June in making the transition without feeling she was abandoning her kids.

June made the decision to retire and rewarded Sterling with an attractive mobile she designed for him. He immediately hung it in his office. June was happy, and he was happy. And the troll continued to expand his paperwork happily.

To commemorate Sterling's new-found use for the principal's private bathroom, his head custodian, who had laughed at Sterling's method of hiding from June Hazel, painted the cover and seat of his toilet in the school's colors—purple and gold.

The Watermelon and the Press

"Grant," Jeannie announced. "David Berry is here to see you. He wants to know if you have a minute."

"David, glad to see you again," Sterling said as he ushered Berry into his office. "How can I help you?"

"Grant, if it's all right with you, I'd like to treat all the kids at Center to a watermelon feed." Berry went on to explain that, along with his many enterprises in the Center community, he had a farm south of the city where, among other fruits and vegetables, he maintained a very large watermelon patch. "I'll furnish the power to cut and serve. How does this sound to you? I think the kids would enjoy this kind of event, and it might help with your efforts to boost school spirit. Whattaya think? Could we make this work?"

Sterling was tickled. "David, sounds great, we'll do it! Would this Friday afternoon at 2:30, just before school dismisses, be okay?"

"We'll be here," David said. "I'll have two large trucks, one to carry the melons and the other for kids to throw their rinds in. I'll also bring sawhorses, boards, and butcher paper to cut and serve the melon sections from."

Sterling laughed, "I like that scene. We'll do the whole thing on the physical education field out back. The kids can spit seeds at each other, and maybe next year we'll have our own patch."

"This is the kind of thing that really brings a school together," he mused after Berry left. "And a really good public relations item. I'm going to call the press and see if we can get some coverage."

Sterling let the faculty and staff know about the watermelon event . . . but students were not to know until he made an announcement at 2:30 that Friday asking everyone to gather on the PE field.

Friday came, 2:30 arrived, and Sterling stood at the intercom microphone. "May I have your attention, please, for this important announcement? Please leave your work and books on your desks. At the sound of the bell, I would like all students, faculty, and staff to report to the PE field for a special event."

He waited a couple of minutes so students and teachers could get their materials put away. He then pushed the master button that bypassed the school's automatic bell timers. The main bells echoed through the halls.

"Jeannie, that bell almost sounded happy!" he laughed. "You come too. Let the phones go unanswered for a while."

As Sterling headed out toward the PE field, he could feel the kids' excitement as they crowded around the watermelon cutting tables. Berry had brought six men with him who were producing surgically measured portions and presenting them with a flourish.

As the kids got their treats, they gathered in small groups throughout the area. As Sterling expected, they spit seeds everywhere, including at each other.

In one corner of the field, there was a monstrous jungle gym, constructed of heavy galvanized steel pipe. Kids sat at different heights to enjoy their portions of melon under a beautiful sunny sky.

Sterling noticed the absence of the TV cameras he had hoped for. But a reporter from the newspaper was interviewing Berry and some of the kids. A photographer was working his way around the field. As Sterling looked over the scene, he saw happy kids, happy teachers—a good picture for a new principal trying to raise school spirit. His exhilaration carried him home that evening.

It was raining gently as Sterling walked out to retrieve the morning paper. A front-page photo showed 11 kids sitting on a jungle gym eating watermelon. The caption read, "Center Junior High School students take time off from classwork. Story on page 21." He hastily thumbed his way to page 21 and read the short, well-written, and factual account. He was pleased that David Berry got credit for the event with the support of Grant Sterling, principal of Center Junior High School.

"Couldn't ask for better publicity," he grinned as he headed for breakfast. "This is a textbook example of a 'feel good' story about schools."

While Sterling was absorbed in patting himself on the back, he failed to notice something about the front-page picture or interpret it in the same manner as his superiors did at their respective breakfasts. He was so close to the school environment and "his kids" at Center that it didn't even occur to him that all the kids in the newspaper photo, perched on the jungle gym and gleefully holding watermelon slices, were black.

When Sterling arrived at his office that morning, he found a note to call the superintendent as soon as possible.

He dialed the superintendent's office. A secretary answered.

"Mrs. Smith, this is Grant Sterling, returning a call from Dr. Boughton."

"Yes, Mr. Sterling, I'll tell him you're on the phone. I know he wants to talk to you."

Almost immediately, the superintendent picked up the call.

"Grant, what in God's name was that picture in this morning's paper all about? My staff is about to have a fit! Do you know what you're doing? All those black kids eating watermelon—sitting on a jungle gym! A school-sponsored event? Please, tell me you have a good explanation for this!"

The connotation that some people might attach to the newspaper photo still hadn't dawned on him. It took a moment for the light to come on and for him to understand what the superintendent was worried about.

"Dr. Boughton," Sterling responded in a quiet voice, "what you have just suggested never crossed my mind. Let me try to give you a better understanding."

He filled Boughton in on the details and reminded him that Berry was a prominent black civic leader. He assured the superintendent that he wouldn't hear anything derogatory from the Center community. He said that if anybody outside the community was concerned, they should contact Sterling or Berry. He respectfully suggested that the superintendent advise his staff to focus on the story, not the picture.

"One last thing," Sterling said. "As you well know, we don't have any control over what the press says or what photographers choose to take pictures of."

"I'll meet with my staff and enlighten them," the superintendent said. "Personally, I think you're on the right track. But to be honest, you scared the hell out of me. I hope we don't get a call from the NAACP. Thanks for returning my call so quickly."

Weeks later, Sterling was still waiting for the first negative call. It never came.

What's an Oreo?

"Grant, Ida Wood is on line 1. Do you have time to talk to her?"

Sterling punched the blinking button on his telephone.

"Ida, what's up?"

"Grant, I noticed Dr. Washington coming out of the building after school yesterday. How well do you know this gentleman?"

"Not well," Sterling answered. "He just stopped by to offer his assistance as director of minority affairs for the school district."

Ida was quick to respond. "Listen, Grant, I know you have to keep the superintendent's office happy, but this gentlemen is known in the Center neighborhood, especially the black community, as an Oreo. He has been more of a problem starter than a problem solver in the past. The community does not want him anywhere near their school or kids, and I agree."

"Ida, thanks for the information. I'll see what I can do about his relationship with Center community. But, I'm sorry, I don't understand the term you used to describe Washington. Oreo is a type of cookie."

"Grant," Ida laughed. "Think black on the outside, white on the inside. He was hired by the 'big house' to keep the black community quiet. He's looked on as 'workin' for the master,' an 'Uncle Tom.' Understand? This minority community doesn't trust him!"

Later that week, Sterling placed a call to Dr. Washington and shared the information he had received from the "community." He didn't feel it necessary to reveal exactly how he got his information. Washington was livid.

"My job description comes directly from the superintendent," Washington angrily explained, "I'm supposed to keep a high profile in the minority community. That includes the Center area."

"I understand the importance of your job," Sterling stressed. "I'm only concerned about your presence at Center Junior High. I'm suggesting that from now on, if we need to communicate with each other, let's do it by phone, or I'll come to your office. And, by the way, my job description also comes from the superintendent."

Washington's normally dynamic voice now sounded pinched. "Are you telling me I'm not welcome at your school?"

Sterling hesitated for a moment, knowing that his response was not going to be readily accepted. "I think that at the present time, yes. I need time to rebuild our image in the community after last year."

If Sterling had wanted to say more to pacify Washington, he didn't have a chance. Washington hung up the phone.

Within the hour, he found himself being summoned to the superintendent's office for a meeting with Dr. Boughton and Washington. Superintendent Boughton, in his predictable cut-to-the-bottom-line style of leadership, began what Sterling fully expected to be an uncomfortable inquisition.

"Grant, I understand from Dr. Washington that you have a problem with him visiting your building. Is that correct?"

"No sir, I don't," Sterling responded. "As I explained to Dr. Washington, my conversation with him was based entirely on a community request. Although I don't wish to get into the specifics of that conversation, I feel that it's in the best interest of Dr. Washington and me, and Center, that any meetings we have should be by phone or in his office, at least temporarily. I fully understand his responsibilities, and I support his role in the school district. I don't want to . . ."

"Enough," Boughton interrupted. "I've heard both sides now. What you're saying, Grant, is that the Center minority community doesn't want to deal with Dr. Washington at this particular time. Thanks for coming in on such short notice, Grant. You probably need to get back to Center now, don't you?"

"Boughton sounded irritated," Sterling thought as he walked to his car. Although he was sure that he was going to be raked over the coals in the next few days, he never heard another word about the matter. In fact, during the rest of the time that he was assigned as principal at Center, he never heard a word from Washington.

Sterling often wondered how Boughton squared it with Washington after he left. He wondered if the topic of the conversation might have centered around something like "let Sterling cook in his own juice."

It's Obvious

Sterling was still worrying about his two recent encounters with the superintendent as he whisked through the papers on his desk.

"Both of those episodes worked out okay," he thought. "I've got to stop worrying about what the folks downtown are thinking. Forecasting yes, worrying no. A cautious attitude will inhibit me when I need to take risks on behalf of Center."

"Mr. Sterling, excuse me. Brenda and I would like to speak with you for a moment." Peggy Woodbine, a school counselor, guided Brenda Huggins, a seventh-grade student, to a chair in Sterling's office. Woodbine gently closed the door.

"Mr. Sterling, Brenda has a problem with a group of seventh-grade boys. She'd like to tell you about it, and hopes that you can help her."

Brenda was a little girl who was clearly physically overdeveloped for her age. It was impossible not to notice her figure. Brenda was crying.

"Brenda, what's happening, what can I do to help you feel better?"

"They're calling me a bad word, that Bobby kid and the others," she said, sniffling.

"Why are they calling you 'a bad word'? What word?" Sterling asked gently.

Brenda looked at the floor.

"I'd be glad to talk to these guys and get them off your case, Brenda. But I gotta know what to talk to them about."

"They're calling me a bad word, Mr. Sterling, I told them to stop, but it's getting worse."

"What word Brenda."

"I can't say it." Brenda was now sobbing.

Every nasty, dirty word or word combination that seventh-grade kids call each other raced through Sterling's mind. He needed to be prepared to handle, with dignity and composure, the horrible thing Brenda or Peggy Woodbine would eventually reveal.

Mrs. Woodbine put her arm around Brenda's shoulder's and looked at Sterling with a partially concealed grin.

"Mr. Sterling," Woodbine started to say something, but was hastily interrupted by Brenda.

"THEY'RE CALLING ME OBVIOUS," she blurted out in a loud sob. "They're calling me obvious because of these!" Brenda pointed to her chest. "I want those boys to stop!"

"Brenda," Sterling was struggling to keep a straight face, "I'll take care of this right away. You won't have any more problems with these guys. I promise. Give Mrs. Woodbine their names, and I'll talk to them. Now, off to the girl's room and dry your eyes. Get a hall pass from the secretary. Any more problems, you let me know right away!"

Woodbine opened the door for Brenda.

"Thanks a lot, Peggy. It was pretty obvious, no pun intended, that you were setting me up to see if I could keep a straight face. Get me the names of these guys, and I'll take care of it." Sterling smiled and pointed his index finger at Peggy. "I'll get even with you though!"

He acted swiftly after learning the names of the boys.

"Gentlemen, very simply . . ."

One of the boys tried to interrupt.

"No, I'll talk, you listen!" he demanded. "I should suspend your butts from school for what you've been calling Brenda. This school will not tolerate that kind of nonsense. Here's my deal, however. The name calling stops now. If anybody else starts calling her names, specifically, 'obvious,' you're all going on a vacation! Understand?"

"Yes sir." The boys knew what Sterling was threatening, and they could tell from his voice that he meant business.

"Thank you, gentlemen. Go back to class. Don't let me down."

"Case closed," he hoped. As he returned to his paperwork, he remembered a magazine cartoon he had seen. A movie director talking to a young girl in a Little Orphan Annie costume who was obviously, like Brenda, overdeveloped for her age. The caption was, "Sorry, Annie, but as a child star you're washed up!"

▬▬▬ The Lord Speaks in Mysterious Ways

Sometimes Sterling worked late. After the night custodial crew left, the building, because of its thick granite and limestone walls, was eerily silent. No creaks and groans; the walls blocked out even loud thunderclaps.

Occasionally, a custodian would leave a ground floor window open or unlocked, causing a late night phone call from the police or school security informing him of an "insecure building." Although he continued to remind the custodial staff of the problem, it was not uncommon for them to forget.

As he started to leave Center one night, close to 11 o'clock, he heard a sound drifting up the staircase from the lower floor.

"Damn it, someone has forgotten to close a window again," he thought. He quietly descended about halfway down the stairs and listened. He heard giggling voices. He moved slowly to the bottom of the stairs and listened again. They were coming from the girls' locker room.

"What the hell!" he muttered under his breath.

He unlocked the door and peeked in. A security light in the girls' physical education office allowed him to see two people, naked, on a pile of gymnastics mats.

"I can't believe what I'm seeing," his mind trying to comprehend the view in the semidark room, "They're having sex!"

He was unable to see the girl's face, but quickly identified the male as Charley Bath, a ninth-grade student.

"This is embarrassing," he thought. "Should I confront them directly, yell at them, and close the door? What's the best way to handle this? This sort of thing isn't covered in any textbook I ever read."

Uncertain about what to do, Sterling eased the door closed and returned to the main office. Suddenly he had an inspiration. He switched on the intercom, lifted the toggle marked "Girls' Locker Room," and positioned the main lever to hear incoming sounds. He could plainly hear the moans of Charley and his unidentified mate. He adjusted the volume for outgoing announcement to level 10, the loudest, switched the main lever to the send-and-receive position, and spoke with a deep authoritative voice into the microphone.

"Charley!"

He could hear the echo of his voice bouncing off the tile walls of the locker room.

After a brief moment of silence, a weak voice stuttered, "Who's that?"

"Charley!" Sterling replied, still in a deep voice, "this is GOD!"

Again, after a moment of silence, Charley responded in a clear but quivering, voice, "Yes sir, God?"

"Charley, you let that girl go right now and get your butt out of this building!"

He could hear the sounds of clothes being recovered, scared and hurried whispers, and, finally, footsteps rapidly stumbling from the area.

"Well, that worked," he chuckled. "I'll visit with Charley tomorrow. And I think some powerful counseling is in order for both him and the young lady. I wonder how they got in the building?"

He turned off the intercom and called it another long and, as usual, interesting day.

Winning and Losing

Sterling expected to get phone calls at home in the evenings and on weekends. He knew it was a part of any principal's job. Warner had warned him that 99% of a school principal's phone calls denote a problem, rather than "I just wanted to call you and tell you what a fine job you are doing!" This evening was no exception.

He looked at the clock as the phone rang—9:30 p.m. Experience had taught him very quickly that this was probably going to be a difficult call. Students wait for their parents to get home from work. If it's a two-parent family, the student will usually tell one parent before dinner. That parent will wait until after dinner to share the problem with the other parent, and a family discussion or argument will ensue. The family will finally get mad enough to muster the courage—or outrage—to call the child's teacher or principal. They almost always want the issue resolved "right now," regardless of the time.

Sterling picked up the phone.

An agitated voice asked, "Is this the Sterling who's the principal at Center?"

"It is," he replied. "How can I help you?"

"What kind of school are you running down there? Why did you allow my daughter's English teacher to lock her in a closet? I want that teacher fired! Who do you people think you are?"

"Well," said Sterling in a nonaggressive tone. "First, who am I talking to?"

"This is Bob Reynolds," the angry voice answered. "You have my daughter Ruby at your school; she's an eighth grader. She came home from school today and told us that one of her teachers, a Mrs. Forester, locked her in a closet in her classroom for no reason, and she didn't let her out until the end of class. My wife and daughter were very upset when I got home from work!"

"Bob," Sterling responded, still in a calm voice, "I don't know what you're talking about, but I want to speak with your daughter first thing in the morning. You folks can come in with her if you wish. I'll speak with Mrs. Forester early tomorrow morning, and then we'll all know what happened, if anything."

"Are you calling my daughter a liar?" Reynolds shot back.

"No, Bob, I didn't mean to imply that. I just need to find out from both parties what happened. I guarantee you, if Mrs. Forester locked Ruby in a closet, I'll be as upset as you. Fair enough?"

"It's gonna cost me money to take time off from work, but I'll bring Ruby in to see you first thing in the morning," Reynolds agreed.

"Good morning Jeannie," Sterling waved as he headed for his office. You're here early today. Listen, would you keep your eye out for Nancy Forester and let me know the minute she comes in? I need to talk with her before school starts."

"She came in about 10 minutes ago, Grant. I think she's in the teachers' lounge."

Sterling unlocked his office, dumped his briefcase, and made a beeline for the lounge.

"Nancy, good morning. Would you take a short walk with me?" Sterling didn't want to discuss his late evening phone call with other teachers listening.

"Nancy, I received a curious phone call from Bob Reynolds, Ruby Reynolds's father, last night. Did you have a problem with Ruby yesterday in 4th-hour class?"

Nancy's ears turned red. "Yes, I did, and I've had it up to here with that girl. For the past month, to get attention, she's been coming to class and going directly into a closet and closing the door. When I call her name during roll call, the door flies open and she takes her seat with a flourish."

"Have you told her to stop?" Sterling asked, one eyebrow raised.

"Yes, but she just ignores me. So I decided to ignore her, figuring she'd get tired of the game."

"Yes, but if she disobeyed you, she was insubordinate. Why didn't you just send her to me?"

"I can handle my own discipline problems, thank you," Nancy said defensively.

Sterling stopped walking. "Okay, Nancy—bottom line. Did you lock her in the closet for the class period yesterday?"

"Yes, I did, for the whole class period!" Nancy, now visibly angry, glared at him. "I hope she learned a lesson. You can tell her parents that she's a pain in the butt!"

Sterling wanted to throw up his hands and tell Nancy how stupid this whole thing was. Nancy may have placed her job in jeopardy if Ruby's parents decided to take action beyond his office.

"Nancy, I'm supposed to meet with Ruby and her parents this morning to explain the reasons for your action. I have to tell you, however, it's going to be difficult. Dad was pretty angry when he called last night."

Nancy started to interrupt.

"Nancy, I'll speak with you again, after I talk with them."

Nancy was shaking. "Let me talk to them, I'll put them straight. They need to teach their daughter some manners. She's a stuck-up little prima donna!"

Sterling responded in a restrained voice, "I'll take care of it. You teach, I'll bail. And by the way, all junior high school kids act like prima donnas."

Reynolds and his daughter were waiting in the reception area when Sterling returned to his office. Ruby's mother was noticeably absent.

"Come in, Ruby, Mr. Reynolds, I just finished visiting with Mrs. Forester. Ruby, tell me, what happened yesterday in your 4th-hour English class?"

As Sterling listened, Ruby laid out her case. She innocently walked in the room, playfully hid in the closet, and, for some mysterious reason, Mrs. Forester locked the closet door with her still in it.

"She's always picking on me. She doesn't like me," Ruby finished her story, neglecting to mention to Sterling or her father that she had done this for at least a month, and that Mrs. Forester had told her to stop.

"Ruby," Sterling said, "haven't you been doing this for about a month now . . . didn't Mrs. Forester ask you to stop?"

"No," Ruby scowled.

"Excuse me just a moment." Sterling got up from his chair. "Mr. Reynolds, would you like some coffee?"

Sterling asked Jeannie to get the coffee as he went to the school's master student schedule ledger and looked up the class roster for Mrs. Forester's 4th-hour English class. He quickly scanned the list of students, closed the ledger, and walked out into the main hall. Students were arriving for classes, and it didn't take him long to spot a student whose name was on the roster he had just examined.

"Hey, Shirley," Sterling motioned her over to him. "May I speak with you for a minute? Shirley, has something been going on between Mrs. Forester and Ruby Reynolds during your 4th-hour English class?"

Shirley's story corroborated Mrs. Forester's version of the events. Sterling thanked her and headed back to his office.

"Ruby, you're not telling your dad or me the complete story. Let me ask you the same questions I asked you before I talked with one of your classmates. Have you been doing this closet thing for about a month, and did Mrs. Forester tell you to stop?"

"Well, maybe . . . all right, yes, Mr. Sterling." Ruby looked at the floor with a conspicuous pout.

"Okay, Ruby, thanks for telling us the whole story. I think you better get to class. Mrs. Petrie will give you a hall pass if you need one."

Sterling closed the door behind Ruby as she left for class.

"Bob, what Mrs. Forester did was wrong. Your daughter baited the teacher, and the teacher reacted. I wish Mrs. Forester had just sent Ruby here to see me. I could have probably stopped Ruby's little game. Unfortunately, Mrs. Forester decided to take another route that led us to this meeting. I tell you what. I'll take care of Mrs. Forester, and you take care of Ruby. Both need a good chewing-out."

Reynolds lowered his eyelids and stared at Sterling. "I want that teacher fired. She has no right to do that kind of stuff to kids!"

"Bob, Mrs. Forester made a mistake. Your daughter was testing her, and Mrs. Forester made a bad decision about how to solve the problem. I'll explain that to Mrs. Forester and let her know, in no uncertain terms, that what she did was wrong, and that if it happens again she could lose her job. I'm not going to recommend that she be fired. She's a good teacher. We all lose our cool occasionally. She won't make that mistake again. You have my word."

"You know, Sterling," Reynolds said as he stood up, "I could contact a board of education member right now, and this teacher would not be here this afternoon."

"I'm not going to respond to that comment, Bob. I just want you to let me handle the problem with Mrs. Forester, and you handle the problem with Ruby. I think that's fair."

"All right, I'll let you win this one. But she better not pick on my daughter again!"

Sterling left a note in Nancy's mailbox to see him during her planning hour. When they met, Nancy, cup of coffee in hand, listened intently as he told her what had taken place—Ruby's lies, her father's anger, and the threat to have Nancy fired.

"Now, Nancy," he leaned forward, "the bottom line is simply this, you made a mistake. You should have sent Ruby to me for discipline, and, clearly, you shouldn't have locked her . . ."

Nancy interrupted him in midsentence.

"You told him what I did was wrong? What I did was wrong? What kind of a principal are you? You're supposed to support your teachers!"

"Nancy, hold on, I did support you. One call from this guy to a board member and you would be downtown for a disciplinary hearing! I could be doing the paperwork right now that would lead to your immediate termination. I was honest with Reynolds, and I'm being honest with you. What you did to resolve this thing with Ruby was wrong. I've taken care of the problem. It's over. It's a dead issue."

Nancy sat silently for a moment, then reached in her purse, pulled out her room keys, stood up, and belligerently dropped her keys on Sterling's desk.

"I quit," she said in a quiet, but forceful voice. "Get a sub for the rest of the day, the rest of the week," her voice noticeably louder, "the rest of the goddamn year!"

Nancy rushed out of the office.

Sterling didn't try to stop her. He was stunned by her response. He picked up the phone and dialed the counselors' office.

"Sylvia, I need you to cover for Forester in her 3rd-hour class. I'll call for a substitute to get here as soon as possible. I'll fill you in later!"

Sterling was upset and angry.

"Did I do something wrong?" he thought. "I don't know what I could have done differently. I saved a teacher's neck and I still lost!"

The term that Forester used to describe Ruby, "prima donna," flashed through his mind.

A Sterling Moment (If the Shoe Fits, Wear It) ▨▨▨▨

"Hey, what's happening, Mr. GQ . . . I mean, Mr. Sterling?"

"What's happening with you?" Sterling responded to Richie Johnstone, one of his students, as he and a group of his friends passed Sterling in the hall.

"Hey, Richie," Sterling inquired, "What's with the Mr. GQ stuff?"

"It's your threads, man . . . it's your threads. That's why we call you Mr. GQ. You know," he explained as his buddies nodded their heads in agreement, "like in *Gentlemen's Quarterly*!"

"*Gentlemen's Quarterly?*" Sterling questioned. "Where do you guys see that magazine?" Sterling couldn't remember if he'd ever seen a copy outside of his barber shop. It was usually the only magazine left on the rack when all the copies of *Field and Stream* and *Popular Mechanics* were already being read.

"We have it in the library, Mr. Sterling. Check it out!" they exclaimed as they headed for their classes.

Later that day, Sterling wandered into the library.

"Lucille, do we subscribe to *Gentlemen's Quarterly?*"

"Sure," was the librarian's reply, "and to *Mademoiselle.* Both magazines are very popular with our students. Center kids may not be able to afford many of the fashions they feature, but they like to keep up with current trends. I hear them talking about your wardrobe quite often. They like the fact that you always wear a suit or sport coat, and they love your wild ties. Why do you ask?"

"Oh, I just wondered," Sterling sheepishly replied. "I think it's great that the kids like those magazines."

"I think you've just heard that they've been calling you Mr. GQ behind your back," Lucille snickered. "They've been doing that ever since you painted those old saddle shoes of yours in the school's colors."

"Really," Sterling said. "You ought to hear the comments I get from teachers and principals from our opponent schools at games."

"Oh, I can imagine," Lucille laughed, "but the kids love them, and, as I've heard you say so many times—kids first."

Sterling continued to wear his purple and gold saddle shoes on game days for his entire tenure at Center. His shoes would undergo a miraculous transformation three more times in his career. From purple and gold, to green and white, to green and gold, to black and gold, and finally, to retirement in the bottom drawer of a file cabinet.

"Mr. GQ . . . hmm. Well, if the shoe fits, wear it."

▬▬▬ You Sound Taller on the Telephone

Two weeks had passed since the last incident with Kelly Roberts. Evidently, Sterling's phone calls to her mother had finally had the desired effect.

For almost a semester now, Sterling had had dozens of telephone conversations with Kelly's mother. Kelly, an eighth grader, had been sent to his office many times for mouthing off to teachers. Sterling and Mrs. Roberts had worked very hard to resolve Kelly's hostile feelings about her teachers and to keep Kelly from being suspended.

"Mrs. Roberts, hi. This is Grant Sterling. Don't panic. I just wanted to call and let you know that you and I may have finally convinced Kelly to control her temper with her teachers. I just wanted you to have some good news from me for a change!"

Sterling could hear Mrs. Roberts sigh with relief. "You did scare me for a moment," she replied. "I'm so glad you called. But I'm only cautiously relieved. Let's keep our fingers crossed. Thanks for your help and understanding."

"No big deal, Mrs. Roberts. Teenagers can get pretty testy, especially when it comes to adult authority. But I think Kelly has finally gotten the message that home and school are equally concerned about her behavior.

"You know," Sterling continued, "we've been talking for almost 5 months now, and we've never met except over the telephone. You have an open invitation to come in for coffee. Please stop in sometime so we can meet personally."

"Thank you, I might," Mrs. Roberts replied.

Sterling wanted as many face-to-face contacts with parents as possible, and frequently ended conversations with an invitation to stop by the school. He thought it unfortunate that few parents ever visited except on open house evenings. "Even then," he noted, "the parents you really need to make eye contact with are seldom the ones who attend!"

A few days later, Jeannie stuck her head around the corner to Sterling's office. "Grant, Mrs. Roberts, Kelly's mother, is here to see you. Said you invited her in for coffee."

"Thanks, Jeannie." Sterling closed the report he was studying and walked out to the main office.

"Mrs. Roberts, I'm Grant Sterling. How nice of you to take me up on my offer. We finally get to meet face to face!"

Roberts eyed Sterling with a puzzled look. "You're the principal? You're Mr. Sterling? I, ah, well, you know . . . you sound . . . well, you sound so much taller on the telephone!"

As Sterling, suddenly feeling even shorter than his 5-foot 6-inch height, escorted Mrs. Roberts into his office, he purposely ignored the stifled giggling of the secretaries. Two teachers who happened to be in the outer office and heard Mrs. Roberts' declaration almost tripped over each other as they scrambled toward the hallway door so that Sterling couldn't hear their uncontrollable laughter.

For the next few weeks, the Center staff gleefully shared with Sterling that they, indeed, agreed with Mrs. Roberts' keen observation.

"You do sound taller on the telephone!"

Sterling took it all in stride. Albeit short strides.

Front Row Seats at the Theater

Sterling shuffled through the call slips carefully positioned at the center of his desk. Classes had resumed following Christmas break. After the holiday, his desk was nearly devoid of the usual paperwork. He had plenty of time, for a change, to return phone calls.

"Mrs. Calkins, Grant Sterling returning your call. How can I help you?"

"Mr. Sterling," she replied nervously, "I know that our son John is not going to be happy about it, but my husband and I want him removed from Mr. Stevens's class. Perhaps to a study hall or something."

"Funny," Sterling thought to himself, "Fred Stevens is one of the strongest teachers at Center." As the music teacher, Stevens had one of the largest and best music programs in the city. Students and parents alike flocked to his concerts and the school musical each year. Problems in his classroom were rare. He was bewildered by Calkins' request.

"May I ask why?"

"I'd rather not discuss our reasons. I wish I could, but I just can't!"

"All right, Mrs. Calkins, I'll refer your request to John's counselor. She'll work with John to find a replacement class or a study period. Does John know about this?"

Calkins told Sterling that she and her husband had agonized about the class change for about a week. They had told John this morning, before school, about their wishes.

"John was very upset," she said. "Especially when we couldn't really discuss our reasons with him either."

Sterling recognized that Mrs. Calkins was upset too, and didn't press the issue further. He assured her that the school would work with John to make the transition as easy as possible. He shared what little information he had gleaned from Mrs. Calkins with John's counselor and went back to his call slips, the question of why still lingering.

During the next few days, Sterling received a number of additional requests from parents to remove their children from Stevens's classes. In each case, parents were hesitant to share any rationale for their request. He asked Stevens what he thought the problem might be. Stevens said he had no idea.

Finally, Gil Martin, father of a seventh-grade band member, was willing, if not eager, to share the problem with Sterling. He also wanted his child "out of that man's reach."

"Well," Martin said. "Anyone who's been arrested in a porno theater for doing what he was doing has no business being around children. I hope you've found somebody to replace Stevens!"

"What do you think he was arrested for?" Sterling asked.

Martin laughed. "I hear that he was sitting in the front row of the Princess Theater, you know, the porn place downtown, masturbating during the movie! Can you believe that?"

Martin continued to report what he had heard as Sterling quietly flipped through his Rolodex for the phone number of police detective Bob Miller. He knew that Miller would give him accurate information.

Miller was unusually formal in his response to Sterling's query. Miller was a member of the juvenile division of the city police department. He and Sterling had worked together with troubled kids for quite a while.

"Grant, as I understand it, the vice guys picked him up the day after Christmas. They had a complaint from the Princess Theater about this guy before. This time they caught him on videotape. I think the charges are indecent exposure in a public place. His brother or somebody posted bail."

"How come nobody from vice called me and filled me in on this situation? How come I've not seen it in the newspaper? They usually go hog-wild with something like this!"

"I'm not sure, but I think the brother knows somebody in vice. I think they're keeping it quiet until the case comes before a judge. Maybe he's just going to plead guilty quietly and pay a fine, rather than go to court. That's really all I know." Sterling thanked Miller and hung up.

"I'm going to have to get some advice on this one," he thought as he slowly closed the door in his office. "If the exodus from Stevens' classes continues and I try to shield Stevens, somebody will leak the Princess incident to the press. Stevens will be fired, and I'll have one hell of a brush fire to put out."

Although he was reluctant to do it, Sterling placed a call to the deputy superintendent for personnel. He guessed correctly where his inquiry would lead.

"Grant, I know this is going to be difficult. This guy's a good teacher. But, well, I'm going to call the chief of police. If the charge is real, I'll call the district attorney to see if he is going to prosecute. If the answers are yes and yes, Stevens is gone. I'll call you back."

Within the next 10 minutes Sterling got the word. The answers were, unfortunately, yes and yes. He sent a message to Stevens to see him right after school. In the meantime, he called the district's supervisor of music and requested the name of a long-term substitute for Stevens.

Fred Stevens appeared within 10 minutes after the final bell of the day sounded. He looked tired, but then, Sterling thought, "Fred always looks tired at the end of the day. He puts everything he has into his work."

"Fred, bad news. The incident during vacation at the Princess has been brought to my attention. I've verified the facts. As you are well aware, a number of parents have called to have their kids transferred from your classes. They knew about the situation. You knew about the situation. I wish you had talked to me about it when I first asked you what you thought the problem was." Sterling was trying to make himself angry to bolster his courage to do what was necessary. It was difficult!

"Fred, I need your keys and your grade book before you leave today. Take any personal belongings with you. You are fired effective today. I understand that you will be paid until the board accepts your termination papers at its next meeting. Damn it, Fred. What a stupid thing to do!"

Fred had no response. He was pale as he left the office. He returned within the hour and gently laid his keys and grade book on the edge of Sterling's desk.

"I'm sorry, Grant."

Stevens left.

Fred and his family left town later that year. Sterling got a few phone calls from some out-of-state school districts during the next school year. Stevens was totally honest with prospective employers. Sterling didn't want to become involved in a negligent hiring case, so when asked, he simply verified the reason Stevens was fired. With each inquiry, however, he added, "This is an exceptional teacher, I hope you will consider giving him a chance."

He knew they probably wouldn't.

You Look Marvelous in Handcuffs

"Big game tonight . . . we're going to take the city championship . . . we're gonna whip the Wilson Wildcats back into their cage," Sterling attempted to sing his thoughts to an elusive melody from *West Side Story* as he returned to Center that evening for the final basketball game of the season. The championship game! He was met at the door by Coach Randol. Randol was obviously distressed.

"Grant, did you suspend Bo Givens from school today?"

"No, what's wrong?"

"He's not here yet. His teammates say his mother won't let him come. I don't understand that!"

"Don't panic, Coach. I know where Bo lives. I'll drive over and see what the problem is."

Bo lived with his mother and little sister about 4 blocks from Center. Their house, with peeling paint and grassless yard, looked like a dump.

Sterling had met Bo's mother before. She worried that her kids would end up like her—an alcoholic who lived on welfare and what little she could pick up on the streets.

Sterling knocked on the door and hollered.

"Ms. Givens! . . . Ms. Givens . . . Bo, anybody home?"

"I'm in here, Mr. Sterling. I can't come to the door."

"Is your mother home, Bo?" Sterling yelled at the door.

"Open the door . . . come in, Mr. Sterling."

Bo sounded frantic. Sterling slowly eased the unlocked door open and peeked in. The place smelled like a tavern. He could see Bo sitting on the floor in what looked to be a bedroom.

"Come back here, Mr. Sterling. I got in trouble with my Mama." Bo had been crying.

"Is she home?" Sterling asked as he cautiously approached the place where Bo was sitting.

"She's right here," Bo pointed at the bed.

Sterling entered the musty room. He could see Ms. Givens sprawled on the bed. He could also see that Bo had a locked handcuff on one wrist with the other end of the cuffs securely attached to the bed frame.

"What's going on Bo, is your mom all right?"

"She's drunk and passed out. We had an argument, and she wouldn't let me play in the game tonight!"

Sterling walked around the bed and shook Ms. Givens. Gently first, then a little harder. No response other than a groan.

"Where's the key to these things, Bo?"

"In her left hand, Mr. Sterling!"

Sterling gently pried her left hand open and retrieved a key. He unlocked the right cuff, leaving the left one hanging from the bed frame. "Let's go kid. We'll take the heat from your mom later!"

Center captured the city championship that evening. Bo Givens had 14 points and 11 assists.

As Sterling took Bo home after the game, he didn't know how he was going to explain his action to Bo's mom. But Ms. Givens just asked how the game went. She evidently didn't remember anything about whatever the problem had been with Bo earlier. Neither Sterling nor Bo brought it up.

"I wonder if parental abuse will outweigh principal kidnapping if Ms. Givens ever remembers this evening and decides to nail my butt," Sterling thought as he drove home. "Thank God Bo didn't foul out in the first quarter!"

A Sterling Moment (Special Delivery)

It was a warm, sunny, spring day, and Sterling was enjoying the sounds of students in rehearsal as he strolled past the choir room. He had spent the last hour casually roaming the halls and peeking in classrooms. "You wear out a lot of shoes in this job," he was thinking as he walked into the lounge located next to the main office for a soda. "I'll be in here for a while," he told Jeannie as he flopped into a well-worn chair. "I've got to get some new furniture and art for this lounge," he thought as he glanced around the room.

"Sorry to disturb your break, Grant," Jeannie said as she walked into the lounge. "Mrs. Gibson is here to see you. She's carrying a colorfully wrapped package in one hand and a shovel in her other hand. Don't ask me," she hastily added, anticipating Sterling's unspoken question.

Mrs. Gibson, a parent of a seventh-grade student at Center, was one of the ladies who had accompanied the notorious Pastor Lewis when he visited Center last August to challenge Sterling. Her daughter was a quiet young lady who always had a smile for Sterling when they passed in the hall.

"Mrs. Gibson, how are you?" Sterling reached to shake her hand as Gibson fumbled with her package and shovel. "I've had folks threaten to hit me, shoot me, or send me to Siberia," he laughed as she finally freed her hand and extended it toward Sterling, "but this is a first. Let me guess," he pointed at the shovel. "You've come to bury me?"

"No, oh no!" she giggled. "Come with me please," she said, holding Sterling's hand as she led him into the hall. "Come outside with me."

"Okay," Sterling said quizzically as he dutifully followed her into the hall and toward the front door. "Here, let me carry the shovel."

"No, you carry this," she said, and handed him the carefully wrapped package.

As they walked out the front door, Sterling noticed a small group of people gathered by the school's flagpole. As Gibson led him closer, Sterling realized that it was the same group that had followed Pastor Lewis into Sterling's office. That had been a day Sterling would never forget.

Sterling was in his usual good mood that afternoon, and immediately started teasing the group with a series of questions and comments.

"All right," he said, "I give up. What did I do wrong this time? The flagpole rope is not strong enough to hold my weight if you're going to string me up! Can I make at least one phone call? Do I know you people?" Sterling was shaking hands with the group as Gibson interrupted his banter.

"Mr. Sterling," she said in a compelling voice that quickly turned compassionate. "We've all been very upset about the way we treated you when you first came to our school. Today we want to extend our apologies to you . . ." She interrupted herself just long enough to hand her shovel to one of the men in the group with the order to "Start digging, right here . . . save the sod, mind you!" She marked the spot with the toe of her shoe as she looked back at Sterling and continued. "We've watched you as you've worked with our children this year. We want you to know that we think you've done a real good job. You've done the Lord's work here, and we ask His forgiveness and yours for allowing ourselves to be drawn into that jumble with Pastor Lewis. Please take this," she put her hand on the package that Sterling was holding for her, "as a token of our friendship and thanks. We know that you have a great sense of humor, and will know what to do with this."

She was grinning as she removed her hand and motioned for Sterling to open his gift. As Sterling quickly thought about how to respond to the group he noticed that they too were grinning. The hole beside the flag pole was getting deeper as Sterling opened the package. As he carefully removed the bow and ribbons and handed them to Gibson, he assured the group that he had dismissed the incident with Lewis and that they should also. He anxiously removed the wrapping and opened the shoebox that had been concealed beneath the paper. He pulled out a well-worn hatchet and triumphantly displayed it to the group, laughing as he went to each of them to display his gratitude with a hug. When he had finished, he twirled the hatchet in his hand, tossed it into the hole, and grabbed the shovel. They were all smiling as Sterling pushed the dirt back where it belonged . . . on top of the hatchet. They all agreed that this was a wonderful way to end a beautiful spring day.

An Affair to Remember

Spring was in the air and the long, exceptionally harsh winter was about over as Sterling reviewed April budget request items. He had come in very early that morning hoping to make some progress on the never-ending paperwork before students arrived. He heard the secretaries arrive and the normal sounds of exchanged greetings as teachers checked their mailboxes before heading for the lounge for morning coffee and gossip.

"Grant, may I talk with you for a moment?"

Sterling looked up from his desk and recognized Beth Adams's husband, Steve, standing in the doorway.

"Come in," Sterling shook his hand and motioned him to a chair.

"Grant, can we close the door?"

Sterling could see that Steve was troubled. "What's up, Steve?"

"This is difficult for me. I'm very angry and upset. I'll try to keep cool. Beth has been having an affair with one of your math teachers for, I think, about 6 months. I suspected something was going on with somebody, and I finally got Beth to admit it last night. She told me she had been seeing Tom Lee."

"Steve, I'm sorry to hear about this, I had no idea . . ."

"Grant, I want you to talk to them both and, if at all possible, transfer Lee to another school."

Sterling turned in his chair, and for a moment, looked out his window. He needed time to think, but he could tell that Steve Adams needed some kind of a response now.

"Steve, I understand what you must be going through. But I gotta tell you, this is a private matter between you, Beth, and Tom. The school can have no interest in this unless it interferes with either Beth or Tom's ability to teach. I've not heard anything about this from other teachers or parents, so they must have done a good job of keeping it hidden. The only thing I can do is to inform Beth and Tom that you and I had a meeting this morning and that you shared this information with me. I will warn them that if this becomes public knowledge, and adversely affects their rapport with parents, students, or other teachers, it could be grounds for dismissal. I'm sorry but that's all I can do."

Steve stood up slowly, still visibly upset, and reached for the doorknob. "Thanks for nothing, Grant."

As Steve walked out of Sterling's office, Tom Lee rounded the corner heading for his mail box. Sterling could see that they were going to cross paths. "What crappy timing on the part of Lee," he thought.

Without warning, and with a single swing, Adams' angry right fist hooked Lee squarely in the jaw. Lee hit the tile-covered concrete floor with a muted thud. Adams didn't miss a step as he continued walking out of the office, out of the building, and to his car. Sterling was glad students weren't around yet to witness the event. But Jeannie was stunned. Her face looked like a distorted question mark. Sterling helped Lee to his feet and suggested that he get an ice pack out of the refrigerator in the lounge.

"We'll talk later," Sterling told Lee as he walked back into his office. He called Jeannie in to explain the problem and advised her to keep the matter private.

During the day, Sterling met separately with Beth Adams and Tom Lee. He advised them that the problem was strictly their business. He tactfully reminded them of their exemplar status as educators and that they could be fired if their private lives became public and interfered with their work. Beth was horribly embarrassed by the unmasked affair and now openly frightened by the critical elevation of the situation. Tom seemed to take the whole event in a cavalier manner, brushing aside Sterling's concern for his teaching position. Sterling almost expected to hear a piglike snort as Tom left the meeting.

"Maybe his jaw is too sore," Sterling shrugged to himself.

One Man's Junk, Another Man's Pleasure

"Probably the only kid in the eighth grade with a full beard and mustache," Sterling observed as he maneuvered his car into his usual parking place next to Center.

Billy Connely had been an eighth grader for 2 years after previously spending 2 years in the seventh grade. Billy usually went to his classes, but rarely made any attempt to do assignments and almost always failed pop quizzes and tests.

"Billy's whole problem stems from the fact that he's still reading at about the fourth-grade level," Mrs. Greely, the school's reading teacher, told Sterling. "I've worked with him since he came to Center 3 years ago. He just lacks motivation."

"Good morning, Billy. Going to class today, or are you just as happy sitting there on the curb?" Sterling shouted as he closed his car door.

"Yep! I'll be in class on time," Billy shouted back. "Just waiting for the bell. You got a problem there with your differential—did ya know that?"

"With my what?" Sterling walked closer.

"Don't you hear that howling noise when you drive slow? Sounds like this." Billy made a low grumbling, moaning sound.

"Is that what that is?" asked Sterling. "I thought it was a tire or something!"

"Nope, pop-out gear. Cost you 20 bucks at a junkyard. Want me to fix it?"

Sterling was surprised that the eighth grader made that offer. "You can do that?" Sterling asked. "Where'd you learn about fixing cars?"

"That's what I do with my uncle. I live with him, and we fix cars. Ain't no problem if you want that fixed. I can do it right where you're parked. Just need some wooden blocks and a socket set. Take about an hour!"

"What class do you have first period, Billy?"

"Math," Billy replied, wrinkling his nose.

"Come with me, Billy. I want to check my calendar to see if I have enough time to take you to a junkyard."

Sterling cleared his calendar, loaded Billy in the car with the "grumbling, moaning sound," and headed toward a junkyard that Billy said would have what they needed. Billy walked up to the grease-stained counter and told the junkman exactly what he wanted. The man left for a moment and returned with a small gear in his hand.

"Nope, wrong one, Jimmy," Billy told the man when he returned.

"Yep, that's it!" He told Jimmy when he returned from his second trip. He took the part from Jimmy and examined it carefully, inspecting each gear tooth with an eye as critical as a dentist's.

"How much?" Billy was still examining the part.

"Twenty-five," Jimmy replied.

"Give him a 20, Mr. Sterling!"

Billy closed the deal by snapping, "That's enough, Jimmy!" Billy was dealing as if he'd been doing this for years.

"Need to borrow a tool. Gonna do the job right here, Jimmy. Okay?"

Jimmy pointed to an empty area between a stack of treadless tires and a rusting, multicolored ice cream truck with no wheels.

Billy snatched a ratchet handle and two sockets from a box on the counter and headed for the assigned repair spot.

"Bring your car, Mr. Sterling," Billy directed.

Billy nudged a couple of old tires under the car, put down a piece of reasonably clean cardboard, and disappeared between the two back wheels. Sterling grabbed a newspaper from his car and carefully laid it over a rusty tractor seat. He climbed up the faded green John Deere, sat, and watched with amazement as Billy performed surgery.

"We need to invent a different track for Billy at school," Sterling thought. "We ought to be able to use Billy's interest and talent in fixing cars as a motivation to learn."

Sterling was anxious to get back to school and share his "Billy" experience with a couple of teachers who, he felt, could put Billy back on the learning curve. "Perhaps we'll invent a new educational program and call it differential learning," he laughed to himself.

Within the next few days, Billy was placed in an extended reading class. He was engrossed in reading automobile, motorcycle, and lawnmower repair manuals Sterling had talked local repair shops into donating to the school.

In addition, Billy was hard at work in the school's metal shop rebuilding the old John Deere that Jimmy the junkman was glad to see hauled away from his junkyard.

Billy later sold the tractor and paid back the school for expenses, according to the debit ledger he learned to keep. With the help of his shop teacher, he spent the remaining profits on a complete set of mechanic's tools and a dozen old two- and four-cycle lawnmowers that needed overhauling.

An added bonus, from Sterling's perspective, was that his car no longer had a grumbling, moaning sound.

Does It Make a Difference if the Gun Is Loaded?

"Sir, excuse me. You can't be here during school hours," Sterling said as he approached a disheveled man standing in the middle of one of the school's outside basketball courts.

The man was arguing with a group of students, and Sterling had been hastily summoned from the cafeteria by one of the teachers supervising the school grounds during lunch. The man ignored Sterling and continued to argue with the students. He wanted to shoot baskets, and he wanted the students to get off the court. Sterling moved closer.

"Sir," he addressed the man in a more forceful voice. "I'm going to have to ask you to leave. You are not authorized to be here during school hours. You can use the court after school hours if you wish."

The man continued to ignore Sterling's attempt to get his attention, and had attracted a crowd of ninth-grade boys, who, at the drop of a hat, could easily have beaten him to a pulp. Sterling moved between the rapidly growing crowd and the "not too smart" uninvited stranger.

"Look, guy." Sterling was in the man's face. "I asked you to leave. Do I need to call the cops and have you arrested?"

"Who the hell are you?" the man asked.

"I'm the principal here, sir, and I want you to leave the school grounds now."

"Fuck you! I kicked my principal's butt years ago," Sterling was swiftly told.

Sterling noticed a gradually intensifying chant from the assembled students. "Hit him Sterling; hit him Sterling; hit him Sterling."

As the chanting grew louder, Sterling was forced to raise his voice. "Look, I want you to leave now, before something happens. I don't think you want me to turn this angry group of students loose on you. I think," he was almost yelling at this point, "that they will beat the crap out of you."

The man must have realized that this was not worth the hassle. He turned abruptly and hurriedly walked to an abandoned house across the street from the school. Just as quickly, the chanting students changed their lyrics and started taunting the man with a rhythmic "chicken shit . . . chicken shit . . ." As Sterling quieted them and sent them back to their lunch-break activities, the man disappeared into the house.

"That idiot should send me a thank-you note. I don't think he fully realized how close he was to being badly hurt."

"Hey, Mr. Sterling." Randy Carlson, one of his ninth-grade students, called him aside. "We've seen that guy around here before. He hangs out in that beat-up old white house over there. He's a pot head. A bunch of them party over there almost every night."

Sterling had noticed the house before. He wondered why the place hadn't been condemned.

"Thanks, Randy," Sterling said as he went back to his supervisory chores in the cafeteria.

He had just stepped inside the cafeteria door when he felt a hand on his shoulder. "Sorry to tell you this, Grant, the guy's back out there again," said the supervisor.

"Okay," Sterling responded as he rushed toward the door. "Have Jeannie call the police, and then come out and help me."

As Sterling approached the playground area, he could see the man waving his arms and hear the obscenities he was yelling at a crowd of students moving toward him. Sterling quickly jumped in front of the crowd and ordered the students to stop. They stopped, but immediately started chanting again. "Chicken shit, chicken shit . . ."

Suddenly, the rapidly growing crowd turned silent. As Sterling turned to confront the stranger once again, he saw what had made the students freeze. The man now held a gun and was waving it at the crowd.

"Okay, now what," he wondered. "Should I challenge this guy? I don't think so. Where are the cops? I don't see them. Is the gun loaded?"

The man stopped waving the gun at the crowd and now pointed it straight at Sterling. "Should I try to reason with this idiot? Should I turn my back to him and see if I can get students to go into the school building?"

It took a moment for him to reach a decision, and he didn't know whether it was the correct one. He turned, faced the crowd, and ordered the students to return to the building. He expected some resistance; however, they quickly complied with his demand. A handful of students stayed with Sterling to make sure he also returned to the building. "We're not leaving unless you come with us, Mr. Sterling."

"All right, guys, show's over," Sterling said as he walked with the lingering students toward the building. "Where are the cops?" he wondered as they reached the front door.

"Who's the chicken shit now," he heard the stranger scream.

"Let it go, guys. Continue to ignore him," Sterling said as he closed the school door behind them. "We'll let the cops take care of it."

Inside the building, students casually went to their lockers and returned to their respective classes. Lunch period was over, and guns in the Center neighborhood were not that big a deal. Center kids lived with violence most of the time. Guns and gunshots in the night were, unfortunately, a fact of life in the community. The school had always been the safest place for them to be. Until today.

The stranger was still standing and yelling in the middle of the street in front of the school when the police arrived. He darted toward the white house and quickly disappeared inside. He evidently continued running through the house and out the back door, because the police could not find him.

Sterling met with police officers to fill out what they called an incident report, and then returned to his normal routine. He continued to worry about the possibility of the stranger returning. The police assured him that they would be patrolling the perimeter of the school for the rest of the afternoon, and would continue tomorrow while detectives tried to find the gun-wielding stranger.

Even though the entire incident lasted only about 15 minutes from the time he was first notified of the man on the playground, Sterling's thought processes were disrupted a number of times that afternoon and evening with a series of introspective questions—all of which started with "What if."

As he returned to school the next morning, he was shocked to see that the dilapidated white house across the street—the house where the stranger allegedly hung out—had burned to the ground.

"Well," he hoped, "that should take care of that problem! The tenants must have gotten carried away with their pot smoking and partying, and accidentally set fire to their own digs . . . or did they?"

For Discussion

General Questions

Using the Sterling paradigm (http://www.corwinpress.com/dunklee.htm) as a model, and speaking from the perspective of a principal, evaluate each episode as follows:

What are the dominant behaviors exhibited by Sterling in this episode?

Is there consensus about this in the class? If not, explain the different viewpoints.

What were the primary actors' individual motives?

How effective was Sterling's behavior in this situation and why?

Can you identify other avenues or approaches that might lead to the same, or a better, conclusion?

If Sterling was a woman,

■ As a female reader, can you identify methodology or behavior that you would change to bring the episode to the same, or similar, closure?

▪ As a male reader, what differences in methodology or behavior would you expect to see?

Specific Questions for Each Episode

Make Sure the Toilet Seat Is Down

1. Does a principal and/or the school district have any special obligation to a long-term teacher or other employee who is becoming less effective?
2. What are your three best time management tools?
3. How can a principal maintain an open door policy and still have time to get desk work done?

What if . . . Sterling had simply barred June from coming to his office each morning?

What if . . . Sterling had ignored June's comment about retirement eligibility?

The Watermelon and the Press

4. Should Sterling have foreseen the possibility of negative interpretation in the publicity generated by this activity?
5. Should the activity have been allowed?
6. What are the salient characteristics of a good public relations story?
7. What actions can a principal take to create a positive relationship with the local press?

What if . . . the community had reacted the same way central office did to the picture in the newspaper?

What's an Oreo?

8. Why did the superintendent support Sterling and not Washington?
9. If Washington perceives that he has been embarrassed by this incident, might Sterling be subjected to some kind of payback in the future?
10. How does a principal determine who has power in the local community?

What if . . . Sterling had simply thanked Ms. Wood for the information about Dr. Washington and then ignored it?

What if . . . the superintendent had ordered Sterling to accept Washington into his school and its community?

It's Obvious

11. At the beginning of this episode, Sterling makes the following statement in reference to the previous two episodes: "I've got to stop worrying about what the folks downtown are thinking." When should a principal consider a superior's viewpoint before making a local decision and when should he or she act independently?

12. The boys' behavior in this episode might be considered sexual harassment under current rules, regulations, policies, or law. What is the policy in your school district, and would you feel compelled to implement that policy in this specific situation?

What if . . . Brenda's parents had called Sterling and demanded that the boys be suspended, in accordance with school district policy, for sexual harassment?

The Lord Speaks in Mysterious Ways

13. Sterling chooses to opt for counseling rather than punishment. Would you have made the same decision?

14. Does Sterling have any legal, ethical, or professional responsibility to talk to the students' parents?

What if . . . the parents of either the girl or the boy involved in this incident had called Sterling and challenged him about the fact that he hadn't notified them about the incident?

Winning and Losing

15. What does the word *support* mean in terms of a principal and his or her teachers?

16. Should a principal ever admit to a parent that a teacher or staff member made a mistake? Why or why not?

17. If Forester contacts her union, what will be her version of the episode?

18. What guidelines, if any, should a principal give teachers about when to handle discipline problems themselves and when to refer a student to an administrator?

A Sterling Moment (If the Shoe Fits, Wear It)

(No specific questions)

You Sound Taller on the Telephone

19. Is a sense of humor an important quality in an effective principal? Why?

20. How important or unimportant is it for an effective principal to be able to see himself or herself through the eyes of others? Why?

21. What are some effective strategies for getting working parents involved in the school?

22. How can principals make their schools welcoming places for parents?

Front Row Seats at the Theater

23. What specific grounds for terminating Stevens might the superintendent present to the board?

24. What possible connection is there between what Stevens did away from school and his ability to teach?

25. When should a principal be concerned about a teacher or other staff member's private life?

26. Do school personnel have an obligation to live morally prudent private lives? Why or why not?

27. What legal obligation does a principal have to reveal why a faculty or staff member left a position?

What if . . . Sterling had refused to allow students to transfer out of Stevens's class without a reason?

What if . . . Sterling had "sat on" the growing situation hoping it would simply go away?

You Look Marvelous in Handcuffs

28. Should a principal become involved in a parent-child dispute off school grounds?

29. Are there circumstances under which you can imagine yourself taking such an action?

30. What steps should school personnel follow in filing child abuse charges? Does this episode provide evidence of child abuse?

What if . . . Ms. Givens had pressed charges?

A Sterling Moment (Special Delivery)

(No specific questions)

An Affair to Remember

31. What, if anything, is different about this situation and the episode that involved a teacher's activities at an adult theater? Why?

32. When should a principal inform a faculty or staff member about gossip that concerns him or her?

What if . . . students had witnessed the altercation between Steve Adams and Tom Lee?

What if . . . after confirming that two of his teachers were having an affair, Sterling had decided to suspend the teachers while recommending their termination to the board?

One Man's Junk, Another Man's Pleasure

33. What kinds of laws, regulations, and/or policies, if any, did Sterling break in his attempt to get this student turned on to learning?

34. Did the end justify the means?

35. Would you use similar methods under the same circumstances? Why?

36. What programs, if any, does your school have to accommodate students such as Billy?

What if . . . Billy had been injured in the process of repairing Sterling's car?

Does It Make a Difference if the Gun Is Loaded?

37. Should Sterling have called for police assistance earlier than he did?

38. What is the principal's role (responsibility) in protecting students on the school grounds during the school day?

What if . . . a student had been hurt or killed in either of the confrontations with the stranger?

3

A Transition

Will the Real Mighty Mouse Please Stand Up?

After 4 years as principal at Center, Sterling found the closing of the school year a routine matter. Student schedules for the next school year were completed, teacher assignments were solidified, and the process of ordering supplies, materials, and equipment was well under way. He'd given the custodial crew its marching orders, and people could be heard moving equipment from rooms, exposing floors and walls for cleaning.

As Sterling examined a stack of purchase orders, wondering again why teachers always wanted more four-drawer file cabinets and coaches continuously ordered additional stopwatches, Bob Wainwright, assistant superintendent for personnel, casually wandered in.

"That's a beautiful mobile you've got hanging over your desk," Wainwright observed. "Got time for lunch? I'll buy."

"You're buying? That's a first. You bet I have time! You probably want to tell me that you've approved all those extra teachers I requested for next year! I can hardly wait!"

At the restaurant, Wainwright presented Sterling with the real reason for the impromptu lunch. "Grant, I've got some great news for you! The superintendent and the board are going to announce at tonight's meeting that you're being transferred to Arthur Junior High School, effective August 1. You've done a great job at Center. You know how happy we are about the way you've turned that place around. We want to provide you with a new challenge."

Sterling was stunned. "The district's highly energetic grapevine hasn't picked up on this," he thought.

Arthur was a suburban school in a wealthy neighborhood, and Sterling had heard that the Arthur community had been petitioning the board to replace the current principal. John Bestinato had been the principal at Arthur for 16 years. But in the past few years, the school had been besieged with drug and gang activity that had led to monumental discipline and vandalism problems.

"Bob, should I look at this as what central office likes to call another vertical step on the ladder to greater things?"

Wainwright laughed. "Look Grant, you and I both know that you're not walking into a bed of roses. But after what you did at Center, we need your expertise there. Let's say that you're moving from one clean-up job to another. The superintendent and the board believe that you're the person for the job. Bottom line: You've got no choice. The board will approve your transfer tonight, and it will hit the news tomorrow morning."

Conversation changed abruptly as the waitress returned to their table with their lunch orders. As Wainwright continued with small talk about the weather, a canceled fishing trip, and the like, Sterling's mind ran through a multitude of concerns and questions. He signaled his acceptance of the new assignment by moving the conversation back to the matter at hand.

"I guess tomorrow is going to be a busy day for me," he said. "I'll have to answer tons of questions from parents and students. My faculty and staff may need some optimistic words. Or maybe they'll be glad to get rid of me. Who's my replacement at Center?"

"We're not ready to make that announcement yet. To be honest with you, we don't have a clue. I can tell you this, though—in strict confidence mind you—because if this word got out early, we'd be in deep trouble. We're going to close Center at the end of next school year. Center kids will go to Bidwell or East River, depending on what the board does with neighborhood attendance lines. We've got to break up the high minority population at Center. The Center community will be notified of the impending closure after the board announces the new principal, probably at the August 1 meeting. Also—again in strict confidence—Arthur, with its almost totally white student population, will be closed for the opposite reason 2 years from now. You'll be at that school only for a short time. The community at Arthur will hear about the closing during the middle of your second year there." Wainwright looked closely at Sterling. "The way I figure," he laughed, "you've got a year to get the place back to educational excellence, a half year to pat yourself on the back, and then all hell will break loose when we announce the closing. Aren't you excited?"

"Geez, Bob, talk about a challenge. Tell me, will I see my effort reflected in my paycheck, in advance, so I can pay off my bills before I'm lynched?"

"As a matter of fact, I have your new contract in my coat pocket. Take a look. I think you'll like the raise. But please don't share with anyone what the board is going to do tonight. I know that's tough, but we have to wait until after it acts."

"I understand," Sterling said, leafing through the papers Wainwright handed him. "I'm looking for the death benefits clause. Is it in here?" Sterling laughed as he signed the contract, tore off his copy, and handed the original back to Wainwright. "You're buying dessert, too, aren't you? The salary increase isn't that generous!"

Later, as Wainwright dropped Sterling off at Center, he saw a new crop of kids playing streetball on the outdoor court.

"Hi guys," Sterling shouted.

"What's up, Mr. Sterling? Wanna play?"

Sterling smiled and waved them off as he opened the spotless main door and slowly walked upstairs to his office, stopping for a moment to run his hand over the worn marble steps.

"Whatja bring me?" Bob Sandinburg hollered over his shoulder as he pushed a cart of cleaning supplies down the hall.

"Good lunch, Grant?" Jeannie asked as he walked by her desk.

"Just fine, Jeannie."

Sterling spent the rest of the afternoon reviewing repair orders and signing off on the school's updated inventory. As he worked, he stopped frequently to jot a note to himself on his ever-present things-to-do list. He wrote down the home phone numbers for Jeannie and Bob Sandinburg and stuck them in a pocket. Sterling intended to call them at home after the board made its announcement. "It'll be easier around the office tomorrow morning if the transfer announcement comes directly from me and not the newspaper."

Sterling fought the melancholy mood he found himself drifting into. His drive home was slower and longer that afternoon as he purposely drove by Arthur Junior High. Although he had been in the school a few times in the past, he had never thought of it as "his school." From the street, he could see the words "Fuck You" spray-painted on the front door.

"Here we go again," he reflected as he drove away. That thought triggered a familiar cartoon character in his memory, and he cheered himself on the way home by quietly singing the character's theme song. "Here I come to save the day, Mighty Mouse is on the way! When there is a wrong to right, Mighty Mouse will join the fight!" In spite of his spirited vocalizing, he soon returned to a somber analysis of the work ahead.

"I've got to get the Center folks psychologically prepared for their new principal, and I've got to get myself mentally and physically primed to tackle Arthur! I'm going to miss Center."

That evening, Sterling tried to relax, but his eyes kept wandering from the clock to the telephone. He'd chosen to skip the board of education meeting that evening in an attempt to avoid reporters. He would deal with them tomorrow. He'd called Lois, the switchboard operator at the central administration building, and asked her to call him at home when the board adjourned for the evening. He was anxious to call Jeannie and Bob as soon as possible, even though he was not looking forward to either conversation.

"I guess I asked for this, didn't I?" Sterling mused. "I suppose my reputation as a 'get-things-done' administrator got started with the 'Greta' incident, shortly after I took over as music supervisor from old C. J. McNabb." He laughed aloud, his thoughts drifting back to that first meeting with the elementary principals. He had been nervous, and the meeting room was hot and crowded. Everyone there was probably wishing to be somewhere else. He had just given his "Hi, here I am . . . I'm here to help you" speech when he had been interrupted by a impatient-sounding questioner from the back of the room. "Who gets Greta this year?"

"I'm sorry, I didn't quite hear you," he'd said, looking for the owner of the voice in the crowded room.

"Who. Gets. Greta. This. Year?" the voice repeated.

"I'm sorry, I don't understand." While he continued to try to locate the source of the question, Ted Summers, president of the elementary principals' association, approached him, pulled him aside, and quickly explained that Greta Thompson, an elementary traveling music teacher, was universally disliked by the principals. "What they want to know," he said, "is which schools she is scheduled to travel to this year; in other words, who gets stuck with her?"

Sterling recognized the awkwardness of the situation as he stepped back to the microphone. "I don't have that information with me—I know that Mr. McNabb made those assignments in late spring, I'll check the file and call whoever is scheduled to have Mrs. Thompson." He hadn't done his homework, and his response was met with a groan of displeasure.

"Boy, I'm really off to a lousy start with those folks," he'd repeated over and over to himself as he looked through the files for a folder marked "Itinerant Music Teacher Assignments."

He'd been surprised to find that McNabb and the elementary principals had set up a rotation schedule for Thompson so that they would have to deal with her only once every 6 years. That revelation caused him to be curious to see what they had said about her on their end-of-year evaluations. He'd driven over to the central administrative office, where copies of all personnel evaluations were housed.

He was amazed to find that over her 15 years in the district, she had never been evaluated as even satisfactory. All her evaluations were, in fact, marked unsatisfactory. In some cases, principals had written "Please don't send her to my school again." He got the impression that nobody ever forced the issue.

He hadn't known what he was going to do to resolve the problem, but had called Greta at home and asked her to drop by and see him. She had shown up first thing the next morning.

"Greta, thanks for stopping by. I'd like to talk with you about your assignment for next school year," he'd said. "Here's the problem as I see it." Then, with no clear intention and not knowing that he was about to stumble into unpredicted success, he had cut to the bottom line and tactlessly said, "Look Greta, I spoke with the elementary principals yesterday and I was shocked to find out that none of them want you at their school. I don't know how to handle that. What do you suggest that I do about this situation?"

"Well! Mr. Sterling," she had huffed, glaring at him with a you're-a-bad-boy stare that he remembered from his own mother. "You certainly get right to the point, don't you?"

"I'm sorry, Greta, I just don't know what to do. I really don't know where to assign you!" he'd said, fumbling words around as he groped for the next thing to say.

"Well," she'd huffed again, "I'm not going where I'm not wanted. This has never happened before. C. J. sent me a note in the spring telling me what schools I'm supposed to travel to! I need a piece of paper and a pen, please!"

A bit puzzled, he'd opened his drawer, fished out a piece of paper, and handed her his pen.

"Please consider this my official resignation from the Greenway Public Schools, effective this date," she had hastily written, then signed and dated the paper and handed it to him.

As he read the document, she walked out of his office boasting, "My husband is a doctor. I don't need to work!"

The board of education had accepted her resignation at its next meeting, and he had become a temporary star in the eyes of the district's elementary principals.

"I really lucked out on that one!" Sterling laughed and leaned forward in his chair. "In retrospect," he grinned and shook his head, "a momentary lack of sensitivity and naive candor is probably what launched my career as a clean-up man."

His memories were abruptly interrupted when the phone rang. "Back to reality," he thought, "that will be 'switchboard Lois' telling me that the board has adjourned and that my next adventure has been matter-of-factly recorded in the minutes of the meeting."

The Center Finale

"Four years. Four extraordinary years," Sterling reflected as he pulled another cardboard box close to his desk. "When I leave this office, all my physical memories of Center will be neatly packed in boxes. My emotional memories will be forever captured in my mind and heart. Even though it wasn't always a picnic, I wouldn't swap my experiences here for anything. I have the feeling that my Center adventures won't—maybe can't is a better word—be matched anywhere else."

Sterling would soon forget the endless days and weekends resolving kid, parent, and staff problems, as well as the hundreds of meetings, events, activities, and district assignments that kept him from having much of a private life. He knew, however, that his time at Center had made him a stronger administrator and that no future challenge would surpass what he had experienced. Still, he was somewhat nervous about the Arthur situation. The curtain was about to open on an entirely new show with an entirely new cast and audience.

As Sterling sorted through his personal files, he found a tattered folder marked "IMPRESSIONS." "My scholarly, and not so scholarly, thoughts about adolescent kids and their parents," he noted. "I don't want to misplace this. Some day these musings are going to materialize in a school program that's specifically designed to meet the real needs of kids who are no longer children but not yet adults."

As he fingered through the collection of anecdotes, his attention was drawn to a poem that a student named Susie Godfrey had given him. He had discovered her crying in the hall one morning before her first class. She told him she had written it on the way to school that morning. It was written with a ballpoint pen, and the smeared ink still revealed evidence of Susie's tears.

> *When I look in the*
> *mirror each day,*
> *I see only me.*
> *Sometimes I wish*
> *it wasn't that way.*

After Sterling had listened to her for a few minutes—that's all she really needed, someone to talk at—she was able to go to class. Her problem that day was one step below the loss of a loved one . . . Susie discovered a pimple on her nose when she got out of bed that morning and neither of her parents had taken time to comfort her. Sterling had taped her poem to a blank sheet of paper and had scribbled below it "Susie's arrived at the age when she cares only for the approval and acceptance of peers. A misplaced pimple can be momentarily devastating to her self-esteem and, in turn, ruin her whole day. While I couldn't make her pimple disappear, maybe I helped her make it through the day."

"Kids are kids, no matter where you are." Sterling tried to comfort himself with that thought as he closed the folder and laid it in a box. "The kids at Arthur will provide me with the same excitement, challenges, and daily surprises that the kids at Center have for the past few years. But even so, it's tough leaving this particular community."

A Sterling Moment (Friday)

Sterling had just finished filling the last box to be moved to Arthur when he heard a familiar tapping on his door.

"Mrs. Gamino! It must be Friday, 4:30 again. You're a sweetheart!"

Mrs. Gamino and her husband, both immigrants from Guatemala, had seven children, one or two of whom were always enrolled at Center. Early in Sterling's first year at Center, Mrs. Gamino started bringing a small paper bag to his office at exactly 4:30 p.m. every Friday. The bag contained a food item that only she could identify by name carefully wrapped in foil. In addition, she always included a can of beer.

"It's our way," she had told Sterling in hesitant English, "to say thank you for teaching our children this week."

Mrs. Gamino had never missed a Friday and today, as Sterling completed his final day at Center, was no exception.

Sterling looked at her with a smile and said, "I'm really going to miss your treats . . . I'm going to miss you too. Oh, wait a minute! Come on now, Mrs. Gamino . . . cut that out! No tears allowed today. You'll make me cry." She did.

For Discussion

General Questions

Using the Sterling paradigm (http://www.corwinpress.com/dunklee.htm) as a model, and speaking from the perspective of a principal, evaluate each episode as follows:

What are the dominant behaviors exhibited by Sterling in this episode?

Is there consensus about this in the class? If not, explain the different viewpoints.

What were the primary actors' individual motives?

How effective was Sterling's behavior in this situation and why?

Can you identify other avenues or approaches that might lead to the same, or a better, conclusion?

If Sterling was a woman,

- As a female reader, can you identify methodology or behavior that you would change to bring the episode to the same, or similar, closure?

- As a male reader, what differences in methodology or behavior would you expect to see?

Specific Questions for Each Episode

Will the Real Mighty Mouse Please Stand Up?

1. Assuming that some steps in everyone's career ladder may be "starting over," what kind of individual mind-set is necessary for personal and professional survival?

2. How much input do middle management administrators usually have on their job assignments or their personal career goals? Why?

3. What would cause a school district to keep a substandard employee in any role?

The Center Finale

4. Do you, like Sterling, believe that "kids are kids, no matter where you are?" Why?

A Sterling Moment (Friday)

(No specific questions)

4 ᐳᐳ

The Arthur Years

Reestablishing a Power Base

Sterling had spent the past few weeks preparing Center for the upcoming school year. He'd wanted the transition to be as smooth as possible for his yet-unnamed successor. He hoped the same courtesy would be extended to him by Arthur's departing principal, John Bestinato.

He'd talked briefly to Bestinato the day after the board of education announced his transfer. Bestinato was angry that he was being reassigned to a nonleadership position in one of the district's counseling offices. He felt that the board hadn't given him the support he needed and that he was being put out to pasture.

"You're welcome to this crappy job," he told Sterling. "I hope you have better luck with this pompous, self-righteous community than I've had the past few years. They don't want a principal here . . . they want a puppet! I've heard about your style, Grant, you'll be lucky to last more than a few months past your honeymoon year! I'll give you 2 years, if you're lucky enough not to get your strings tangled." Bestinato hadn't been told that the school was going to close in 2 years.

Sterling had made an appointment to meet with Bestinato to get the basic information he needed about Arthur. Bestinato pledged to continue normal organizational activities until the day Sterling was scheduled to take over.

Assured that Bestinato was handling the fall planning for Arthur, Sterling continued the necessary routine of getting Center ready for the fall semester. In addition, he initiated the same preplanning strategy for Arthur that he had crafted when he first went to Center. He met with program-area supervisors to discuss Arthur's faculty and program strengths and weaknesses. He also visited with as many central office personnel and Arthur community leaders as possible. His job for the final 5 weeks, he'd felt, would be threefold: keeping Center on track; learning as much as he could about Arthur; and, hardest of all, responding to the Center community's apprehension about a new principal.

"I know they'll choose the right person for this job. Don't worry, everything will be all right. I'm sorry, but I have to go. I'll miss you all." Sterling could be sure of only the latter as he'd responded to people's anxiety.

Sterling's interaction with the community was made more difficult when he learned that Center community phone calls to the superintendent's office protesting his transfer were seemingly being ignored. He found out later that the calls were being forwarded to the office of Dr. Washington. Washington was director of minority affairs and the person Ida Wood had labeled an Oreo early in Sterling's career at Center. Washington was now playing "get even" with Sterling for not including him in Center activities. He was purposely avoiding the community's calls.

A flurry of formal requests from a number of Center teachers wanting to be transferred to Arthur was also a problem. Sterling could respond to them only by stating that all requests would be placed on file and, if Arthur had any openings, the requests would be considered. He knew, however, that he would not break up the strong faculty team he had worked so hard to develop at Center.

A new principal for Center was finally selected; Gene Hathaway was named to succeed Sterling. Hathaway had been a high school coach and athletic director and was a vice principal at one of the district's high schools. He had the reputation of being a tough disciplinarian with a hair-trigger temper.

"I hope this guy knows how to love. The Center community doesn't need to be told how to line up." Sterling had doubts about Hathaway's ability to succeed with the Center community. "But, a whole bunch of people thought the same about me when I came to Center." Sterling kept his reservations about Hathaway to himself.

After a series of meetings with Hathaway, Sterling handed his keys to his successor, said good-bye to his summer staff, and headed out the door. He turned and looked at the Center building for a moment. "This has been a difficult, but fun experience," he thought. "I'll be able to use my experiences at Center as a frame of reference, but I know that reforming Arthur will require building a personal power base all over again. I'm going to have to use my personality to sell myself and my methods of leadership to an entirely different community."

He couldn't help recalling, as he thought about Arthur, the admonition of his high school counselor when he told her that he planned to go to college to get a degree in education. "I want to teach," he had told her.

"Forget college," she had coldly responded. "Your aptitude test scores show that you don't have any talent in that area. But, with your personality, you might become a good salesman." Sterling liked what she said about his salesman personality, but her declaration about his ambition to teach became a lifelong "eat crow" challenge.

Turning a minus into a plus, a challenge into a victory, had always been a part of Sterling's nature. Maybe it was his style of life or his personality, but he felt the drive to overcome weakness or adversity as a creative force in his work. He knew that creativity, when successfully combined with personality, usually resulted in what he called personal power—the ability to influence others, apart from organizational skills or the power given automatically with a position of leadership, was his personal power. He also knew that the community and organizational climate at Arthur were dictated by a community with power—that is, a community of wealth that served as the power elite for the rest of the city. Anyone who was anyone lived in the Arthur school community and believed that they possessed the right to set the rules and run "their" school.

Although the Center adventure had been a great learning experience for him, Sterling knew that each school's problems were unique and that the situation at Arthur was quite different than the one he had inherited at Center. Some things were the same, however. Like Center, Arthur had been without real leadership in the past few years. Sterling would, again, have to exert strong leadership and convince the community that the school was in good hands. To do this, he'd need to build a base of support.

He remembered a warning that Wainwright had given him when they first discussed the Arthur position. "Anytime anything went wrong at Center," he had said, "the folks confronted you face to face. In schools like Arthur, when things go wrong, they'll stab you from behind. You won't hear their grievances directly . . . you'll hear them secondhand from the superintendent or president of the board."

As Sterling approached Arthur's front door, he thought, "At Center it was fire, ready, and then aim. The new game plan may be ready, check the politics. Aim, recheck the politics. Then fire and prepare for the political recoil."

Old Melody, New Lyric, and a Surprise Turn of Events

The situation at Arthur was typical of a school that had lacked administrative direction. One of the first things Sterling noticed was the lack of custodial pride in the building. "Every so often," he grumbled to himself, "custodians have to be reminded that there's more to a school building than shiny floors. They need to be prompted to look up to see walls, windows, ceilings, and light fixtures." Clearly, this was something that this school's crew had not been told.

Arthur's head secretary, Peggy Landry, had anticipated what Sterling would want to examine first. She met Sterling at the office door with a notebook filled with pertinent information she thought Sterling would need to ensure a smooth administrative transition.

"Peggy, you're Bill Landry's sister-in-law aren't you? Your husband is a coach at Moundview, isn't he?" Sterling smiled as he greeted her. Bill Landry was principal at Milestone Junior High. Landry and Sterling had been appointed to their first principalships at the same time.

"Yes, and yes," Landry responded. "I've heard a lot about you, Mr. Sterling," she continued. "In fact, I just got off the phone with Jeannie at Center. I wanted to go over this notebook with her to see if I had guessed right on what you would want to look at right away."

"Fantastic," Sterling said as he shook her hand. "So tell me, did you guess right?"

"I think so," she beamed as she handed the notebook to Sterling. "Here, let me show you your new office."

"I can only stay for a few minutes today," Sterling said. "I'll take the notebook with me and study it this evening. We'll talk about it tomorrow. I have a meeting with Mr. Bestinato later this morning, and then I've been summoned to a conference with Associate Superintendent Robb at 1 o'clock. I think, however, that I'd like to meet the head custodian and take a short tour of the building before I go."

"Sounds like you've got a busy day ahead of you, Mr. Sterling," she said as she walked over to the main intercom and pushed the master bell button twice. "He'll respond to the bell and be here in a minute. Have you met him?"

"No, I haven't," Sterling said. "Please call me Grant, Peggy."

"His name is Ralph Saxton, Grant. He's been with us for just a short time. His predecessor had been here since the building opened and retired last year. Ralph's been having some problems, and I'm sure he'll want to discuss those with you right away."

"You rang?" Saxton asked has he opened the office door.

"Ralph, this is Grant Sterling, our new principal."

"Mr. Sterling, happy to meet you. Welcome to Arthur."

Sterling shook his hand. "I'm glad to meet you Ralph. Please call me Grant. I can only stay for a little while this morning. Do you have a few minutes to show me around the building?"

As Saxton escorted Sterling around the building, he seemed to be apologizing continuously that this hadn't been done yet or that hadn't been fixed yet. Sterling finally interrupted him.

"Ralph, do you realize that you haven't told me anything positive about the building yet? What's the real problem?"

"Well," Ralph hesitated for a moment and then the dam broke. "We've been eating up all the time that we should be spending on cleaning putting things back together. This spring's graduating ninth graders decided to get even with Mr. Bestinato for screwing up their spring party. He got fed up with their discipline, or attitude, or something, and canceled it at the last minute. They were really angry! To get even, I guess, they brought screwdrivers and pliers to school during the last few days of the school year and unscrewed or unbolted almost everything in the building. Desks, tables, light switch and socket covers, you name it, they dismantled it. They managed to sabotage everything they could before the last day of school. They were either really sneaky about it or teachers ignored it—maybe both, I don't know. All I know is that my crew and I have our hands full putting stuff back together before we can start cleaning."

"Let me see if I can get you some help," Sterling said. "I'll let you know tomorrow. If I can, I'll want you and your crew to concentrate on getting the building in tip-top shape for the start of school. Fair enough?"

Ralph could hardly turn down a deal like that.

Sterling excused himself to leave for his meeting with Bestinato, who had requested that Sterling come to his house for the meeting. He didn't want to meet him at Arthur, and Sterling now knew why.

The meeting with Bestinato was not helpful. His bitterness about his transfer was still apparent and overshadowed anything constructive that Sterling could use to become better acquainted with the Arthur community.

"Maybe the man just needs to retire," Sterling thought as he left and headed toward the central administration building. He wanted to get there a few minutes early so he could contact Steve Burgess, his administrative contact at the school district shop. He'd ask Burgess to send a crew out to repair the damage done by the ninth-grade class and remove or repaint any areas covered with graffiti. He knew that Burgess would follow through with his request without any problem. He had sent Burgess a number of complimentary letters, purposely forwarding copies to the superintendent, about his cooperation with Sterling at Center.

After reaching a quick agreement with Burgess, Sterling waited outside the associate superintendent's office for the 1:00 conference. He had just started to peruse the notebook Landry had given him that morning when he was interrupted.

"Have I got a deal for you," Howard Robb boasted as he ushered Sterling into his office and closed the door. "You know, you're going to have an easy time the next 2 years at Arthur," he said. "No more of that welfare and race relations stuff. You're on the west side now, where you've got good kids and good parents."

Although he found Robb's comment appalling, Sterling was not surprised. Robb had never worked anywhere except in predominately white schools, and his view of urban schools was biased, if not outright prejudiced. In addition, he'd been in central office so long that he had no idea what a modern principalship was all about. In his day, the school office was a proverbial ivory tower, where the biggest problem was deciding with which community club group he should have lunch that day for so-called public relations purposes.

"He should be assigned to Center for about a week for inservice training," Sterling thought. "But that wouldn't be fair to the kids!"

"Look, you're going to have some spare time at Arthur," Robb continued, "and there's a special project I want you to work on for me. Now, what I'm going to share with you is confidential. I know that Wainwright told you that Arthur is going to be closed in 2 years. What he didn't tell you, however, is the rest of the plan."

Robb explained that the board was secretly studying, and would most likely approve, a much larger plan than the mere closing of Arthur. "At the end of next year, the superintendent and the board will announce that half of the district's junior high schools will be closed at the end of the next school term. Those remaining will be converted from a junior high format to a middle school format. In other words," he continued, "we're going to switch to a middle school program with appropriate curricular and extracurricular offerings. We hope to move all ninth-grade classes to the high school and all sixth-grade classes to the new middle schools. Instead of the current 7, 8, 9 configuration, we'll have a 6, 7, 8 configuration."

Sterling was elated at what he was hearing. He'd advocated a change to middle school concepts for 2 years. He felt that junior highs were rapidly becoming miniature high schools. When kids got to high school, it was nothing but a repeat of what they had done in junior high school—same curricular offerings, same extracurricular activities, including sports and cheerleaders.

"Maybe someone finally heard me," he momentarily thought.

"We're losing enrollment all along the line," Robb declared, "and we need to close some schools. This is the easiest way to do it. We can really save some big bucks with this plan."

"So," Sterling injudiciously reacted. "This is not really about providing adolescent kids with the kind of education they need, but rather a way to save money?"

"Come on, Grant, don't look at it that way. We can do both. This is an opportunity to make some of the things you've been talking about for the past few years come true!"

Not wishing to debate the rationale for the move further, Sterling simply promised his support and asked what he could do to assist.

"Well, Grant, we—the superintendent and I—want you to develop a program of studies and a profile of middle school activities for us to present to the board and, eventually, to the community. Make it a 5-year developmental plan and synthesize as complete a picture as possible. We need something in black and white that we can use to market our rationale for school closings. I promise you, in return, that we will give you complete freedom to pilot your program at your next school. You can be the first in the district to have a middle school that you've designed."

"Can I choose the school?" Sterling laughingly asked. Robb didn't bother to respond.

"I'll have a plan for you to examine as soon as possible," Sterling promised as he got up to leave. "I've got to get my feet on the ground at Arthur first, but you'll be pleased with the presentation materials I'm going to develop for you later this fall."

As he drove away from the administration building that afternoon, he knew he had his hands full. Clean up Arthur while developing a clandestine plan for redevelopment of the district's entire middle education program. This may, in fact, be a job for Mighty Mouse!

"Isn't it amazing," he pondered, "that school districts seldom decide to make major changes because it's good for kids. Too often, change happens because it's 'budgetarily expedient.' "

Off Again

The building was starting to take shape, with school district maintenance personnel and custodians working toward the moment when the bell would ring announcing the first day of school. Sterling had his annual welcome-back letter in the mail and had finished his traditional one-on-one meetings with teachers and staff. He was ready and anxious for the first faculty meeting so he could lay out his plan for the school year.

His biggest problem this year, he felt, would be to protect faculty, staff, and kids from the inevitable rumors concerning the closing of Arthur in 2 years. In the meantime, he would manage the school in the same manner he had at Center. Teachers teach, students learn, and everybody has fun doing just that.

He could see no other major problems. He had a good faculty, for the most part, and a population of students that had good guidance at home. Most of the previous problems at Arthur had been the result of poor management that led to remarkably diminished student and faculty morale. Sterling was confident he could resolve that situation easily. He felt that his experiences at Center had more than prepared him for any problems at Arthur, except for next year's announcement of the closing of the school and the obvious negative effects that would have on morale. In the meantime, he would manage the facilities and budget, guide and nurture teachers and parents, help students survive their adolescent propensity to screw up, and develop a *sub rosa* strategy for the district's transition from junior high to middle school. Although he had a logical plan for Arthur, he expected it would be continuously interrupted. He had his ducks in a row, waiting for the tide that would send them drifting in every direction.

The first faculty meeting before school officially started went smoothly, with the usual "what ifs . . . how are we going tos . . ." asked and answered.

Sterling's first meeting with students was also smooth, followed by the usual hubbub in the halls with kids trying to find their lockers, identify their classrooms, and visit with long-lost friends. Sterling and the faculty patrolled the halls, comforting seventh graders who couldn't figure out how combination locks work or where their classrooms were located.

Sterling had scheduled his first parent meeting that same evening. From what he had heard from parents and teachers, the school's auditorium would be packed. Parents in the Arthur community readily attended such functions, and he knew that his prepared remarks needed to be concentrated and energetic. During the meeting, Sterling carefully laid out his goals for the year and asked parents for their support and guidance. He announced his open door policy, invited parents to visit the school and the principal at any time, and assured them that he welcomed their inquiries.

He also presented a list of special equipment he thought the school ought to have. He told parents that he had asked the Arthur faculty to present him with wish lists outlining any items of equipment that would assist them and students in the teaching-learning process.

"When all their lists were put together, and I had marked out a few items that might be considered frivolous," Sterling announced, "I was surprised at the amount of money I would need to fulfill their requests. $13,000! I was able to meet $5,000 of their requests. That leaves me $8,000 yet to raise. You can expect some major fund-raising projects this year," he laughed.

After the meeting, Sterling was mingling with parents when a man pulled him aside. "I want to write you a check, a donation," he said. "Should I make this out to Arthur Junior High? Would you please send me a receipt for this? I'm Richard Gordon," he announced. "My daughter Shelly is a seventh grader at your school this year."

"Mr. Gordon, I'm pleased to meet you, and I look forward to meeting your daughter," Sterling said as he shook Gordon's hand. "Thank you for your consideration. I hope my remarks about raising money didn't sound like begging."

"Oh, no," Gordon casually replied. "You just hit me at the right time. My tax attorney told me just today that my company could use some additional tax write-offs. Here, maybe this will help both of us."

Sterling thanked him again, folded the check, and placed it in his pocket. He returned to his schmoozing, and could be heard repeating himself over and over as he moved from one group of parents to another. "Hi, I'm Grant Sterling, glad you could make it tonight. Hi, I'm Grant Sterling . . ."

"What a long day!" Sterling was tired as he returned to his office after the building emptied. "Let's get this show finally on the road. Tomorrow the routine starts, and I'm more than ready." He started to turn off his office lights when he remembered the check from Mr. Gordon. "I'd better leave this here in a safe place tonight. I'll give it to Peggy tomorrow for her to deposit." Sterling unfolded the check and read the amount. "Eight thousand dollars? EIGHT THOUSAND!" Sterling couldn't believe what he was seeing. "This is clearly not the Center community," he reflected. "Wow, this is really something!"

Although he was excited by the day's successes, he couldn't help feeling, as he drove home that night, that he was misleading kids, faculty, and parents. He couldn't tell them that their school was slated for mothballing. Instead of his Center experience of long-range planning and building, he would be pretending to plan the school's growth while secretly planning its demise.

For Discussion

General Questions

Using the Sterling paradigm (http://www.corwinpress.com/dunklee.htm) as a model, and speaking from the perspective of a principal, evaluate each episode as follows:

What are the dominant behaviors exhibited by Sterling in this episode?

Is there consensus about this in the class? If not, explain the different viewpoints.

What were the primary actors' individual motives?

How effective was Sterling's behavior in this situation and why?

Can you identify other avenues or approaches that might lead to the same, or a better, conclusion?

If Sterling was a woman,

▪ As a female reader, can you identify methodology or behavior that you would change to bring the episode to the same, or similar, closure?

▪ As a male reader, what differences in methodology or behavior would you expect to see?

Specific Questions for Each Episode

Reestablishing a Power Base

1. What sources of power available to a principal do you think are the most effective? Why?

2. How much influence do you think a community can exercise on the climate of a school?

3. Why did Washington ignore the Center community's phone calls?

4. Is the maintenance of a working teacher team more important than an individual teacher's request for a transfer? Why or why not?

What if . . . Sterling had chosen to take his core team of teachers with him when he moved from Center to Arthur, and central office had allowed him to do so?

Old Melody, New Lyric, and a Surprise Turn of Events

5. Do you agree with Sterling's assessment that school districts often make important decisions not on the basis of what's good for students but rather for budgetary or political expedience?

6. If Sterling had not been interested in developing the middle school program, could he have graciously declined the offer? Explain.

Off Again

7. What does this episode illustrate about the complex role of a principal or other middle manager?

A Stitch in Time?

"Grant, I need you right now! In my classroom! We've got a problem!"

Roxie Caldwell, a ninth-grade English teacher, was standing at the office door demanding attention. She was livid. Fearing the worst, Sterling dropped what he was doing and followed Caldwell as she huffed and stomped down the hall.

"Roxie, what's up?"

"You'll see, you'll see!" She snapped out her words with conspicuous anger. "I've had it with these kids, just had it!" She yelled over her shoulder at Sterling who was trying his best to keep up with her combative pace. "Look, just look," Caldwell glared at Sterling as he entered her classroom.

Maybe it was the time of day, maybe it was his eyesight; Sterling looked at the classroom and saw 25 or so students sitting erect and very attentive in their neatly arranged desks. The room was silent except for the intensifying prodding by Caldwell for Sterling to "see what they've done, can't you see it, just look!"

Sterling was beginning to think that Caldwell had lost it. He walked slowly toward the first row of students.

"Who can tell me what's going on?" he asked. The room remained silent as he started down an aisle. Suddenly he felt a resistance across his thighs causing him to jump back.

"What the hell was that?" he thought as he kneeled down to get a better look at whatever was keeping him from walking between the aisles of student desks. All eyes were focused on him as he slowly proceeded with his detective work.

"Now, I see what's going on here." He had found the problem—a length of heavy-duty black nylon fishing line securely attached. No, not attached, he discovered, peering along the line, but strung from desk frame to desk frame throughout the room.

His mind raced to a conclusion. Somebody had brought a large spool of almost invisible fishing line to school today, tied one end to his or her desk, and the class had spent the rest of the period secretly passing the spool from desk to desk. The class had managed to weave a giant web of 500-pound thread that was now preventing them from leaving Caldwell's meticulously arranged rows of student desks.

Sterling suddenly found himself overwhelmed with the ridiculousness of the scene. While Caldwell made huffing noises in the background, the students looked straight at him with sweet, innocent, if not a bit sheepish, expressions on their faces. They were clearly waiting for him to say something. The class change bell had rung, and a new batch of students stood in the hall waiting to come into the room, wondering what was going on. Sterling needed to act!

He could not control himself any longer and he broke out in laughter. This was the funniest scene he had ever witnessed in a school classroom. "This class should get an award for innovation," he thought as he opened Caldwell's desk drawer and grabbed a pair of scissors.

Caldwell stomped out of the room, pushing students who were now trying to peek into the room out of her way. The class was stunned by Sterling's outburst, but remained stoic waiting for the inevitable ax to fall.

Sterling gently handed the scissors to a student in the front row. "Start cutting, and pass the scissors around," Sterling said in a now very authoritative voice. "I assume that this will never happen again, and that you understand you would have been in big trouble if we had to evacuate the building for a fire or something. Although I think what you did was clever, if anyone else at Arthur attempts to copy your actions, I will hold this entire class responsible, and punishment will be fast and unpleasant. Get the word out!"

After clearing the room and getting Caldwell's next class in place, Sterling located Caldwell. He had guessed right. She was grouching to anyone who would listen in the teachers' lounge.

"Your next class is waiting, Roxie. I talked with the kids about the fishing line stuff and it won't happen again. Just pretend it didn't happen today!"

Sterling knew that Caldwell would never forget the incident. "Oh," he reasoned, "she'll soon forget about what the kids did, but she'll never forget my immediate response. She'll be angry at me for years, but when she tries to tell the story to anyone else, they're gonna see the humor in it and laugh. *C'est la vie.*"

Hold the Phone

The ninth-grade spring party is going well, Sterling thought as he left the gym. The kids had picked a good disc jockey and were gyrating happily to the music. He felt he had enough supervision at the party to allow him to take a few minutes to catch up on paperwork in his office. He had just opened a folder on his desk when he heard the office door open.

"Grant, you in here? We've got a problem."

"What's up, Tom?" Sterling closed the folder as Tom Bennett, one of the teachers supervising the party, stuck his head in the door.

"Gloria and I have Ruby Washburn in the girls' restroom down by the gym," Bennett said. "She's barfing up most of the pint of vodka Gloria found her with in the girls' locker room." Gloria Levy was also an Arthur teacher supervising the party.

"All right," sighed Sterling, "I'll call her parents." Bennett couldn't help laughing at Sterling's disgusted expression.

"What are you laughing about?" Sterling shot a grinning glare at Bennett.

"I'm just glad it's you that has to deal with her parents and not me," Bennett replied sympathetically. Bennett and Sterling both knew that Ruby's parents were not going to receive the news about Ruby calmly. Following past practice, they would probably look for some way to blame the school.

Confident that Ruby was being taken care of by Levy and Bennett, Sterling looked up the Washburns' phone number and prepared for the worst. Sterling had never been able to develop a working rapport with the Washburns. Ruby was immature for her age and had emotional problems. She spent a lot of time in the school counselor's office for a continuous string of conflicts with teachers and students. Ruby's father was president of a local college, and her mother was a full-time socialite. They acted like Ruby was an embarrassment to them.

Earlier in the year, Sterling had suspended Ruby from school for calling one of her teachers a "bitch." The parents blamed the teacher and Sterling. Dr. Washburn had called each member of the board of education to complain about the "mistreatment" of his daughter at Arthur and to demand Sterling's transfer. Sterling spent hours on the phone with the superintendent and others while they tried to pacify Ruby's parents.

"Here we go again," Sterling was thinking as the phone rang at the Washburn residence.

"No, I'm sorry, Mr. Sterling. Dr. and Mrs. Washburn aren't here," said the Washburns' maid. "May I take a message?"

"Ma'am," Sterling continued, "it's very important that I reach them immediately; we have an emergency with Ruby at school."

"I can't give you the number where they are, Mr. Sterling. I'll see if I can reach them and have them call you. May I have your number?"

As Sterling waited for the call from Ruby's parents, he worried about Ruby. "She's going to get triple punishment," he feared. "She's going to be in trouble for drinking, in trouble for getting suspended from school again, and she's probably going to get caught in the middle of her parents' ongoing conflict with the school."

Within 10 minutes the phone rang.

"How dare you interrupt us . . . chasing us down through our housekeeper . . . getting her all upset about a so-called emergency. Is this another attempt on your part to embarrass us?"

Sterling hesitated for a moment, fighting off the urge to respond with something like, "Of course, you pompous dipshit. Why else would I call you?"

"Dr. Washburn, thanks for your prompt attention to my call. It seems that Ruby got hold of a bottle of vodka and is very drunk and very sick. I need to have you pick her up as soon as possible."

Washburn replied quickly and angrily to Sterling's announcement. "You little son of a bitch. Ruby doesn't drink. What kind of a stupid game are you playing this time?"

"Dr. Washburn, you must pick Ruby up now. She's very ill and needs to go home. I'll be glad, if you're too busy, to call an ambulance and have her transported to the emergency room. You could pick her up there if that would be easier." Sterling was now fighting the impulse to sound sarcastic. He knew he needed to be extremely careful and very professional.

Just then he saw Gloria Levy walk by the office door supporting Ruby as she stumbled toward the school clinic.

"Hold the phone, Dr. Washburn. I'll see if Ruby can talk to you."

"Gloria," Sterling hollered, "bring Ruby in here, please, so she can talk to her dad."

"Ruby," Sterling handed the phone to Ruby as he supported her with his left hand. "I have your dad on the phone. He wants to talk to you."

Ruby dropped the receiver on the counter, laid her head beside it and half slurred, half whimpered in a soprano voice, "Daddy, I'm not drunk." Suddenly, as if on cue, she let loose with a long piercing burp followed by a series of gagging sounds as she threw up all over the receiver and the counter.

Sterling gingerly picked up the receiver with two fingers. "Dr. Washburn, I rest my case. Come pick up your daughter now, please!"

Sterling gently laid the receiver on the phone, got some paper towels and cleaned up the phone and the counter as he waited to see if Ruby's parents would come for her. He alerted Gloria to watch for them and help get Ruby into the car. About 30 minutes later, he watched through the office window as Gloria and Dr. Washburn helped Ruby to the car.

"Maybe she'll barf all over his tuxedo," Sterling hoped as they drove away.

Before returning to the gym to join the kids in their fun, he called the superintendent to apprise him of the situation and to warn him of the possibility of another confrontation. Later, as the kids struggled to teach Sterling a new dance, he couldn't help thinking, "These kids have no idea they are associating with a 'little S.O.B.' "

Ruby was suspended from school for the remainder of the semester. Sterling was relieved that Washburn didn't attempt to get him transferred as he had with the previous incident. Sterling wasn't surprised to hear that Washburn's contract wasn't going to be renewed at the college at the end of that year. "Anybody with that kind of temper and insensitivity shouldn't be in education," he thought. He hoped that Ruby was getting some help.

Kids Deserve the Best

"Ben, I've made four visits to the gym at various times during the past few weeks to observe your classes. And to be honest with you, I'm not pleased with what I've seen. Answer a couple of questions for me, and perhaps I'll feel better."

"Fire away, Grant," Ben Edwards said with a puzzled expression on his face as he sat in Sterling's office. Edwards was in his second year at Arthur, and his previous evaluations had been marginal. Sterling had heard from his former PE teachers at Center that Edwards was lazy and very immature. He had also heard from some Arthur parents that the only reason Edwards was hired was that his father, Howard Edwards, was the principal of one of the district's elementary schools and a personal friend of Arthur's former principal, John Bestinato. Sterling was not interested in ancestry or secondhand information today; he simply wanted Ben Edwards to respond to the two questions he was about to ask.

"Each time I've visited your classes, your students have been playing dodge ball, or bombardment, or whatever you call it," Sterling said. "Hasn't that activity been declared dangerous, and haven't you PE folks been told by your district supervisor that this is an improper class activity?"

"Well, I don't know if he ever told us that," Edwards responded. "All I know is that the kids beg me all the time to let them play it. It's good physical activity."

"Yeah, but don't you agree it's a dangerous activity?" Sterling asked.

"Oh, I don't think so, Grant! I've never had anybody hurt bad."

"What does 'hurt bad' mean?" Sterling retorted.

"Well . . . you know. I've never had a kid break a bone or need stitches or anything like that."

"And you're telling me," Sterling quickened the pace of his probing, "your district supervisor has never told physical education teachers not to play this game. Is that right? Do you ever do anything else in PE besides play this game? Is this game included in your curriculum guide for either seventh-, eighth-, or ninth-grade coursework? Come on, Ben, stop with the BS, and stop letting kids talk you into playing this game. You're the teacher, not them. I want to see you following the curriculum guide and really teaching physical education rather than disorganized grab-ass! Do we have an agreement?"

Edwards looked as if Sterling had ruined his lesson plans for the rest of the year as he quietly responded, "Yes, sir."

"Good. Now we can deal with my second question," Sterling said. "Why is it that each time I've paid a visit, or just looked in the door as I walk by, you're always sitting in a folding metal chair over by the drinking fountain? Is that what good PE teachers do, sit on their butts all day and bark commands at their students? Did they teach you this at your university? Don't answer, Ben. I think you'll come up with the right response when you return to the gym. Get these problems solved now. And let's get back to teaching basic physical education."

"You got it, Grant. I'll take care of it," Edwards said as he hurriedly left Sterling's office.

Sterling could only be half sure of two things: Both dodge ball and the chair would probably disappear. He wasn't sure, however, that Edwards was really capable of teaching. He would continue to pay unscheduled visits to Edwards' classes.

By the end of the first semester, Sterling had collected quite a bit of evidence concerning Edwards' flimsy attempts to teach. He continued to meet with Edwards to provide suggestions on how he might improve, but he was already making plans to ask for his resignation effective at the end of the current school year. Because Edwards was also Arthur's head basketball coach, he would wait to talk to him about resigning until after the end of basketball season. He knew, however, that if Edwards had a winning season, his ability to negotiate a resignation would be much more difficult. He also knew that Edwards was going to be blessed with excellent players this season, and that there was talk in the community about the possibility of a city championship for Arthur this year.

By the fifth game of the season, Sterling knew that a city championship in basketball was not in the cards for Arthur. Although the kids played the best they could, the coaching was lousy. After a game, it had become commonplace for referees to whisper to Sterling that he needed a new coach next year. Although Sterling felt free to talk to Edwards about his classroom activities, he had always refrained from interfering with coaching activities. Whether the Arthur team won or lost, unless Edwards did something unprofessional, Sterling would let the season play out; then they would talk.

During the eighth game of the season, Sterling noticed something unusual. After the half-time break, Edwards didn't return to the gym with the team. The assistant coach was directing the play as Sterling headed for the locker room to find out what the problem was. As he entered the room, he could hear Edwards talking on the telephone. He moved closer to the locker room office where the phone was located and eavesdropped.

"That turkey is talking to a girlfriend while his kids are involved in a tough game upstairs!" Sterling positioned himself so he could hear better, and determined that Edwards was making a date for after the game.

"Edwards!" Sterling shouted in the door. "What the hell are you doing? Your team is on the court!"

Edwards put his hand over the receiver. "I'll be there in just a minute, Grant."

Sterling waited in muted anger and amazement as Edwards casually finished his conversation, hung up, and started out the door of the locker room office.

"I'm on my way, boss!" Edwards nonchalantly said as he brushed by Sterling.

"Wait, Ben." Sterling grabbed him by the arm. "Go to your all-important date now. I don't want you to return to the gym. Your assistant coach can handle the rest of the game. We'll talk about this tomorrow morning. You won't, however, be coaching for the rest of the school year. Go out the back door, get in your car, and leave. You've just demonstrated to me that your love life is far more important to you than your players."

Sterling was prepared for Edwards to do something. Argue, call him names, punch him out . . . something. Edwards just grabbed his coat from the office and left.

"What a wimp," Sterling fumed as he returned to the gym and told the assistant coach that the rest of the game was in his hands. Arthur lost 63 to 21 that evening.

Edwards reported to Sterling's office first thing the next morning. He began to apologize, but Sterling interrupted him.

"Ben, nothing you can say to me, to your team, or to the parents, can make last night's fiasco disappear. I'll pay you for the remainder of your coaching contract, but you're through coaching. I'll let you continue to teach PE for the rest of the school year. But Ben, I want your resignation from both teaching and coaching, dated the last day of your contract year, on my desk by the end of the day today. If you decide you don't want to do this, I'll start due processing you tomorrow, and believe me, you'll be fired at the end of the semester. If you have hopes of teaching somewhere else in the future, don't test me on this. Any questions?"

Edwards looked like a little boy who had just been scolded as he got up and left Sterling's office without a word. At the end of the day, Edwards gave him a hand-written resignation. In it he included the following: "I think that teaching is really the wrong job for me anyway. I'm going to look for something else."

Sterling started processing the resignation immediately. He knew he might hear from Edwards' attorney or the teachers' union claiming that he had coerced Edwards into resigning. He'd deal with that if and when it happened. Right now, he needed to find a coach for the basketball team as soon as possible.

"We've got seven games left," he said to Tim Richards that afternoon. Richards was the team's assistant coach. "I can't pay you more than your coaching contract is now because I have to honor Edwards' remaining contract, but I'd like to name you as interim head coach, and have you lead the team for the rest of the season. How about it?"

"I understand and support what you've done, Grant. I'll help in any way I can, but you've got to know that I'm not a good basketball coach. My forte is football and wrestling."

"You're not telling me that you're worse than what the kids have already had, are you?" Sterling smiled.

"Oh, I don't think so," Richards laughed.

That evening, Sterling got a call from the local newspaper's sports editor. "The word is out, Grant. An Arthur parent called me a few minutes ago. He seemed to be quite happy that you'd canned your basketball coach. Thought it might make good copy. So, tell me, are you starting a new trend in junior high sports, replacing a coach in midseason like the NBA?" Buck Thompson, a respected writer, was giggling like a kid as he presented his question to Sterling.

"There's no story for you here, Buck," Sterling firmly replied. "This is strictly a personnel matter that I don't want to see in the paper. I'll give you the whole story on this after the situation is stone cold. You'll have to trust me on this one. No press, please."

After a little more discussion, Thompson agreed. Sterling's annual breakfast for the local press corps, a tradition that he started while at Center, continued to pay off.

Richards quickly pulled the team together, and, with the help of some of the district's other basketball coaches who volunteered their expertise for some late evening practices, Arthur's basketball team won six of its remaining games.

Although the team didn't qualify for the city championship play-offs, it finished the season with self-respect. None of the players ever questioned, or even mentioned, the midseason coaching change directly to Sterling. Their thumbs-up gestures to him when they passed in the halls were enough to tell him that they agreed with what he had done.

Power Prerogative

Dear Mr. Sterling:
I am
sorry for teasing
my teachers
Which I probably
should apologize to
Please forgive me
but it was fun
to see the look on
their faces.
                                    Larry Smith, seventh grade

Notes like the one from Larry Smith that typify the "they don't understand me" world of the adolescent gave impetus to Sterling's rigorous desire to reform junior highs. Larry was characteristic of the majority of his peers. They liked to test adults.

Sterling worked feverishly in his spare time putting together a comprehensive plan for converting the district's junior high schools to middle schools. He needed to have his work in Associate Superintendent Howard Robb's hands before the board and Superintendent Boughton made the announcement about the school closings and the change from junior high to middle school. In addition, he had been promised that whatever school he was assigned, when Arthur closed, would become the model for his plan, and the rest of the middle schools in the district would follow suit.

Sterling was particularly interested in studying the format of schools before the junior high school concept evolved. He scoured university libraries and corresponded with education professionals throughout the country. Although he could find the background to support his basic concepts, he couldn't find a vehicle or mechanism that would translate his concepts into action. He needed to find a working model, if there was one. Otherwise, he was going to have to invent a whole new framework on which to base his program.

During his research, he stumbled on the name of a young university professor in Florida who, with the cooperation of a local school district, had developed what some authorities had identified as the middle school of the future. He called the professor and went to Florida to see the school firsthand. After spending a few days observing and taking notes, he felt sure he had his model. He had found the vehicle that, with some modifications, could convey his concepts to reality. He needed only to develop a marketing package that Robb, the district, and the board would adopt.

He became a closet zealot as he designed, on paper and in his mind, what he considered to be "his school." When he finished, he had developed a highly confidential 124-page manuscript titled *Most Asked Questions: A Convergence Plan—Junior High School to Middle School* and explanatory exhibits, overheads, and charts. Most important, he developed a districtwide middle school plan to be implemented in a 5-year time span and a model for the school to which he would be assigned after Arthur closed.

He called Robb to announce that he had finished the project and was anxious to present the plan to him.

"Great," Robb replied. "Let's do it this week if possible. I'll have my secretary call you with a time and date."

Sterling told Robb that he'd need to set aside about 2 hours so that he could give him a complete overview of the package. He wanted to do a thorough job of selling his proposal and still provide ample time for discussion and revision, if necessary.

The program Sterling had designed wasn't limited to just the identification of concepts or how the school would work. He had also developed a model philosophy, public relations strategies, and proposal to eliminate or redesign almost all current junior high methodology. His presentation was designed to cover all the bases.

As he entered the board of education building later that week for the meeting with Robb, Sterling was ready to provide Robb with all the facts, information, and ammunition he would need to sell the middle school concept to the superintendent, the board of education, and the community. As he walked down the hall to Robb's office, he passed by the district's boardroom. He couldn't help noticing that the door, usually open when the room wasn't being used, was closed and the window in the door was covered. A sign on the door said, "Meeting in Progress—Do Not Disturb."

"Grant, you're right on time as usual. Let me get my note pad; we're meeting in the boardroom," Robb said as he grabbed a pad from his desk. "We've got more room and privacy in there, and I had my secretary set up the display tripod and overhead projector you requested. I'm looking forward to your presentation."

Sterling was excited as he entered the room and walked to the front to set up his displays and prepare his overheads. His excitement quickly turned to nervousness as he suddenly realized that Robb had invited all the district's associate, assistant, and area superintendents to the meeting. Instead of a presentation to an audience of 1, he was going to be making a presentation to all 12 of the district's top honchos. "Oops, make that 13," he noted to himself as Superintendent Boughton strolled in and joined Sterling at the front of the room.

"Grant," Boughton said. "I'm aware of the hard work that you and Howard Robb have put into collecting information for this presentation. I appreciate the fact that both of you have spent many long hours preparing for our district's move to the middle school concept. We thank you both for your hard work."

"What is this 'you and Howard crap'?" Sterling thought to himself as the superintendent continued.

"Now, ladies and gentlemen," Boughton said, "I don't need to remind you that the information you're going to receive today has not yet been presented to the board, and we're not ready to release this information outside of this room. I trust you to handle what Howard and Grant are going to say today with utmost confidentiality. Howard, Grant, the floor is yours."

Robb stepped forward. "I'm going to let Grant do the presentation today. Go ahead, Grant."

As Sterling took his place at the front of the room, he was momentarily tempted to say, "Oh, no, please Howard, you did *all* the work on this, *you* should make the presentation!" Sterling bit his tongue.

After his formal presentation, Sterling was battered by questions and concerns, but the feeling in the room was remarkably positive, and he felt that middle schools in the district were imminent.

After the room emptied, Robb asked Sterling for the overheads, charts, and any other notes that Sterling had produced. "I want to use these for my presentation to the board," he said. "I'll let you know when the presentation is scheduled. I want you to be there to help me answer any questions they might have. We work well together, Grant!"

Sterling had just gotten his first taste of the misappropriation of credit. "A power prerogative?" he wondered as he drove back to Arthur. He would get his second taste a few weeks later.

"Dr. Robb, the board congratulates you on the formidable work you've done on the middle school proposal for our district and the presentation you've given us tonight. All in favor of Dr. Robb's plan to convert our junior highs to middle schools say 'aye'—opposed 'nay.'" Middle school development in the district was approved, and Sterling, seated in the audience, was pleased. Local papers carried the story of the board's decision and Associate Superintendent Howard Robb's presentation. Robb quickly became a featured guest over the next few weeks on local radio and television talk shows. Sterling's vision had officially become "Dr. Robb's plan."

Sterling was reminded of something he heard frequently as a musician. "Once you present your performance to the public, it's no longer yours. They will decide what to do with it. If it's acclaimed, accept it. If it's rejected, move on. You gave your best, it's theirs now—that's all you can do."

"I got want I wanted," Sterling thought. "Robb can take all the credit he wants, but he still needs me to put 'his' plan into action. I hope he doesn't forget his pledge to allow me to implement the model for the district." His professional respect for Robb, already anemic at best, was now completely gone, and his association with him in the future would be circumspect.

Sterling's manuscript, *Most Asked Questions: A Convergence Plan—Junior High School to Middle School,* would be modified 2 years later and distributed nationwide by professional education associations under the title, *How to Grow a Cat: From Junior High to Middle School* with Sterling's name, sans Robb's, displayed on the cover.

"Maybe now," Sterling thought, "teachers, parents, and school administrators will be able to understand the needs of adolescent kids better."

Dear Mr. Sterling:
There seems a time
in everyone's life
when no one
understands.
And when you reached
out your hand to
give some understanding
I didn't want it.
But a person must
understand for herself.
Thank you for understanding!
                    Mary Ann McGuire, former student

Do you remember me?

So, What Is the Past Tense of Stick It?

"So what you're telling us, Mr. Sterling, is that you dismissed Mr. Prosser because he refused to turn on the lights in his classroom. Is that correct?"

"Partly," Sterling said in response to the question posed by the mediator for the labor relations board.

"Oh? Were there other reasons?" the mediator asked.

"Yes sir. I believe they're listed in detail in the affidavit you have in your possession."

"I'm well aware of that, Mr. Sterling. I've read them, and I've taken notes. I'd really like to hear them directly from you, however. In your own words, if you don't mind."

Sterling looked at the school district's attorney for approval to proceed. He nodded.

"As I understand it, Erwin Prosser was an excellent English teacher at Sumpter Junior High School," Sterling began. "I further understand that he suffered a nervous breakdown and was hospitalized at a local private facility for a year as an inpatient, and another year as an outpatient. Sometime this past summer, I got a call from the assistant superintendent for personnel asking me if I could find a place for Prosser on my faculty. We discussed his situation and determined we would start him off with a small class of students needing remedial help in English."

"Why a small class, and why remedial students?" the mediator interrupted.

"We felt it would be in the best interest of Prosser if we started him back slowly with a small group of select students who needed individual help. In addition, I already had a full complement of faculty and really couldn't place him in our regular schedule."

"Continue, please," the mediator said.

"So, the faculty and I welcomed Prosser to Arthur and helped him prepare his room and materials for the school year. Shortly after the beginning of the semester, Prosser brought a student to my office for discipline. It seems Prosser had told the student to sit down and get ready for class to begin and the student told him to 'fuck off.'

"Prosser went back to class, and I proceeded to get the student's side of the story. He admitted that he didn't like the teacher and that he had told Prosser, 'fuck off.' While I was questioning the student, he continually shook his head and brushed some kind of white powder out of his hair. When I asked him what the stuff was, he told me that Prosser had grabbed him, put him in a full nelson, and rammed his head through a plasterboard wall in the classroom. I summoned the school nurse to examine him while I left to check out his story.

"Prosser told me that indeed he had grabbed the student in an attempt to get him to sit down, and that they tussled and the student bumped the wall. I examined the wall and found a head-sized hole punched in the plasterboard.

"I returned to my office, checked with the nurse, found that the student was uninjured, and called his parents. They immediately wanted to file charges against Prosser, and I told them that they had every right to do so. After I explained their son's actions and that suspension from school was imminent, however, we negotiated an agreement. Their son would face restrictions at home, and I would assign him to another teacher. In addition, I would present Prosser with a formal letter of reprimand."

"Did the parents restrict their son, and did you follow through on your end of the deal?" the mediator asked.

"I don't know what the parents did; however, I moved the student to another class, and I had a long talk with Prosser that I followed with a letter of reprimand. The day after Prosser received the letter, he sent me a response. You should have a copy of both my letter and his response in your folder."

"Were you satisfied with his response, Mr. Sterling?"

"Well, Prosser wasn't required to respond, so I didn't measure his reaction as satisfactory or unsatisfactory. He made it quite clear to me, however, that he really didn't understand the gravity of the situation. He wrote that he would do it again under the same circumstances."

"Didn't this make you angry at Mr. Prosser?"

"No sir, I took it as a warning that Prosser might still be suffering some problems and that I should watch him closely for any other actions that might endanger students.

I reported the incident to his psychiatrist and asked her for assistance. I knew that she was meeting with Prosser on a regular basis."

"What happened then, Mr. Sterling?"

"About 3 weeks later—you have the exact date and time in my affidavit—a teacher witnessed a situation in the cafeteria and brought it to my attention. It seems that Prosser broke into the lunch line by pushing a group of students aside. He yelled at them 'teachers come first.' When one of the students was slow to move, Prosser kicked the student's legs out from under him, causing him to fall. When I questioned Prosser about the alleged incident, he told me that the student had called him a name. 'Besides,' Prosser said, 'kids need to learn that adults are more important.' I told Prosser again that this was inappropriate behavior and that I was going to add another letter of reprimand to his file. In addition, I informed him that if anything like this happened again, I was going to suspend him, pending an examination of his capability to continue as a teacher at Arthur."

"But you did suspend him, Mr. Sterling. Did he fail to follow your directive? Did he strike another student? You not only suspended him, you're recommending that he be fired." The mediator shook his pencil at Sterling. "How did we get to this point?"

"Shortly after the cafeteria incident, Prosser's students started asking their counselors to allow them to transfer to another class. They claimed Prosser didn't like them and was cruel. He yelled at them constantly for no apparent reason, and assigned them additional homework as discipline."

"Maybe, Mr. Sterling," the mediator scowled, "those 'select students,' as you called them, were kids that no other teachers wanted in their classes. Maybe you dealt Mr. Prosser a losing hand to start with."

The school district's attorney immediately objected to the mediator's statement, and advised Sterling not to respond.

"Well, okay then," the mediator pulled in his horns. "What happened next?"

"I walked by Prosser's classroom one morning and noticed that the room was dark. Prosser was lecturing to his students in a pitch-black room. His room had no windows, so with the light off, the only light available was from the hall. I reached around the corner and switched the lights on. If he was about to show a film or something, I was prepared to turn them off again. He wasn't, and he yelled at me to turn them off. He said, 'The kids pay more attention to me in the dark!'

"I spoke with Prosser in the hall and told him that I wanted the lights on in his room at all times unless he was showing a film or videotape. He told me to tend to my job and stay out of his business. I sent him a follow-up note demanding compliance with my request. He came in after school that day with a written response to my note. He tossed it on my desk and left. The note, and you have a copy of it, simply said: 'Stick It!' "

"I'll bet that made you angry, didn't it Mr. Sterling?"

"No sir, I don't have time to get angry in my profession." Sterling stifled the urge to add, "just get even!" "I made a point of going to Prosser's classroom right after the first tardy bell the next morning. The room was dark, Prosser was yelling at his students, and I removed him from the classroom immediately. His classes were covered by a substitute for the rest of that day, and to this date. I immediately suspended Prosser for insubordination and notified the personnel office of my action. I recommended that he be terminated immediately."

"So, let me get this straight," the mediator said as he shuffled through the papers piled in front of him. "We're here today because you told Mr. Prosser to turn the lights on in his classroom, and he didn't do it. Is that all there is to this case?"

"I don't think so," Sterling responded. "That represents, maybe, the final straw. The bottom line, at least in my mind, is do you want this gentleman teaching your kids?"

Sterling was dismissed from the room, leaving the final haggling to be done by the mediator and the school district's attorney. It was their problem now. He had gotten Prosser out of Arthur, and even if the mediator ruled against the district, he felt certain that he would not be asked to take Prosser back. He had had sympathy for Prosser at first; however, he felt that he had given him a fair chance. Now, he was just converting Prosser's words into action. He had stuck it, but not where Prosser intended.

The mediator ruled in favor of the district, and Prosser was fired.

An Adjunct Lecture

"Man, that's a cold wind!" Sterling pulled his collar around his neck as he walked across the campus to the education building. "I wish I could convince Dr. Hopkins to schedule this lecture for late spring, not February."

Sterling had made this trek many times before, both as a graduate student working on his master's degree and now as a regular guest lecturer in Hopkins's education leadership class. It was his obligation, he felt, to make himself available to speak with students who aspired to become school administrators. He didn't need notes for his presentation this evening. This was the fifth time he had been asked by Hopkins to return to the campus, and he knew from past experience that student questions tended to be practice based rather than purely academic.

"Ladies and gentlemen, I'd like to introduce and thank Mr. Grant Sterling for coming out on this bitter-cold night. Mr. Sterling was the principal at Center Junior High for 4 years and now is the principal at Arthur Junior High.

"He's also a graduate of our education leadership program, although he claims that we forced him out so that we could have peace and quiet," Hopkins chuckled. "Grant, the class is yours."

"Thank you for inviting me, Dr. Hopkins. It's a pleasure, notwithstanding the weather, to be here," Sterling said as he turned to the class. "Folks, rather than hearing me lecture, which would probably be quite boring to both you and me, let's just open the floor to questions."

"Yes ma'am," Sterling said, recognizing a young lady sitting to his left.

"Mr. Sterling, we've been studying a lot of different theories and styles of leadership. How would you define your style of leadership?"

"Survival and manipulation! I lead to survive—I live to manipulate." Sterling quickly retorted with a broad grin. "No, really," he continued. "I'll give you an unpretentious definition in a minute, but first let me ask the class to help me in developing the foundation for my response.

"In this section of the blackboard, let's list as many leadership theories or styles as we can. I'll start us off," Sterling said as he picked up a piece of chalk and scribbled the words "Seagull Intermittent" on the board.

"I . . . I don't think we recognize that theory, Mr. Sterling," one class member said in a hesitant voice.

"Oh, I'm sorry," Sterling laughed. "That's the theory of leadership that describes the action or style exhibited when the boss flies over your work station and drops a . . . well, for lack of a better word, an excrement on your desk and promptly flies away, leaving you to clean up the mess. Now, you folks put some theories up here."

The humor seemed to work as students, chalk dust flying, listed some of the theories and styles they had recently studied. Sterling could tell, as he scanned the developing list, that they, like most students and some professors, frequently confused simple human behaviors with theory or styles. When they finished, they had created the following list:

Dictatorial, Authoritative, Autocratic, Micro-, Achievement Motivation Theory,
Delegation, Empowerment, Enabling, Teamwork,
Consensus Building, Laissez Faire, Loose Coupled,
Tight Coupled, Visionary, Hesitant, Indecisive,
Persuasive, Need Hierarchy Theory,
Motivation-Hygiene Theory, Equity Theory,
Expectancy Theory, Goal-Setting Theory,
Management by Objectives, Situational Leadership,
Behavior Modification and Operant Learning,
Work Redesign Theory, Theory X and Theory Y,
Contingency Theory, Path-Goal Theory,
Theory of Participative Leadership,
Influence-Power Continuum.

"Wow, I'm really impressed." Sterling smiled as he went back to the board. "Now, let's briefly analyze each of these." When the class and Sterling had finished, the class was pretty sure that what it thought were leadership theories or styles were, in fact, mostly management behaviors.

"That's right," Sterling continued. "These are mostly management behaviors, or roles that people assume, to direct others to get the job done! For the most part, these are not descriptive of leadership behaviors or roles.

"It's been my experience," he continued, "both as a practitioner and as an observer, that most theories of leadership really address management. For example, the theory called situational leadership really describes a kind of instantaneous managerial behavior that's needed to facilitate the resolution of an immediate problem.

"Now, one more board exercise, then I promise I'll answer your question. Please take the chalk again, and in this space write any role you think you've ever assumed to get someone to do something for you. Now, these have to be roles that you've acted out—not real behaviors, just pretending. Purposeful, but controlled."

The class, amid much laughter and teasing, hurriedly scribbled the following:

angry, frenzied, enraged, irritated, evil, spiteful, cranky, grumpy, bitchy, bureaucratic, political, big, powerful, shy, reserved, knowledgeable, controlling, stupid, dictatorial, laissez faire, compromising, disappointed, unhappy, befuddled, confused, serious, creative, entrepreneurial, loyal, trustworthy, authoritarian, know-it-all, braggart, capable, incapable, naive, innocent, curious, tense, loose, easy, hardened, resigned, happy, silly, buffoon, joker, playful, sexy, cold, warm, loving, affectionate, friendly, admiring, kind, considerate, pompous, smooth, courteous, debonair, jealous.

"Now you've got it!" Sterling joined in their frivolity. "You've stumbled on my leadership style. Except, perhaps, sexy. I don't think I've ever had to act that role!

"My leadership style is a combination of almost everything you've written on the board . . . theories, styles, and roles. I lead by what I call aggregate impression. Over the years, people have seen me in most of those roles. They don't know at the time whether I'm acting or not. They tend to believe that that's the real me, and over time they build, in their minds, an aggregate impression of who I am based on a composite picture that they develop. I believe that an effective leader is an effective actor, and that the playing of all these roles creates an aggregate impression.

"Now, back to your first list—the list of theories or styles that I labeled as behaviors. These are not roles, not things that you act out. These are real behavioral methods that you implement to get a job done. These are the tools that the actor uses as props.

"In answer to your question, if you put behavioral theory, styles, and role-playing together, you have my leadership style, at least what others think my style is based on the aggregate impression they have of me while I'm on the job."

Sterling looked at the young lady who asked the original question. "Aren't you glad you asked that question?" Sterling laughed.

"Mr. Sterling." A hand shot up in the back of the room. "You use the word 'effective,' as do many of the professional journal articles we have read in this class. My question is simply this. What does effective mean to you, in terms of effective schools?"

"Good question, sir. To me, an effective school has the following characteristics. If we look at the school under a microscope, we see leaders leading, managers managing, and followers following. We see that the climate of the school is comfortable and promotes success; employees and students are functioning at expected or above levels of productivity; employees and students look forward to coming to the workplace each day; the environment is inviting, secure, happy, and physically comfortable; and we note that minimum time is spent with the 5% or less who create discipline problems, while maximum time is spent with the other 95+%.

"As a result," Sterling continued, "students are successful and comfortable with learning and feel a sense of pride in their work and accomplishments. Teachers teach well and feel a sense of pride in their work and accomplishments. The school runs efficiently and cost-effectively. Parents and patrons are pleased with the school program, and last, the central office and the school board are also pleased with the school program.

"Now," Sterling continued, "let me elaborate on part of what I just said, and give you my definition of leaders, managers, and followers.

"Good leaders make the organization move forward to greater success. Good leaders may or may not be good managers. Effective leaders are both good leaders and good managers, however. Leadership is a means of marshaling the proper emotions or convictions in others to enable and encourage them to do what needs to be done.

"Effective managers may or may not be good leaders. Managers keep the organization running smoothly. They possess the means to get specific pieces of work done effectively. They plan, direct, and delegate the work of others.

"Good followers do just that . . . follow. On the other hand, effective followers understand and support what leaders and managers are attempting to achieve. They never follow blindly, they follow analytically. They see the bigger picture. They see the whole school from the community and district perspective, not from just their own perspective or specific role. Dr. Hopkins, you had a question?"

"Yes, Grant. After we take a short break, would you answer the question, what are the sources of a leader's power?"

After coffee, Sterling was prepared to tackle Hopkins' question, although he wasn't so sure of the class's readiness. He had already given them a lot to assimilate and, he hoped, to discuss later.

"I think," Sterling began, "that all the power that effective leaders need comes automatically with the role they've been assigned. This authority is substantially enhanced by the power of knowledge when leaders are experts in their field.

"If you're not an effective leader, however, then the power proffered by your position or knowledge isn't worth a hoot," Sterling continued. "The ineffective leader has to turn to what I call the power to punish . . . 'do this or else.' Ineffective leaders also often revert to using reflective power . . . 'my personal friend the superintendent will fully support me on this issue so you better watch out.'

"Let me add one more power base that most effective principals cultivate. For lack of a better term, I call it a kind of sphere of protective power or support. Effective principals surround themselves with strong and influential people from within the school and from the community, and actively involve them in key decision-making activities . . . what did I leave out, Dr. Hopkins?"

"What about charisma, Grant?"

"Easiest question so far this evening," Sterling smiled. "You'd better have natural charisma, or you'd better inspire it through awfully good acting!

"We have time for just one more question, then I'll stick around after class for any of you who want to discuss anything I've said tonight in more depth. Make it an easy one, will you? You've overtaxed my brain tonight, and remember—I have to get up early in the morning to practice my charisma act before I get to my office . . . Yes, ma'am."

"Mr. Sterling, what do you see as the major roadblock for women wanting to be leaders?"

"Wait a minute," Sterling responded. "I thought I asked for an easy question. If I answer your question honestly, I will probably have to flee from the building after class instead of hanging around for another cup of coffee! Are you sure you want to hear my answer?"

"Yes, sir," the lady replied.

"All right," Sterling smiled. "This is my opinion, mind you . . . Women tend to be viewed more as managers because their main focus seems to be the welfare of the organization and getting things done. Men tend to focus on self-promotion and are viewed as leaders because they are more frequently seen directing the work of others.

"In other words, it seems that women work for the organization; men work for themselves. Women need to learn to practice leading in addition to doing. Did anyone ever wonder where the expression, 'if you want the job done right, give it to a woman,' came from? Something to think about, isn't it? Clearly, I'm leaving you this evening with a wide open can of worms.

"Thank you for inviting me to visit with you. Please feel free to stop in at Arthur any time you're in the neighborhood. I'll stick around for a few minutes if any of you have any other questions."

Expediting the Ironic

"Horace, you are clearly the most presumptuous and arrogant person I've ever known," Sterling yelled into the phone. "How dare you send your 'vultures' to my school, during school hours, to inventory stuff they'd like to have at Moundview next year! Do you realize what kind of an impact this stupid incident has had on faculty and student morale today . . . and maybe the rest of the semester? Where's your brain anyway? Did you even think about calling me first? We could have made arrangements for some of your people to come over here in the evening. Who told you you could do this anyway? Why do you think you're going to get anything when this building closes? Horace, I'm sorry . . . I know this isn't professional, but you're really an S.O.B."

"Are you finished, Grant?" Horace Krupt, the principal at Moundview Junior High, asked in his usual pompous tone.

"I just want an explanation, Horace. That's all."

"I don't believe I owe you anything after that outburst," Krupt responded.

"Okay, I apologize," Sterling said curtly. "Now, talk to me, you supercilious ex-jock! Either talk to me, or have your area superintendent call me and tell me that he approved it." Sterling doubted if Krupt's boss even knew about Krupt's action, much less approved it.

"Well, I'm sorry," Krupt said with much less resistance in his voice. "I just thought that with your school closing . . . you know . . . and all that equipment has to be transferred somewhere . . . that I would turn in a list of things we could use at my school."

"And who do you think you'd be turning that list in to?" Sterling asked, anger still obvious in his tone of voice.

"Oh, I don't know . . . probably your area superintendent," Krupt guessed.

"I gotta tell you, Horace . . . in case you couldn't already tell . . . I'm so ticked off at you right now that if I have anything to say about it, you'll be lucky to get so much as a single roll of toilet paper from this building. Don't do this again! Have I made my point?"

"I'm sorry you feel that way, Grant. After all, I'm only trying to expedite."

"And I'm only trying to run a school, Horace. Expedite that if you can," Sterling said as he abruptly hung up the phone.

"Grant, is everything all right?" Peggy asked as she cautiously opened the door to Sterling's office. "You sounded awfully upset. Was it about those teachers from Moundview who were here a while ago?"

"Yes, Peggy, it was. I just unloaded on Horace Krupt."

"I'm glad you did. That was really demoralizing, but then those Moundview folks didn't look too happy when you escorted them out the front door," she laughed. "By the way, Howard Robb would like to meet with you tomorrow at 2:00. My copy of your calendar shows you free then. You want me to call his secretary back and confirm?"

"That'll be fine, Peggy. You have any idea what the meeting's about?"

"Sorry, Grant. His secretary just said he wanted to meet with you."

The next day, as he parked his car at the district's administration building, Sterling huffed to himself, "I hate meeting when I don't know the subject matter. Howard probably wants me to design another program for him so he can take credit for it."

"Good afternoon, Grant. How's it going? 'Bout ready to close Arthur down? Heard you had a tussle with your colleague over at Moundview yesterday. You and

Horace have never gotten along, have you? Well, don't worry about it. You and I are going to solve some of those problems today. Sit down please. I've got a list of things I want to cover.

"First," Robb continued, "the board has accepted the superintendent's plan to use Arthur for a special education center. All the equipment, materials, and supplies at Arthur will remain in the building when you close it at the end of the school year. Clyde Benning will be calling you in the next few days, and you and he can set up some kind of a transfer inventory. He has blueprints of the building so he can start redesigning rooms and spaces. He won't need to visit your school before the end of the semester. You've worked too hard with the community to ensure a smooth closing. I don't want anyone to upset the apple cart.

"By the way, one of the Moundview teachers you kicked out of Arthur yesterday plays bridge with my wife. The teacher said Horace was beet red and fit to be tied when they returned to Moundview. The secretary said you had called and read Horace the riot act. Well, it won't happen again. I'm sending a memo to all district administrators about the new special services center tomorrow morning. Do you believe in irony?"

"You mean like a twist of fate or something like that?" Sterling asked.

"Yeah, I think it's ironic that Horace Krupt did what he did yesterday."

Sterling look puzzled. "You lost me, Howard. I don't understand."

"Of course you don't," Robb laughed, "and neither does Krupt! That's what's so weird. The board's not ready to announce this yet, but Krupt's going to be transferred to the regional vocational education center as a counselor, and you're going to replace him as principal at Moundview. In addition, Moundview is going to be the district's first pilot middle school."

"Howard, that's really great! I couldn't be happier!"

"This is just between us for the time being," Robb cautioned. "The superintendent wanted you to know now so you can begin making plans. The rest of the district, including Krupt, won't be told until after school is out in June."

As Sterling left the administration building, it was beginning to spit snow. He turned on his windshield wipers, wishing spring would get here. The snow had begun to accumulate by the time he got back to Arthur. Looking at the dark sky, Sterling thought, "The CIA could use this school district as a training center for espionage." Sterling pulled the collar up on his trench coat and stepped out of his car. He glanced around and facetiously wondered if Krupt had any agents lurking in the bushes.

Señor Sterling, Ayuda a Mi Hijo, Por Favor! ▬

"Grant, some lady named Mrs. Ortiz is on the phone. She needs to talk with you right away. I'm having difficulty understanding her. She sounds pretty upset. I think she's trying to tell me that her son needs help."

"Thanks, Peggy. I'll talk to her right now," Sterling said as he ushered a couple of students out and closed the door.

He had graduated two of Mrs. Ortiz's children from Center. Both of them were high achievers and had served the school as members of the student council. Clardy, her third child and his favorite, was now a ninth grader at Center. He'd spent many hours with the kid trying to help him control his temper. Clardy suffered from low self-esteem largely because he was part Hispanic and part Caucasian. His Caucasian father had left home years ago. He was a city champion wrestler and an excellent student, but was often sent to the office for challenging other students to fight and then beating the tar out of them. Sterling had developed a paternal relationship with the kid.

"Mrs. Ortiz, what a surprise to hear from you. How can I help . . ." He was abruptly interrupted by a flurry of words that he couldn't quite understand.

"Mrs. Ortiz," he said, "Wait . . . wait please . . . slow down. You're talking too fast and mixing Spanish with English."

"I'm sorry, Mr. Sterling," she cried. "I'm so upset. The new principal at Center, Mr. Hathaway, first he suspended my Clardy and now he just called and told me that he had decided to expel him for the rest of the year."

"What was the reason, Mrs. Ortiz?"

"Clardy got in a fight with a student and got sent to the office. Mr. Hathaway said that Clardy then threatened him. What am I going to do? I can't keep Clardy at home during the day. He'll go out and get in trouble and get arrested and . . ."

"Wait, Mrs. Ortiz. Let me call Mr. Hathaway and talk to him. I'll call you back in a little while. Give me your phone number."

"Damn!" Sterling muttered as he hung up the phone. "I don't want that kid to fail. He's got too much potential."

"Jeannie! Hi," Sterling said as a familiar voice answered the phone at Center. "I need to talk to Gene Hathaway. Is he available?"

"I'll connect you, Grant. I can guess why you're calling," she whispered. "Clardy needs you!"

"Hi, Gene, Grant here. I just wanted to call and tell you that we're going to whip your butt in football next week. Care to make a friendly bet?"

"You don't have a chance in hell, Sterling. Why don't you just forfeit the game now and spare us all the embarrassment?"

"We're not going to forfeit, but I would like to hear about Clardy Dawson, Mrs. Ortiz's son. What happened?" Sterling asked.

Hathaway gave Sterling a clear picture of what had taken place prior to Clardy's suspension and then what had led to his decision to expel Clardy for the rest of the school year.

"No student is going to threaten to pound me into hamburger and then expect to get leniency from me," he said in a challenging voice. "How did you hear about this anyway?"

"His mother just called me, Gene. Tell you what," said Sterling, groping for a solution, "we won't forfeit the game with you next week, but I'll yell a little less loudly in the stands on one condition—that you withdraw your expulsion and work with me on a transfer for Clardy to Arthur."

"Get serious Grant! You know I can't withdraw Clardy's expulsion, and even if I could, he doesn't live anywhere near your district boundaries. We'd never get a transfer approved. We'd be breaking policy all over the place. Look, the kid's a psycho. Let him get in trouble outside of school so that social welfare or the cops can place him somewhere where he can't hurt anybody."

"Gene, I'll be the first to agree that the kid needs help. I was able to keep him under control most of the time, however, and he was getting better as he matured. Let me continue to work with him. Just say yes, and let me try to finagle the details with the powers that be. Fair enough?"

"And you won't yell as loud at the football game?"

"You got it, Gene."

"All right, go ahead, Grant, but I think you're crazy."

Sterling needed to work quickly. He was acting on Hathaway's inexperience as a principal and his lack of expertise in what Sterling called "the fine art of foreseeability." First, he knew that all expulsions crossed the desk of David Washington, the district's director of minority affairs. Clardy's expulsion notice would have just arrived on his desk. Just as Washington could approve a transfer, he could also bury that notice. Second, Sterling wanted Clardy safely back under his wing before Hathaway figured out that, if Sterling was able to pull this off, other students at Center might use it as a way to avoid suspensions or expulsions. They'd simply request a transfer to Arthur. He didn't want that to happen, but he did want Clardy back in school. He could tell by Hathaway's voice as he talked about Clardy that trying to get him back into school at Center was not an option.

It was after 5 o'clock—standard quitting time at central administration—but Sterling, hoping he might still catch Washington, placed a call to his office.

As he waited to see if the phone would be answered, he worried. "I hope Washington has finally cooled down from my confrontation with him about the Oreo thing. Maybe not dealing with the calls about my transfer to Arthur has satisfied his desire to get even." Washington answered the phone himself.

"Working overtime today?" Sterling laughed.

"Yes," Washington answered in a formal tone. "We're always busy in this office. Who's calling please, and how can I assist you?"

"David, it's Grant Sterling at Arthur. I need your help."

Dead silence.

"David, are you still there?" Sterling asked.

"I'm here, Sterling. How can I help you?" Washington's short response was frigid.

Sterling proceeded to give Washington the full story on Clardy Dawson, emphasizing his Hispanic heritage. "Here's an opportunity to help a minority kid stay in school. Hathaway and I have reached an agreement. All we need is your blessing," he concluded.

"And you think I'm going to approve this after the embarrassment you caused me with the Center community? You think I'm willing suddenly just to forgive and forget?"

Sterling really thought that Washington would lay the past aside, at least for a moment, and think about a kid in trouble. He could tell by the tone of Washington's voice that he might have to be as petty and offensive as Washington was to pull this deal off.

"Yes, David. I think we should work together in this case. I think you should forget the Center situation, just as I'm willing to forget about all those calls from anxious parents concerned about my transfer from Center. You remember, the ones the superintendent forwarded to your office that you didn't return for some reason? Come on, dammit, we've got a kid in trouble here, and I'm willing to stick my neck out for him. Now, I'll stop playing tough guy if you will. It's not a role that I like to play."

After a long moment of silence, Washington must have decided that he didn't want to test Sterling. "Okay," he said. "Put through the transfer paperwork and I'll approve it. I'll send the expulsion notice back to Hathaway. Will you contact the kid's parents?"

"Yes David, thanks. I'll take care of the paperwork."

Washington abruptly hung up the phone.

Sterling called Mrs. Ortiz and gave her the news. He wanted to meet with Clardy and her the next morning. He called Hathaway at home that evening to advise him of the transfer approval and to remind him to nullify Clardy's expulsion.

"So, Clardy," Sterling said after he'd gotten Mrs. Ortiz a cup of coffee. "Here's your choice. Sit home and watch *As The World Turns* on TV, or start back to school here. What's it going to be? No—never mind, kid. I'll tell you what you're going to do. You're going to start school today . . . at Arthur. You're stuck with me again for the rest of the year. Sorry, you've got no choice. Remember, however, that if you step out of line now, it's not just your butt in a sling, but mine too! I really stuck my neck out a long way for you this time . . . don't you dare let me down!"

Clardy's facial expression turned from serious to warm as he smiled and said, "Yes sir, Mr. Dad . . . excuse me, I mean, Mr. Principal."

Clardy fit in comfortably at Arthur and was, much to Sterling's and Mrs. Ortiz's delight, a model student and gentleman. He went on to finish high school and college, and graduated with honors from law school. He currently practices juvenile law with a firm in another city.

Sterling never felt comfortable about having to threaten Washington with blackmail; however, Clardy was more important at the moment than Washington's bruised ego. As far as Hathaway's situation at Center was concerned . . . no students attempted to use Clardy's transfer as a means to avoid discipline.

Some observers might think that Clardy got off scott free from his behavior at Center. Because he transferred from Center to Arthur after the school term began, however, he lost his state athletic association eligibility to compete, and was barred from defending his city championship in wrestling.

Nothing Unusual, Just the Daily In-Basket

"Paperwork, paperwork, paperwork . . . does it ever end in this business?" Sterling complained as he sat down at his desk and surveyed the usual collection of incoming messages.

"Bob, come in. How can I help you?" Sterling was interrupted by Bob Allen, one of his industrial arts teachers.

"Oh, really nothing, Grant," Allen said. "I just had a few minutes to kill before my planning period ends and thought I'd drop in and see how you're doing."

"I'm doing fine, Bob. I'm about ready to plow into this stack of messages and see if I can whittle them down a bit before . . ."

"I've often wondered," Allen interrupted, "how you principal types handle all the paperwork that's thrown at you each day, and still have time to run the school?"

"Oh, I guess it's a bit like being a traffic cop. Some of it I handle myself, some of it I delegate, some of it I disregard. The object of the game is to try to keep up with it. To do that, you have to be pretty decisive. Quick but good decision making is the key. I try to get a lot of it done before you guys get to work in the morning and school starts; and I finish as much as possible during the day or after school. I avoid, as much as possible, having to take much work home with me. I like to have a life outside of work."

"I can relate to that, Grant. Talk to you later . . . I'm off to class."

"Let's see how many of these I can deal with before my next distraction," Sterling thought as Allen left the room.

Dear Mr. Sterling,

Please give me some guidance on this. My daughter Susan is in Ms. Albright's PE class. I talked to Ms. Albright last night by phone to state my concern for the physical and emotional abuse Susan and others are suffering in PE. It seems that any time any of the girls do something that Ms. Albright thinks is wrong, she makes them do pushups. As a former math teacher, I would never have required my students to do X number of math problems as a punishment for anything. In addition, Susan is not a physically strong young girl, and when she can't do all the pushups, others in the class, including the teacher, tease her. In my conversation with Ms. Albright, she said that all the students know what the punishment is for not paying attention in class, which is what she is accusing Susan of. She says that the punishment will remain the same, and that Susan just needs to settle down. Would you look into this please?

Thanks, Gwen Taylor

Grant: I think we may have a problem developing!

I've noticed that some of our students are starting to use smokeless tobacco or what I used to call chewing tobacco. They're spitting it on the floors and in restroom sinks. You might want to do something about this.

Pat

Grant,

Could I see you sometime today? My husband was notified yesterday that he is being promoted and transferred to a position out of state. He needs to report to his new position in 2 weeks and would like me to go with him. I really hate to leave, and would like to stay until at least the end of the school term. He wants me to go with him now. I need your advice! My planning period is 4th hour, or I could see you after school today.

Thanks
Billie

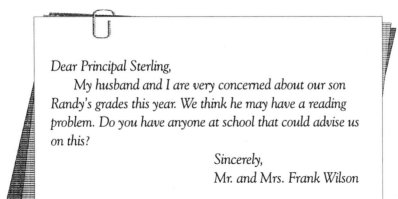

Dear Principal Sterling,

My husband and I are very concerned about our son Randy's grades this year. We think he may have a reading problem. Do you have anyone at school that could advise us on this?

Sincerely,
Mr. and Mrs. Frank Wilson

Telephone Message

For: Grant
From: Mr. Greenway
Time: 4:55 yesterday.

Please call him at 746-3432 this morning as soon as possible.

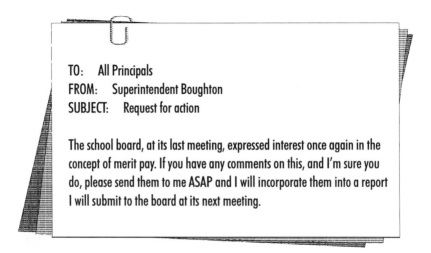

TO: All Principals
FROM: Superintendent Boughton
SUBJECT: Request for action

The school board, at its last meeting, expressed interest once again in the concept of merit pay. If you have any comments on this, and I'm sure you do, please send them to me **ASAP** and I will incorporate them into a report I will submit to the board at its next meeting.

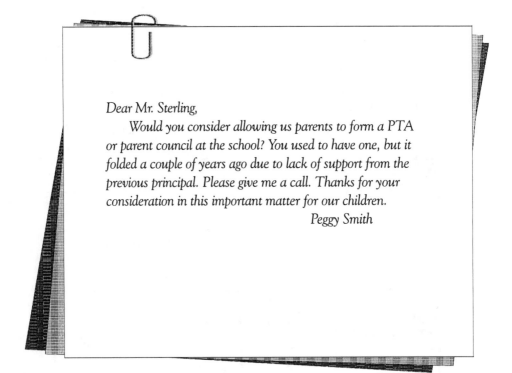

Dear Mr. Sterling,
    Would you consider allowing us parents to form a PTA
or parent council at the school? You used to have one, but it
folded a couple of years ago due to lack of support from the
previous principal. Please give me a call. Thanks for your
consideration in this important matter for our children.
                                                    Peggy Smith

Dear Mr. Sterling:
    Please accept this letter as a formal request to conduct a study
at your school site. My proposal to determine if there is a significant
difference between students' study habits and their parents'
marital status has been approved by my doctoral committee.
I'd like to talk to you about this and get started as soon as possible.
Please call me at 395-6521.
                            Thank you,
                            Frederick Monroe
                            Doctoral Student
                            State University

Grant Sterling
    For your information. The water will be turned off from 1:00 to 2:30 today so that the city can replace a water main at the corner of Allen and Eastern Ave.
                City Water Department

Dear Principal:
    I live at the corner of Allen and Eastern Ave., and your kids cut through my yard on the way to school each day. They continually trample or pull up my flowers. Please tell them to stop. I've tried, but they scare me.
                Thank you
                Alice Lamont
                1152 Eastern Ave.

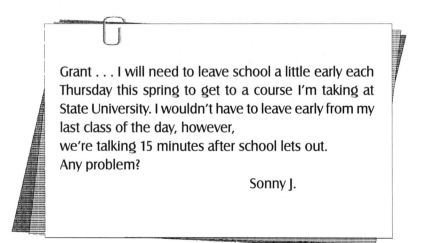

Grant . . . I will need to leave school a little early each Thursday this spring to get to a course I'm taking at State University. I wouldn't have to leave early from my last class of the day, however,
we're talking 15 minutes after school lets out.
Any problem?
              Sonny J.

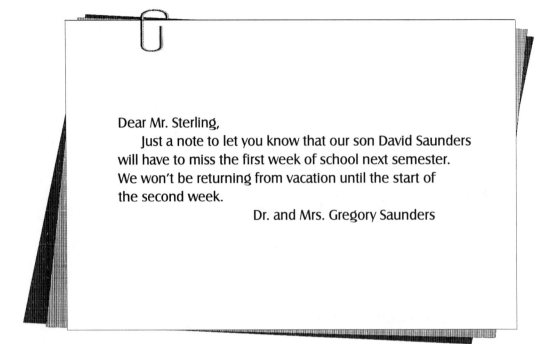

Dear Mr. Sterling,

Just a note to let you know that our son David Saunders will have to miss the first week of school next semester. We won't be returning from vacation until the start of the second week.

Dr. and Mrs. Gregory Saunders

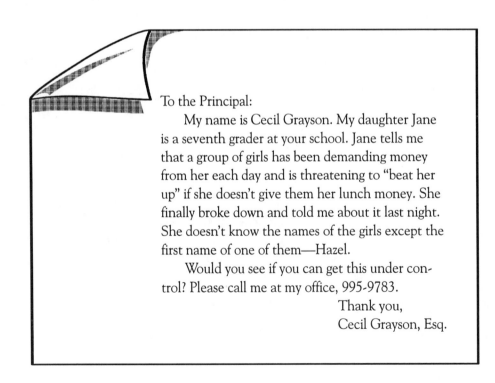

To the Principal:

My name is Cecil Grayson. My daughter Jane is a seventh grader at your school. Jane tells me that a group of girls has been demanding money from her each day and is threatening to "beat her up" if she doesn't give them her lunch money. She finally broke down and told me about it last night. She doesn't know the names of the girls except the first name of one of them—Hazel.

Would you see if you can get this under control? Please call me at my office, 995-9783.

Thank you,
Cecil Grayson, Esq.

Grant: My eighth grade government class would like to sponsor schoolwide elections concurrent with the national and state elections this fall. They want to conduct it as much like the actual elections as possible with campaign posters, speakers, buttons, preregistration, etc. Will you support this? I've talked with some teachers already and am getting a mixed reaction. Let me know.

Larry

Dear Mr. Sterling:

Our church, Trinity Baptist, is preparing a presentation that depicts the Biblical account of the Christmas story. We would like to provide this production, free of charge, to your students in an assembly just before your winter break. Would you be so kind as to provide us with some dates and times so that we can schedule this event for the students and faculty at your school? We bring all our equipment and props with us.

Very sincerely
Kevin Smally, Pastor

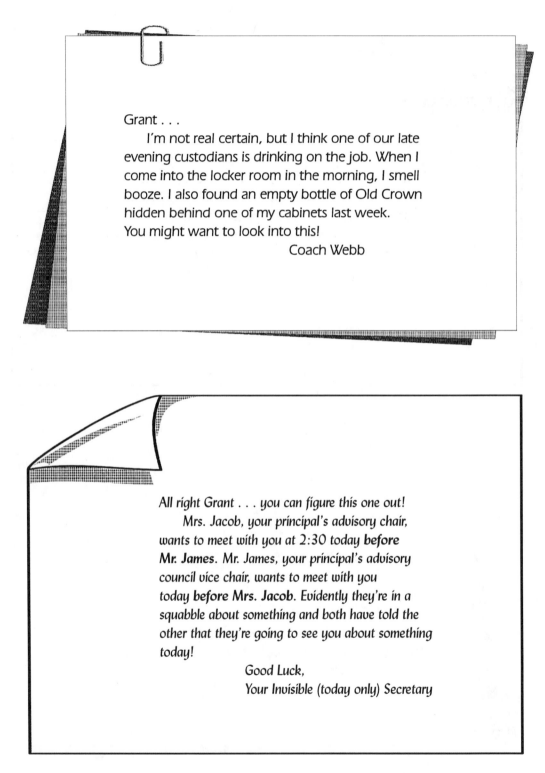

Grant . . .

I'm not real certain, but I think one of our late evening custodians is drinking on the job. When I come into the locker room in the morning, I smell booze. I also found an empty bottle of Old Crown hidden behind one of my cabinets last week. You might want to look into this!

Coach Webb

All right Grant . . . you can figure this one out!

Mrs. Jacob, your principal's advisory chair, wants to meet with you at 2:30 today **before Mr. James**. Mr. James, your principal's advisory council vice chair, wants to meet with you today **before Mrs. Jacob**. Evidently they're in a squabble about something and both have told the other that they're going to see you about something today!

Good Luck,
Your Invisible (today only) Secretary

Dear Mr. Sterling,
    I have just started as a substitute teacher in your school's area. I hope to be asked to come to your school when the need arises. I am writing this note to you and other area principals to let you, and them, know that I will insist that absent teachers provide me with a complete set of lesson plans for the day they are gone. Thank you in advance for your attention to this important matter!
    Betty Lou Adamson

Mr. Sterling . . . Grant,
    We need to have teachers to crack down on litter in the halls and classrooms. Also, students have been using the opening provided for notebooks and textbooks below their seats for wastebaskets. Also, we're getting low on toilet paper. I'm not sure we budgeted enough money for supplies this year!
                        Your custodial staff

Mr. Sterling,
Is it okay for one of your teachers to be dating a high school student? Do you know about this?

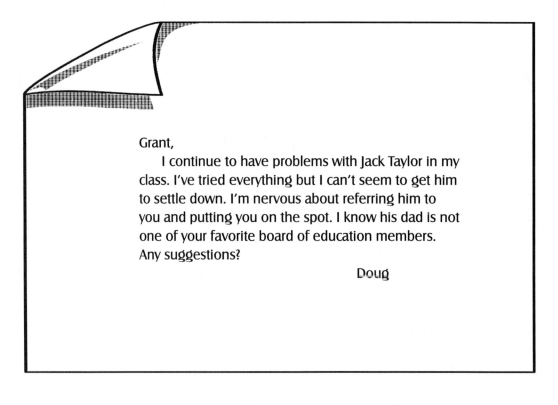

Grant,

    I continue to have problems with Jack Taylor in my class. I've tried everything but I can't seem to get him to settle down. I'm nervous about referring him to you and putting you on the spot. I know his dad is not one of your favorite board of education members. Any suggestions?

Doug

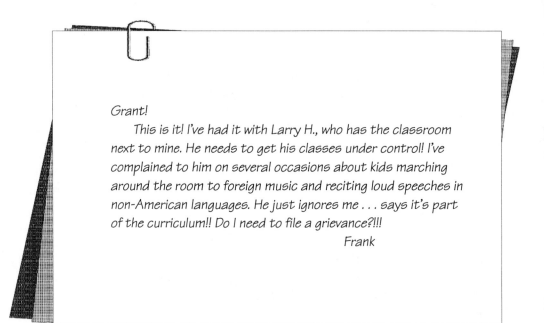

Grant!

    This is it! I've had it with Larry H., who has the classroom next to mine. He needs to get his classes under control! I've complained to him on several occasions about kids marching around the room to foreign music and reciting loud speeches in non-American languages. He just ignores me . . . says it's part of the curriculum!! Do I need to file a grievance?!!!

Frank

Grant,

Can you get Frank off my back? Just because he's such a boring teacher doesn't mean I have to be. He keeps interrupting my classes because he thinks I'm not teaching correctly (decorum, he calls it). He told me he was going to write you a letter about it today, so here's my response.

Thanks
Larry

Dear Principal Sterling,

My son Gary brought a library book home last night that he checked out of your media center. I'm shocked at the amount of foul language and graphically described sex in the book. The book is Green Stars and Lollipops *by Ellen Groverly. I think this book should be removed immediately.*

I'm going to drop the copy that Gary checked out by your office today. You might want to read it.

Very sincerely,
Lorraine Moran

Grant:

I've received a batch of political buttons from the campaign manager for Les Gordon, candidate for governor. Can I go ahead and distribute these to students today?

Thanks, Mary

Mr. Sterling,

We are ahead of budget in the cafeteria. I would like to thank those students who buy their lunch from the cafeteria by giving them a free dessert next Tuesday. Maybe we can entice some of the kids who bring their own lunch to start buying from us. I cannot include those students who qualify for free or reduced cost lunch. I can't afford that.

Is this OK with you?

Betty

Grant . . .

I want to take a day of personal leave next Friday. That day is a religious holiday for my faith. I know that the following Monday is an official school holiday and that the policy says that no one can take personal leave on a workday before an official holiday, but I think I qualify for special consideration. Can you help me with this?

Bill

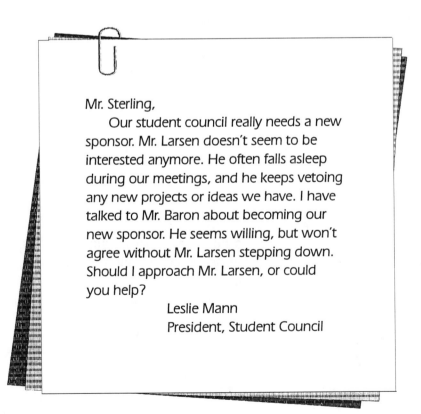

Mr. Sterling,

Our student council really needs a new sponsor. Mr. Larsen doesn't seem to be interested anymore. He often falls asleep during our meetings, and he keeps vetoing any new projects or ideas we have. I have talked to Mr. Baron about becoming our new sponsor. He seems willing, but won't agree without Mr. Larsen stepping down. Should I approach Mr. Larsen, or could you help?

Leslie Mann
President, Student Council

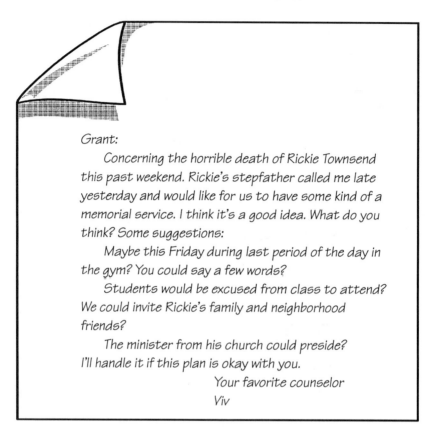

Grant:

Concerning the horrible death of Rickie Townsend this past weekend. Rickie's stepfather called me late yesterday and would like for us to have some kind of a memorial service. I think it's a good idea. What do you think? Some suggestions:

Maybe this Friday during last period of the day in the gym? You could say a few words?

Students would be excused from class to attend? We could invite Rickie's family and neighborhood friends?

The minister from his church could preside? I'll handle it if this plan is okay with you.

Your favorite counselor
Viv

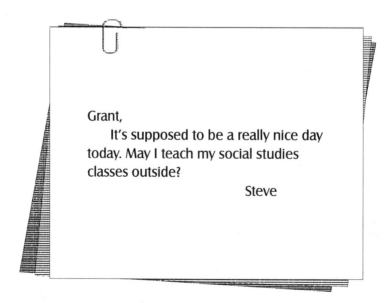

Grant,

It's supposed to be a really nice day today. May I teach my social studies classes outside?

Steve

Grant:

I understand that my classroom is scheduled to be painted next week. The smell will last for weeks afterward. Don't forget that I'm pregnant. I won't go back to that room at least until after the baby is born. Do we have to paint now?

Liz

Boss . . . Potential problem!!!

We have a home football game this Friday evening at the high school stadium. Students are talking that the scumbags that blew away Rickie Townsend are students at the high school where we'll be playing. There may be problems in the stands or in the parking lot. Would you consider moving the game to Saturday afternoon so it would be in the daylight? I've talked to the activity director at our opponent school, and he says it's all right with him. I also called the high school, and the stadium is available Saturday afternoon. I need to know right away!

Your <u>*overworked & underpaid*</u> Activity Director

Grant, sorry to interrupt you. Your 10:30 appointment is here.

For Discussion

General Questions

Using the Sterling paradigm (http://www.corwinpress.com/dunklee.htm) as a model, and speaking from the perspective of a principal, evaluate each episode as follows:

What are the dominant behaviors exhibited by Sterling in this episode?

Is there consensus about this in the class? If not, explain the different viewpoints.

What were the primary actors' individual motives?

How effective was Sterling's behavior in this situation and why?

Can you identify other avenues or approaches that might lead to the same, or a better, conclusion?

If Sterling was a woman,

■ As a female reader, can you identify methodology or behavior that you would change to bring the episode to the same, or similar, closure?

■ As a male reader, what differences in methodology or behavior would you expect to see?

Specific Questions for Each Episode

A Stitch in Time?

1. Do teachers and principals have a mutual responsibility to support the others' efforts to maintain discipline and decorum? If you were a teacher at Arthur, whose side would you take regarding this incident, Caldwell's or Sterling's? Why?

2. What will the students in Caldwell's class most remember about this incident?

What if . . . Caldwell had filed a grievance with the teachers' union or the superintendent claiming Sterling had failed to support her as he should have?

Hold the Phone

What if . . . Washburn had filed a negligence complaint with the board of education or a similar complaint in a court of law?

Kids Deserve the Best

3. What kind of role does school athletics play in the school environment, and how does Sterling's view of that role affect his actions and decisions?

What if . . . Sterling had chosen to ignore Edwards' late arrival to the second half?
What if . . . Edwards had filed a grievance through the teachers' union that he had been coerced into resigning?

Power Prerogative

4. What does this episode illustrate about the complex role of the principal and other middle managers?
5. What role should principals play in curriculum innovation, development, or implementation?
6. What advantage, if any, would Robb gain if he gave Sterling credit for the work?
7. How important is self-promotion?

What if . . . Sterling had stepped forward in the administrators' meeting or the board meeting and claimed full credit for the middle school plan?

So, What Is the Past Tense of Stick It?

8. What constitutes due process when dealing with a poor teacher? How are the rights of students and teachers balanced under the laws and/or school district policies?

What if . . . Sterling had been less politic in his responses to the mediator's questions?

An Adjunct Lecture

9. At times, a person's quick and first response to a question can be quite revealing. Do you think that there's any basis for Sterling's supposedly facetious response about survival and manipulation?
10. Explain, in your own words, Sterling's theory of leadership by aggregate impression. Does his theory have merit? Why or why not?
11. Can effective leaders facilitate the development of effective followers? Explain.

12. Do you agree with Sterling's statement that "women work for the organization; men work for themselves"? What would your central argument be if you thought the statement to be inaccurate?

Expediting the Ironic

13. Is it common practice for school districts to have a strategic plan for placing administrative personnel?

14. Are such plans often held in confidence by the superintendent and board over an extended period of time?

Señor Sterling, Ayuda a Mi Hijo, Por Favor!

15. Explain the following excerpt from this episode: "Sterling needed to act quickly. He was acting on Hathaway's inexperience as a principal as well as his lack of expertise in what Sterling called the fine art of foreseeability."

16. Should policies ever be sidestepped or negotiated to help individual students? If you break a policy or procedure, can you explain how it might open a "floodgate" or lead to litigation?

17. Sterling mentions "blackmail" in this episode. Blackmail is usually considered in negative terms. On the other hand, leverage is considered an acceptable persuasion tool in day-to-day negotiations. Is Sterling using blackmail, or is he using leverage in his conversation with Washington? Is there a difference?

What if . . . Washington had refused Sterling's request?

Nothing Unusual, Just the Daily In-Basket

18. This episode deals with professional and personal time management and the daily routine of in-basket items. Be prepared to discuss the importance of overall time management.

19. In a sentence or two, state your resolution to each of the 32 in-basket examples. Follow each resolution with a brief rationale (Why I made this particular decision).

5

A Transition

Which Comes First, the Rumor or the Grapevine?

The car started instantly and idled smoothly, as it always did after Rick Rosen, Sterling's friend who repaired cars for a hobby, got his hands under the hood. For a six-pack of beer, a couple of off-color jokes, and an evening of simple banter, Rick was willing to keep his friends on the road and happy. Nearly all the trees were showing green, and the snow had retreated for another year. It was one of Sterling's favorite times of the day. The 15 or so minutes it took for him to drive to Arthur provided one of the only quiet, reflective periods of his day. He was always a bit mindless on the drive home, still burdened with the after-thoughts of the day's activities or of that night's meeting, concert, game, or whatever. But in the morning, the day was ahead. He could think, organize his mind, enjoy the radio, the view . . . or deliberately daydream.

As he got closer to the school, he shifted his thoughts to the schedule ahead and started the process of thinking like a principal. He knew he had a number of little problems he needed to deal with today . . . but nothing big. He parked in his allotted space, got out, and headed for the building.

"So . . . Grant, where are they going to put you next year? I heard that you were going to the central office." Ed Overly, an Arthur parent who had just dropped off his daughter, yelled out his car window. "Suzy will be attending Moundview . . . any chance you'll be transferred over there? We'd sure like for her to finish out her junior high experience with you."

"Thanks, Ed. Your daughter's a sweetheart. I'd love to be there when she finishes, but your guess is as good as mine as to where I'll be. I'm betting that the board won't announce districtwide administrative changes until, at least, June."

Sterling didn't like the kinds of political games that one sometimes had to play in school administration. It would have been much easier to just tell Overly that he looked forward to working with Suzy at Moundview.

"It's funny," Sterling thought as he entered the building. "The grapevine has me going to a number of different places next fall. The underground bet-board has me slated to go to the one of the high schools . . . the odds are fixed at about 20 to 1, last time I heard. Nobody has identified Moundview as even a remote possibility. They think that Krupt has that job locked up for life." As Sterling reached the main hall leading to his office, he noticed Ralph polishing the glass on the school's display cabinet.

"Hey, Ralph," Sterling said as he approached his head custodian. "Good work there. You know, I'm really pleased with what you've done with this building since I've been here. By the way, just out of curiosity, you got any money on the bet-board over at the shop about where some of us administrator-type folks are going to be next year?"

"Oh, yeah . . . I got Murray going to Swift; Goldblat going to central office; I got five bucks on you going to South High. Why, you got a hot tip for me today?"

"No, not today, Ralph. But here's a sawbuck and a fiver. Let's mess with people's heads a bit. Call this in for me, will ya? Let's start a new slot on the board. Ten bucks on me being named to replace David Washington as the district's director of minority affairs. Five bucks that Washington is going to be transferred to director of transportation. Make sure the guys at the shop know the bet came from me. Let's see what the grapevine does with that. Maybe we can make Washington a bit uncomfortable," Sterling grinned.

"You got it, boss," Ralph chuckled.

"Hi Carrie! Good morning. 'scuse me, Ralph, looks like Carrie needs to talk to me."

"Grant, can I visit with you for a minute . . . now, if that's possible?"

"Sure, Carrie, come in. What's up?" Carrie Phillips was new at Arthur, having replaced a teacher whose spouse had been transferred to another city. Carrie had just graduated from college at midsemester when Sterling hired her for Arthur's ever-expanding special education department.

"Well, Grant, it's like this . . . I've got this IEP, you know . . . individualized education plan meeting this afternoon with an incoming seventh grader's parents, and I hear through the grapevine that they are bringing Illa Kinyon with them. This is only the third IEP I've done, and I'm scared to death of this lady! Even though I'm new here, I've heard a lot of horror stories about this person. Carolyn O'Hara said she would attend as department head, and I appreciate her support . . . but she said that I need to conduct the meeting so I can establish a strong relationship and credibility with the family from the start. She also mentioned that, even though she serves as your administrative designee at all IEP meetings, sometimes you attend. Remember, you said when you hired me that I could come to you if I ever felt I needed help? Well, today I feel like I need help. Can you come to the IEP?"

Carrie was usually a very calm individual. It was one of the characteristics that Sterling looked for in special education teachers. "Not true today," Sterling noted as he listened to her concerns.

"I guess, Carrie, if Illa is coming, I can come too. When's the meeting, and where?"

"Oh, Grant, I'm so relieved! It's at 2 o'clock in the guidance department conference room. I'm so relieved," she repeated.

"What issue or issues do you think might cause contention? What do you know about the child's special education needs?" Sterling asked, attempting to prepare himself for whatever might be discussed.

"Well, from what the previous teacher told me, the new student is a boy . . . uh . . . Bobby Becker. Bobby falls squarely in the middle of the mild range of retardation on his IQ tests. He apparently has some aggressive tendencies or something, however, because his teacher said that she hoped we had better luck coming up with an effective behavior management program than she'd had. She said that Bobby was a tough, strong kid, and she had the bruises to prove it. Because I don't really know this teacher, I'm not sure if her comments reflect accurately on the kid's behavior or rather on her own skill with behavior management. I don't know what she's tried in the past. But she mentioned that he receives speech, OT, and PT services presently, and that his parents are feverish proponents of full inclusion."

"Excuse me just a moment, Carrie. Peggy's trying to get my attention. What is it, Peggy?" Sterling asked.

"The superintendent's on line 2 . . . says he needs to talk to you as soon as possible."

"I'll take it, Peggy, thanks. Carrie, sit tight for a minute."

"Yes sir, good morning," Sterling said as he picked up the phone.

Superintendent Boughton, in his usual bottom-line voice, was calling to inform Sterling that he and Associate Superintendent Robb had just met with Horace Krupt, the current principal at Moundview. They'd informed him that Sterling would be replacing him in June and that the board would make the announcement soon. In the meantime, Krupt was to keep the transfer under wraps. The superintendent also noted that Krupt was not a happy camper when he left the meeting.

"Thank you for the update, Dr. Boughton. I'm in conference with a teacher right now . . . but I appreciate your call. Do I need to call you back? . . . Okay, thank you, again, Dr. Boughton. See you at the board meeting next Monday," Sterling said as he hung up the phone.

"Now, Carrie, where were we?"

"Well, his former teacher said that his parents were always asking for more opportunities for their child to be in general education classes. She also sounded relieved to be rid of the whole family, and sent her condolences that Illa was part of their 'attack team,' as she called it. She said that Illa dominated all meetings she attended, and the parents sat quietly while Illa ranted. Oops, there's my bell. I'll see you at 2 o'clock. And again . . . thanks Grant."

From all that Sterling had heard about Illa Kinyon, she was a bear. Kinyon had been part of the parents' movement that had struggled to obtain basic educational opportunities for disabled children 25 years ago, before PL 94-142 was passed in the mid-seventies. She had advocated aggressively for her son, who had emotional problems, and she had driven several special education teachers to seek other careers. According to the rumor mill, Kinyon was an articulate, intelligent woman who had a basic distrust of anyone who worked for the school district. About 5 years ago, she had developed a private consulting business that dealt exclusively in advocating for parents, and she kept popping up in IEPs around the region.

"Sending Phillips into an IEP unprotected is like sending a lamb to sure slaughter," he thought. "I'm not even sure O'Hara is up to the task of controlling a meeting where Kinyon might be the dominant participant. But then, I've never met Kinyon . . . maybe I'm in trouble too!"

"Grant, your 9 o'clock meeting is here. Judy Hammond . . . from the newspaper. She knows she's early, but she happened to be in the neighborhood so . . ."

"Peggy, I need to take my usual walk through the halls. My God, it's only 8:15. Please tell her I'll be with her in a few minutes. I need to let the troops know I'm alive and on the job." Sterling didn't like missing any opportunities to get out of his office. "Administration by walking around," he called it.

When he returned, he ushered Hammond into his office. Judy Hammond was the wife of a prominent district court judge. Although her reputation was one of a rambling writer and a poor reporter, she maintained her position with the paper because, according to rumor, of her husband's influence.

"Thank you for seeing me, Mr. Sterling. I suppose I should begin . . . I know you're a busy man," Hammond said forcefully, her eyes concentrating on an old microscope Sterling had salvaged from the trash and placed prominently on the credenza behind his desk. She paused, cleared her throat, and smoothed out an unseen wrinkle on her skirt.

"I've heard through my sources that you and other principals in the city have kids sitting in class stoned out of their minds on drugs and that teachers don't even recognize it right under their noses."

"Mrs. Hammond, I don't know who your sources are, and I really don't care. But your information is dead wrong. Need I say more?"

"Well, I'd like you to expand on that if you would."

"Expand? Expand on what, Mrs. Hammond? How can I expand on something that doesn't exist?"

"Are you saying that you don't have any drug problems at—what school is this—oh, of course—Arthur?"

"No, we're no different than any other school. We have a few kids who experiment with drugs, alcohol . . . you name it. We identify those kids quickly and effectively, and get them help. If they become a disturbance, we suspend, and sometimes expel, them from school."

"May I quote you on that?"

"In what context? Oh . . . never mind. Of course you can quote me, Mrs. Hammond."

"I understand the board's going to change this place into some kind of a resource center next year. Is that for kids with drug problems?"

"I don't have any information on that, Mrs. Hammond . . . but I doubt it very much."

"And what's the board going to do with you? I heard that you were going to be transferred to some kind of a supervisory position."

"That's funny, Mrs. Hammond. Actually, I'm thinking about taking the position, and this is just rumor mind you, that's going to be offered to me by your newspaper. Something like city editor, or whatever."

"Oh." Hammond smoothed out her skirt again. "Do you have a degree in journalism?"

"Is that a qualification?" Sterling leaned back in his chair.

"Well, thank you, Mr. Sterling. I'm going to be late for my next appointment. I'll call you if I have any other questions."

Sterling closed his office door behind her as she left. "Another stupid entry for the book I'm going to write someday. I think I'll title the book *What the Hell Was That All About?*"

The rest of the day moved along at a normal pace. There were no food fights in the cafeteria during lunch, nobody punched out anybody else, and Sterling made sure he arrived for Bobby Becker's IEP on time.

"I'm glad all of you were able to make the meeting this afternoon," Carrie Phillips announced after everyone had been introduced. "Here's the way I like to handle IEPs," she continued. "First, I'd like to hear from the school psychologist and the sending school counselor. Then, I'd like to visit with Bobby's parents, Mr. and Mrs. Becker. Now, Mrs. Kinyon, I know you're here serving in the capacity of 'parent's advocate.' I appreciate that, and I'm sure that Mr. and Mrs. Becker do also. The way I understand the role of an advocate, however, is simply that if the parents need any assistance, then they can turn to you for advice. If they don't, then your role, again as I understand it, is one of monitoring. The IEP will be built on what's best for Bobby as agreed on by the Beckers and myself. Okay, with that out of the way, let's begin."

Sterling sat quietly at the table pretending to take notes. "Wow," he thought. "I gotta get whatever pills she's taken since I met with her this morning."

"Well, *I'm* sorry," Illa Kinyon interrupted. "That's *not* the way I understand my role in an IEP . . . and I've been involved in a lot of them, young lady."

Sterling bit his lip. "Aha, here it comes, Carrie. Watch out," he wanted to say.

"Just so I understand what you've just said," Kinyon continued . . ."you're telling me that *your* rules—and they seem to be just that, *your* rules—prohibit me from speaking unless the parents ask me about something. Is that what you're trying to say?"

"Now, Carrie . . . now! Go for the jugular. Kick butt, lady!" Sterling was having a hard time remaining quiet, and his lip was starting to hurt.

"Mrs. Kinyon," Carrie responded. "As I said before, I appreciate the fact that you're here today. I'm sure Bobby's parents appreciate it too. But the only people who are ultimately responsible for Bobby's special education placement and education are his parents and me. So all I'm asking for is the opportunity for that process to begin. If we have any problems along the way, then there will be opportunities for any and all at this table to assist. It's not 'rules,' Mrs. Kinyon, it's a professional request."

"Well, I'm just going to have to object," Kinyon said. "I feel that my . . ."

"Mrs. Kinyon," Sterling said in a quiet but forceful tone, "I think Ms. Phillips has stated her position clearly. Perhaps you'll have an opportunity for input later. In the meantime, let's get on with this, please . . . Bobby needs our help."

The meeting was concluded an hour and a half later. Carrie Phillips, with a little support from her department chair and an occasional smile from Sterling, managed to keep Kinyon under control. Most important, Bobby had a new IEP, and his parents seemed to be pleased when they left the meeting.

Now that Sterling had met Kinyon, he too would be in a position to add a little more scuttlebutt to the Kinyon mystique. He stuck a note in his pocket to remind himself to have flowers delivered to Carrie's classroom the next day.

Driving home that afternoon, Sterling decided to detour into the countryside. He drove instinctively and without thought for what he was doing or where he was going. His newly tuned-up engine was responsive, and he imagined it too would enjoy an opportunity to exhaust some frustrations. He couldn't drive too far . . . he needed to be at an all-school track meet that evening.

He slowed down and pulled into a roadside picnic area.

"All in all," he thought, "the past 2 years at Arthur have been good. It started out looking like an impossible situation . . . or series of situations. Some I solved. Some just seemed to solve themselves."

Sterling opened the car door and got out. It was a beautiful day. It was peaceful. He stretched, walked over to a small stream, and stared at the gently flowing water.

"Another few weeks and my assignment at Arthur will end. Ninth-grade kids will be promoted to the high school, and seventh and eighth graders will be transferred to other schools in the area. The faculty will be split up and sent to who-knows-where. I'll be off to new challenges and more premature gray hair."

Sterling took a deep breath, inhaled the fresh country air . . . and smiled. "My IEP is about to be modified again."

▬▬▬ The Arthur Finale

The entire west wall of the library was glass, almost floor to ceiling, and the 3:45 sun was beaming heat across the room. Betty Curry, Arthur's librarian, was closing the drapes as Sterling entered.

"This faculty and staff look tired," he thought as he crossed the room to a table on the far side, moved some materials, and perched himself in the space he'd cleared.

"Three more days and school will be out," he said, getting everyone's attention. "And 3 days after that you're free spirits again. For the kids," he continued, "it's been a great year; for their parents . . . it's been a great year. For us . . . well, we all have reason to be tired . . . and we are. I want to take a moment to thank you for making the Arthur closing as painless as possible for our kids and parents, and I want to commend each of you for the strength you've shown through the process of finding new professional homes. As of yesterday, each of you has received notification of your new assignment for next year, and I understand that, in most cases, it was your first-choice school."

"Did you get your first-choice school, Grant, or will we be hearing about you doing something with central administration?" Larry Rafael asked from the back of the library.

"Thank you for asking, Larry . . . but you know I'm not at liberty yet to disclose what my next assignment is going to be."

"Aha! Then you know where you're going to be next year!" he challenged.

"I do, Larry. But we'll wait for the board to announce it. It'll be in the paper, I guess, in about 2 weeks or so."

"Grant?" Marline Hammersmith asked in a subdued voice. "Is it an assignment you'll be happy with?"

"Speak up, Marline," somebody hollered from the back of the room.

"She asked if it's an assignment that I'm going to be happy with," Sterling repeated for the room. "Marline, if it's with kids, I'll be happy; if it's with teachers like you and the rest of the folks in this room, I'll be ecstatic. Oh! Look folks, Marline's blushing." The tired room came alive with laughter.

"Now, listen up, folks. We need to make these last days as smooth as possible. Just to review the schedule . . . Thursday's the last full day for classes. Make sure kids have turned in books and other school-owned stuff. Sixth hour will be shortened so that we can supervise kids in the usual locker clean-out and inevitable mess. Yes, I know, Mrs. Curry . . . we'll be on the lookout for library books! Friday, seventh and eighth graders will report to school at 9:00 and gather in the auditorium. Parents have been invited to attend if they wish. I'm just going wish them the best as they go to their new schools next year. I'm not going to march each kid across the stage like we do with our ninth graders, and I've prepared a kind of diploma, with each student's name on it that officially announces to the world, at least to *their* world, that they were among the elite that made up the last class to finish at this school. Then I'm going to—actually, some of our ninth-grade student council members have agreed to help—I'm going to ask the kids to move either to the right or the left of the main aisle, depending on which of the two schools they've been assigned to. Two cheerleaders in uniform from each school will enter the auditorium from the back and attempt—note that I said attempt—to lead the kids in a cheer for their new school. Then I'm going to announce that each of the schools has agreed to include one of Arthur's school colors in their official logos, and flags, and banners, and whatever. Our kids will take a bit of Arthur with them to their new school next year and for years to come. This should help the transition. My speech will be brief—no tears, Marline—and we should be out of there by 10 . . . 10:15. The building should be cleared by 10:45, and I understand we're all going to lunch at Robbie's restaurant. We need to be back at Arthur no later than 1:00. Then at 2:00, we're going to graduate our ninth graders. Any questions, so far?"

"Yeah, Grant. I think dividing the kids according to their new school is a great idea," Mark Waite, one of Arthur's industrial arts teachers commented. "But," he continued, "what if they get too wrapped up and start yelling slurs at each other, or get into one big rivalry-type fight?"

"Mark, that's why *I'm* on the stage and you good folks are supervising in the audience. What the hell do you think I'm paying you for?" Sterling said with a grin.

"Okay," Sterling continued. "The ninth-grade promotion will run just as all the others in the past. Music, pomp, ceremony, parents crying, and all that. We should be finished by 3:30. Monday, Tuesday, and Wednesday next week . . . let's clean this place up, pack up our stuff, and celebrate the successful closure of another year, another chapter in our lives. Dress code is grubby, attitude is positive! Now, it's 4:15 . . . let's go home!"

Sterling didn't take his usual drive around the Arthur campus that afternoon. He liked to check on the looks of the grounds; he liked to see the late afternoon activity on the playing fields. This afternoon, however, he felt emotionally and physically drained. Arthur had been a good assignment. He had learned about the not-too-subtle differences between an inner-city school like Center and a suburban school like Arthur. He had reinforced his belief that kids are kids wherever, and that parents, regardless of their socioeconomic status, send schools the very best kids they have to offer. And he had learned that the principal's job is the same . . . take names, kick butts, and keep the lid on the place. He'd continue that role next year at Moundview.

"Hey, Mr. Sterling!" A group of kids yelled as he turned the corner and headed away from the school.

"Hey, yourselves!" he yelled back.

▬▬▬ For Discussion

General Questions

Using the Sterling paradigm (http://www.corwinpress.com/dunklee.htm) as a model, and speaking from the perspective of a principal, evaluate each episode as follows:

What are the dominant behaviors exhibited by Sterling in this episode?

Is there consensus about this in the class? If not, explain the different viewpoints.

What were the primary actors' individual motives?

How effective was Sterling's behavior in this situation and why?

Can you identify other avenues or approaches that might lead to the same, or a better, conclusion?

If Sterling was a woman,

■ As a female reader, can you identify methodology or behavior that you would change to bring the episode to the same, or similar, closure?

■ As a male reader, what differences in methodology or behavior would you expect to see?

Specific Questions for Each Episode

Which Comes First, the Rumor or the Grapevine?

What effect can the ever-present rumors and grapevine have on the day-to-day operations of a school or school district?

The Arthur Finale

(No specific questions)

6

The Moundview Years

Change: An Intricate Science

Using the same methodology he had used at Center and Arthur, Sterling had sold himself to the Moundview community and staff. He now felt confident enough with his administrative standing and rapport to start the process of selling his middle school concept and converting Moundview from an unexceptional junior high school to what he hoped would be an exemplary middle school.

He had the model plan; he had the authority and position power. He had the desire; he had the responsibility; but he didn't have the *influence* power. He knew he was going to have to build a foundation for change by *borrowing* the influence of others. If he tried to change the present junior high system, which was firmly entrenched at Moundview, without community, teacher, and staff "buy-in," his chances for short-range success were minimal. His chances for long-term implementation were scant. Bottom line: Sterling knew he wasn't going to bring about change at Moundview all by himself.

Clearly, he had the support of central administration and the board of education in whatever he decided to do. It wasn't their support he needed at this juncture, however; it was the Moundview community's. He'd be asking the community to be actively involved in many hours of planning, discussing, and developing new curricular and cocurricular activities. The job would require collective thinking and lots of elbow grease.

His challenge was to promote and implement change from the "miniature high school" structure and mindset, where programs are more important than student needs, to a middle school concept, where student needs take precedence over programs. It was critical, he felt, to have some kind of an empowerment structure that would place his teachers, staff, parents, and students in substantial planning and organizational positions.

Sterling knew that if he micromanaged the change process, his overall management and political leadership would be jeopardized. He had to limit his role to design counsel and visionary leader. He wanted to empower key master teachers, staff members, and prominent representative members of the school's community to play important roles in the development of the master plan. He needed their influence to balance that of those who might resist the changes.

In addition, he wanted to create two new administrative positions at Moundview. He lacked administrative managers to supervise the development process, manage the implementation, and be in charge of making the entire program materialize. He wanted people in those positions who could help others adapt; who possessed effective nonlinear skills; who were willing to think beyond the thinkable and reconceptualize procedures, programs, personnel, and purposes; and, most important, who were capable of making substantial change happen. They would supervise work teams charged with the task of implementing Sterling's vision while incorporating their own ideas. These teams would develop final program elements for him to fine-tune and implement at the appropriate time.

His job was to lead the change effort; to market the newly developed Moundview middle school program to a potentially resistant community; and to assure teachers, staff, and students that change is not scary or confusing. His objective was to modify the culture of Moundview from how it was to how it was going to be, and from "but we've never done it that way before!" to "wow, that's really terrific!" He didn't want merely to change and implement programs. He had to change the methods and motives of the people who would be affected.

If Grant's empowerment strategies worked, Moundview would be reorganized from a traditional hierarchical structure to a participatory environment. Teams of teachers would have the authority to decide how they could best teach and guide adolescent students. After the implementation of the middle school program, Sterling wanted his teachers and staff to continue to be actively involved in significant educational decisions. Teachers and staff are the front line of success in any school organization, he believed. He wanted them to continue to design and re-design, implement, and evaluate all phases of the education process: grading, grouping of learners, curriculum content and development, textbook and supplementary material selection, parent conferencing, goal development, space use, and staff development. He wanted to develop follower-leaders rather than traditional leader-followers.

His position of principal or "boss" would shift from the traditional role of controlling to one of keeping managers and teams trained and flexible enough to achieve their new and continuously evolving goals and objectives. He knew full well the difficulties of leading while managing the diverse problems that can derail a school at any time. He would, of course, continue to manage day-to-day administrative operations. His primary goal, however, would be to motivate others to excel professionally.

He also knew that change would be difficult for some people to accept, and that deviation from a routine, no matter how small, requires a specialized approach to ensure a positive outcome. Because there was no single, foolproof list of steps, he knew he'd have to customize and experiment throughout the change process. He'd have to play the roles of change leader, discoverer, and inventor all at the same time. And, to add a bit more stress to everyone's workload, while all this was taking place, Sterling, his teachers, and his staff would have to tend to the linear business as usual. School was in session.

"So, Grant, how's the transition going?" Associate Superintendent Howard Robb asked as he leaned back in a chair in Sterling's office.

"Well, Howard," Sterling responded, "I've got a good plan; I'm involving lots of other people in the work; I've put respected people in charge of the process; I've created multiple planning and transition teams; I'm providing training in new values and behavior; I'm in the process of developing newsletters, logos, and community events; school is in session; and I'm damned tired. But Howard, you're in a much better position to answer that question than I am. Any complaints at the district office?"

"As a matter of fact, none whatsoever. Your community has been remarkably quiet," Robb noted.

"So, then," Sterling quipped, "my teachers, staff, and I can expect that long overdue Christmas bonus?"

"Right," Robb quickly retorted. "You and me both! Sorry, Sterling, no Christmas bonus. That's an aspect of public service culture you'll never be able to change—or even influence."

For Discussion

General Questions

Using the Sterling paradigm (http://www.corwinpress.com/dunklee.htm) as a model, and speaking from the perspective of a principal, evaluate this episode as follows:

What are the dominant behaviors exhibited by Sterling in this episode?

Is there consensus about this in the class? If not, explain the different viewpoints.

What were the primary actors' individual motives?

How effective was Sterling's behavior in this situation and why?

Can you identify other avenues or approaches that might lead to the same, or a better, conclusion?

If Sterling was a woman,

- As a female reader, can you identify methodology or behavior that you would change to bring the episode to the same, or similar, closure?

- As a male reader, what differences in methodology or behavior would you expect to see?

Specific Questions for Each Episode

Change: An Intricate Science

1. What is position power?

2. What is influence power? Explain the concept of borrowing influence power.

3. Explain the concept of culture. Describe the culture of your own organization.

4. What does Sterling mean when he states that he wants to develop follower-leaders rather than leader-followers?

5. Define the role of change leader. What are some of the key elements leaders need to incorporate to ensure the success of any change?

What if . . . Sterling used his position power and authority simply to dictate "this is the plan, procedures, methodology, and schedule . . . implement immediately"?

When Lip Gloss Becomes Lip Glow

Every school building has distinctive scents. The industrial arts area is identified by the aromas of sawdust, metal shavings, and oil. The science rooms emit the noxious smell of formaldehyde; the library always seems musty; custodial storage areas can be found by following the scent of mop oil and cleaning agents; and the gym and locker room areas sport the familiar fragrance of dirty sweat socks. One scent usually missing from the perfume of the school, except perhaps in the nurse's clinic, is the smell of alcohol.

For about 3 months, teachers and others had complained that the hallway where seventh graders were assigned lockers carried the distinctive bouquet of liquor before school started and after the lunch hour each day. Subsequent locker searches revealed nothing more than some overdue library books and a couple of squirt guns. It was a mystery that begged to be unraveled, but remained stubbornly unsolved until Annie Johnson, a sweet, petite seventh-grade girl with a broad smile and shy disposition, appeared in the school's office one morning.

Annie was the last person Sterling would ever expect to see waiting for him with a discipline referral in her hand. As Sterling walked by her, he gently removed the slip from Annie's hand and read the teacher's note.

"Annie giggled her way through the first 15 minutes of class—I had to tell her three times to quiet down and get to work. I think she needs to hear some 'words of wisdom' from the principal!"

Sterling frowned at Annie as she huddled in a semifetal position in an office chair. "Annie, I think we need to talk about this."

Annie followed Sterling into his office and again assumed her huddled posture.

"Annie, Annie, Annie!" Sterling feigned anguish. "I'm really having a hard time believing that you, of all people, are in trouble with a teacher. I think you better tell me about it."

"It wasn't my idea, Mr. Sterling. I don't know why we did it. It just seemed like fun. Please don't tell my parents. I wouldn't do it anymore!"

Annie was crying as Sterling reread the discipline slip, searching for some correlation between what Annie was saying and what the slip implied.

"Annie, please explain." Sterling and Annie were still reading from different scripts as Annie continued.

"We stop at Mary Ellen's house each day on our way to school. Her parents always leave for work before we come to walk with her, and we go in her house and put liquor from her parents' cabinet in our lip-gloss bottles. Just a little bit!" Sterling handed Annie a tissue to wipe the tears now starting to flow down her cheeks.

"You mean those little lip balm-lipstick-type tubes that you use for chapped lips?" Sterling asked.

"Yes," Annie whimpered. "They don't hold very much and we just put it on our lips and lick it off!"

"Who is the 'we' you're talking about?" Sterling set the discipline slip aside and started jotting down notes. Annie listed a total of 12 seventh-grade girls, including herself and Mary Ellen Janoski.

"Okay, Annie, you just sit here for a minute. I've got to think about this. I'll be right back."

Sterling walked out to the main office, leaving Annie with a fistful of tissues to dab her tears. He gently closed the door behind him. "Phyllis, please send call-slips for all these young ladies to see me immediately."

Sterling picked up Phyllis's phone and pressed the numbers for both of the school's counselors, Fran Winters and Bob Grimm. "I need you in my office now," he told them. "We've got a little problem that I think you need to be involved with."

Sterling glanced at the master schedule and identified a room that wouldn't have a class in it for another 30 minutes. As the girls and counselors arrived, he escorted them and Annie down the hall to room 104. He had told Annie to act as if she had been called out of class as the others had and not to talk with her friends about the conversation she had had with him. "We don't want you singled out as a 'snitch,' do we?"

"Young ladies, let's talk about your lip gloss bottles," Sterling began.

There was a shocked silence, and the girls' complexions paled. One by one, each girl began to cry. The counselors, leaning against the wall at the side of the room, had no clue what Sterling had said to set off this frenzy of anguish.

"All right, young ladies, this is what I know. I know that you have been stopping by Mary Ellen's house each morning and filling lip gloss bottles with booze. I know that you have been bringing the bottles to school and wiping the booze on your lips and licking it off. I know that you thought that this was a cool thing to do and I know that you have been caught and now think maybe that this was not so cool. Well, it's not a cool thing to do and you're in trouble. I'm going to let you think about your predicament for a few minutes while I talk with your counselors. We'll be right back."

Sterling motioned the counselors into the hall and closed the classroom door. The girls' crying followed them out.

"Well, counselors, how do you want to handle this?" he asked.

Fran and Bob looked at Sterling. Their facial expressions clearly said, "What do you mean, us?"

"Any suggestions?" he probed. Their facial expressions remained impassive.

"All right then, let's go back in the room; thanks for your scholarly guidance in this matter," Sterling grinned at them and shook his head. He liked to get his counselors involved in these kinds of things, but he knew from past experience that they really didn't like to get into problem solving until they had a chance to examine what they called "the root cause." He didn't have time for that today.

"Young ladies, here's what you're going to do. You're going to go home after school today and tell your folks the whole and honest story about your lip gloss escapade, including this meeting. You're going to tell them that you can't come back to school tomorrow until they call me. I'm going to give you a phone number where your folks can reach me this evening. After they call me to let me know that you've shared this information with them, all of you and I are going to meet again and decide what your punishment, as far as school is concerned, is going to be. Any questions?"

The room was silent except for the desolate sound of sniffling.

"Go to your lockers and bring your lip gloss bottles to me, and then return to class. I'll be standing outside the main office door."

One by one, the girls met Sterling and the counselors in the hall and sheepishly traded their now infamous lip gloss bottles for a card with Sterling's home phone number on it. Later, each one's parents called Sterling to let him know that their daughter had shared the problem with them. Each parent was upset and prepared to support the school in whatever Sterling decided to do. The parents also shared with him the prescription for punishment they had developed for their daughters at home. Earlier that day, Sterling and the counselors had worked out a plan that he was able to share with parents when they called. School district policy required that the girls be suspended. Because each girl had been truthful with her parents, however, Sterling reduced the mandatory 10-day suspension to 3 days. Each girl would spend 2 days at home and 1 day in a community alcohol awareness seminar. The real punishment, Sterling felt, had been forcing the girls to tell their parents the story and having their parents make the phone call to him that evening. He considered that as time served.

Mary Ellen's parents installed a lock on their liquor cabinet, and Sterling was able to send a note back to the teacher who sent Annie to the office for giggling in class. The note simply stated:

Re: Annie's problem—Annie assures me that it won't happen again!

Good Intentions, Good Results, Bad Choice

Greg Baldwin was one of the best art teachers in the district, and Sterling felt privileged to have him on the Moundview faculty. His classes overflowed with eager students each year.

Sterling enjoyed visiting Baldwin's classroom often to see what new things kids were creating. He had just stepped in the art room door when Baldwin approached him. He knew from the look on Baldwin's face that he was about to hear something exciting.

"Grant, have I got a proposition for you. You know that I do part-time work as a projectionist for the Argyle Theater. Well," he continued, "the night manager down there is an excellent cartoonist and impressionistic painter. I've seen some of his work, and it's really great stuff. He doesn't work during the day, and he's willing to volunteer to come to Moundview each day and work with our kids and me—like a second teacher for free! What do you think?"

Sterling could hear the excitement in Baldwin's voice.

"Greg, invite him in to observe your classes for a day and then bring him in to meet me. I need to talk to the gentleman first. It sounds too good to be true."

Sterling always welcomed parent volunteers at the school; however, he'd never had any experience with a nonparent volunteer, and was a bit puzzled by this overture.

Later that same week, Baldwin introduced Sterling to his friend Harvey Green, night and weekend manager at the Argyle Theater and art aficionado. Green had just finished spending the day in Baldwin's classes.

"Mr. Green, as I understand it, you want to volunteer to work with Greg here at Moundview. Is that correct?"

Green's affirmative answer was followed by a verbal resume of his interest and involvement with art. Green, a portly man about 40 years old, was well dressed and groomed and spoke with authority about art and about his love for children.

Sterling was so impressed with Green's interest that he presented Green with some basic do's and don'ts and gave his blessing to the arrangement that Baldwin and Green had worked out. Within a short time, he noticed the affection Baldwin's students developed for Green as they worked together on special projects. Green unquestionably filled the role of a second full-time teacher in the art room and, in addition, volunteered to work with the English and music departments on scenery for school plays, concerts, and musicals. Teachers, students, and parents quickly warmed to Green's enthusiasm for art and his gentleness with kids, and Baldwin and Sterling were thrilled at their stroke of luck.

The auditorium was packed at the final evening music concert of the school year. Green and a group of hand-picked students had created a spectacular spring backdrop for the stage. Sterling stood at the back of the auditorium with a group of teachers, enjoying the performance. Green, who was now winding up 7 months at Moundview, stood beside Baldwin beaming with pride at the kids on the stage.

As usual, the district's school security office had been notified that the building was going to be used that evening. Security required such notice so that they could be aware of late evening crowds around school buildings. Marvin Bonnert, chief of security for the school district, decided to drop by. He said hello to Sterling, then stood just inside the door listening to the performance. It was not unusual for Bonnert to stop by the school. He and Sterling had been friends for years. He enjoyed seeing kids at their best as an occasional break from seeing some of them at their worst. Bonnert listened for a while then worked his way over to Sterling, stopping along the way to greet teachers. He was smiling as he approached and reached out to shake Sterling's hand.

"Great show! The kids are really good! But I need to talk with you. Outside. Now!" Bonnert was still shaking Sterling's hand as he punctuated his words with a series of hard squeezes. He was still smiling as Sterling followed him into the hall. As they reached the hall, his expression immediately turned serious.

"What the hell is Harvey Green doing here?" Bonnert's voice was quiet but demanding. "Grant, do you know that guy?"

"He's been a volunteer in our art classes for about 7 months now, Marvin. He's great! What's the problem?"

"Green is a convicted pedophile. He's been in and out of jail for years. Last I heard of him he was an outpatient from the mental ward at the Veterans' Hospital. Look, I'm gonna use your telephone and find out his current status. I'll get back to you in a few minutes."

"Marvin? . . ."

"I'll be discreet about this. You go back inside. I'll get right back with you." He knew that Sterling could be in trouble. He knew that Sterling sensed the depth of that trouble.

As promised, within a few minutes, Bonnert motioned Sterling back to the hall.

"No wants or warrants, Grant, but he's a court-ordered outpatient. He's forbidden to have any association with juveniles. He's got to go, Grant! We need to meet with him right away and order him to stay away from here!"

"I'll take care of it as soon as the program ends tonight," promised Sterling. "You might want to sit in. I'm going to have one very surprised and upset art teacher, and I imagine that Green is going to be pretty upset also. Do you mind hanging around?"

At the end of the program, Sterling caught Baldwin and Green in the hall and asked them to meet him in his office for a moment. After spending a few minutes saying goodnight to parents, he took a deep breath and loosened his tie in anticipation of a difficult encounter.

"Come in, gentlemen. We need to talk for a minute. This is Marvin Bonnert, chief of school security. I invited him in to listen to what I have to say."

Greg Baldwin looked totally confused.

"Harvey," Sterling looked him straight in the eyes, "Maybe I didn't ask the right questions when I first met you. Maybe if I had, and you had answered them truthfully, you wouldn't have had this opportunity at Moundview. The bottom line is this. I've just been informed about your problems with juveniles, your problems with the court, and your status at Veterans' Hospital. Greg, do you have any idea about what I'm talking about?"

Greg gave Sterling a scared, puzzled look.

"No, sir," he said hesitantly.

"Harvey, do you want to explain your situation to Greg or do you want me to?"

Green started to cry. "Please, I can't talk about it; you tell him if you have to. I'm sorry, Mr. Sterling and Greg, I'm really sorry."

Sterling walked to the window and looked at parents and their kids walking and driving away from the school.

"Harvey, listen to me," Sterling turned and said in a soft, but assertive, voice. "I want to thank you for the really neat stuff you've done for kids and teachers at Moundview these past months. We really appreciate your efforts. We all like you very much. Now, Officer Bonnert is going to walk you out to your car and explain to you that you can't come back to Moundview or have any further contact with Moundview kids. I'm really sorry about this, Harvey. Go with Officer Bonnert now, please."

Green got up slowly, his head still bowed. Bonnert opened the door and followed him out. "I'll be back in a minute," he said.

"You can relax now, Greg. We really screwed up, and it's my fault. I should have checked this guy out more intensively than I did."

When Bonnert returned, he and Sterling explained the whole situation to Greg. Even though Sterling told him not to worry, Greg blamed himself for the situation as he left. Sterling thanked Bonnert and went back to his window, wishing that this wonderful experience for the kids hadn't come to such a negative end.

Two days later, Bonnert reported back to Sterling, "During the 7 months that Harvey Green worked with kids at Moundview there were no reports of child abuse or incidents attributed to him anywhere in the city. For the first time in 15 years, Green was happy, according to his psychiatrist at the hospital. The psychiatrist didn't know why."

Bonnert later reported that, almost immediately after the end of Green's tenure at Moundview, he left town without the court's permission and was arrested in a city about 200 miles from Moundview for soliciting a minor. "The police found hundreds of kiddie-porn photographs in his rented room," Bonnert said. "I met with the police and went over all the pictures. I was relieved to find that none of the pictures were of local kids, especially Moundview kids." Sterling and Baldwin were also relieved.

Title Censored ▨▨▨▨

Sterling looked at the return address on the envelope marked "Confidential." He guessed that the senders, Mr. and Mrs. Markem Curtis, might be the parents of Amy Curtis, one of his new seventh-grade students.

September 1

Mr. Grant Sterling
Principal
Moundview Junior High School
1504 W. Greenview

Dear Principal Sterling,

  I am writing to you in regard to my daughter Amy Curtis, a seventh grader at your school. We are very concerned about ensuring that Amy gets not only a good education, but an education that is right. Her father (Markem) and I wish to request your assistance in helping us ensure that Amy is not subjected to any testing that might be used to determine her psychological needs or her feelings toward her personal or family life. In addition, any outside-of-classroom testing, evaluations, or meetings with school counselors, psychologists, or social workers do not meet with our approval. Also, we are quite concerned that Amy not be involved in the discussion of morals or values, in genealogical research, or in sensitivity activities.

  Please inform Amy's teachers of our desires and assure them that we are ready to assist them in any way. To ensure that we, your school, and its teachers are working together in Amy's best interests, we would like for you to require your teachers to provide us with copies of any materials, outside of the textbooks, that they will be using in class. We would like to have such materials at least 1 week in advance. Finally, we are aware that public schools include exposure to different kinds of religions in their curriculum, and that your school library provides teachers with videotapes and movies concerning other areas of our society that we do not wish to have Amy exposed to. We have visited your school's library (media center), and have talked with your media specialist. Attached to this letter please find a list of tapes, movies, books, and other print material that you have in your library, or that teachers will be using in their classrooms, that Amy may not be exposed to without our express permission. In addition, please find some articles from a publication that we subscribe to that you may find inspiring.

(Continued)

Sterling folded the cover letter back and examined the attached list. He took a deep breath, sighed, and continued reading.

If we object to any of the materials that Amy will be exposed to, we do not give permission for Amy to be removed from that class or class period. We have been advised by our church that our rights in this matter have been given us through the United States Supreme Court in the case of *Mendis v. Dobson Unified School District #225*, which states that we have the right to insist that the material be removed from the curriculum. We sincerely hope that we can work together on this matter, and that Amy's education will be a cooperative one between you, Amy's teachers, and us.

Sincerely,

Mrs. Markem Curtis

Sterling turned in his chair and reached for one of the few books he had kept from his graduate school coursework.

"I wonder if this case is cited in my old education law book?" he thought as he ran his finger down the index page. He found the case with references to prayer and religion, but none of the other things that Mrs. Curtis had mentioned as concerns.

He opened the school district's policy book and found the following statement:

In the event that a child or his or her legal guardian objects to any teaching materials (print or nonprint) or books (text, reference, or library), Form 1256 is to be provided to them.

Although he had only had to use the form once before, Sterling knew that Form 1256 was most commonly used when a parent or student objected to a library book or a film. School principals were advised to hand or mail the form to them, and then the complaining party was to mail the form directly to the superintendent's office. "Maybe I should make a couple hundred copies of these and just mail them to Amy's parents, without comment," he laughed.

He knew, however, that this situation needed to be handled with extreme care and that, whatever he did, he needed to protect Amy from being caught in a conflict between the school and home. In addition, he needed to limit awareness of the problem to his office so that teachers and counselors wouldn't start to worry and practice unwarranted restraint in working with Amy or any other students. He knew that, every now and then, some people seemed to need a reason to get hysterical. This challenge might provide just such a reason.

He picked up the phone and called two other principals. Neither had ever experienced such a demand. They both suggested that Sterling wait until the parents march in and demand that something be changed, then hand them Form 1256 and see what happens.

Although he was hesitant to do it, he called the superintendent's office and explained the situation to Associate Superintendent Howard Robb.

"Send me a copy of the letter and attachments, and I'll refer them to our attorney," Robb responded. "What kind of nuts are these people?"

Sterling ignored the question and simply replied that he would send a copy of the material today. He knew that he would not receive a reply from either Robb or the attorney for weeks, if at all. The school district had a tendency not to react to potential problems but to wait until after an explosion to take action. Sterling called this *"ex post facto* crisis management." He knew that if he wanted to head off this potential problem, he would have to do it himself.

He called the Curtis home that evening and invited Mr. and Mrs. Curtis in for a "mutual interest" meeting the next morning. Up to this point, he had suppressed his personal thoughts about the letter. Although he felt the requests were ridiculous and unwarranted, he knew that playing with the Curtis's personal values was a dangerous game. He would try to be neutral and seek some kind of a compromise for Amy's sake.

Mr. and Mrs. Curtis arrived at the agreed-on time the next morning. They brought three people with them whom they identified as friends from their church.

"As you know from our telephone conversation last night, I received your letter and attachments yesterday. Help me understand what the school needs to do to ensure that we are meeting Amy's needs," Sterling said in his most professional voice. He was hoping that they would be less assertive in this face-to-face meeting than they had been in their letter. They weren't. What they had proscribed for Amy in their letter was based on strongly held beliefs. Sterling could hear no room for compromise as he listened.

"All right," he said as they finished explaining their position. "Here's the dilemma as I see it. Although I agree with your right to ask that the school adhere to your wishes, I cannot agree with the methods you have outlined for the school to follow in providing a continuing education for Amy. I can agree, because it's part of my job, to monitor the curriculum and instructional methods here at Moundview. I can't agree, however, to alter anything just to respond to your blanket request. The best that I can do is to offer you these alternatives." He provided the Curtises with an explanation and a copy of Form 1256. In addition, he suggested that perhaps a private or parochial school might fit their particular family needs better than Moundview could.

"But," he said, "I'd like you to give us a try first. You and Amy are just starting at this school, and I want you to know that I want Amy, and you, to be happy here. The door to my office is always open. So when you or Amy have a question or concern about school, feel free to call me or come in so that we can discuss it. Fair enough?"

"You'll notify Amy's teachers of our concerns?" Mr. Curtis asked.

"No," Sterling replied. "I don't want Amy treated differently from other students. I don't think that would be fair to Amy. I'm also not going to place your letter or any of the attachments in Amy's file. Again, I don't think that this would be in Amy's best interest. Can we work together on this for Amy's sake?"

"Thank you for seeing us today, we'll be in touch," Mr. Curtis said coldly. Sterling shook hands with each of them as he escorted them to the door.

Just in case the Curtis family decided to bypass him and send a letter directly to the teachers, Sterling included a note in his weekly memo to faculty and staff that, if they received any requests from parents or others to alter the curriculum or their teaching methods or materials, he was to be notified immediately. He didn't believe in *ex post facto* management.

Amy had a successful stay at Moundview and was active in a variety of extracurricular activities. Amy's parents never used Form 1256 or called Sterling with any additional concerns about Amy's education. Guidance from the associate superintendent or counsel from the school district's attorney never came.

A Classic Snow Job

"Lynn, with the adoption of a new text for eighth-grade social studies, the district will pay for one teacher from each school to attend a 2-day conference sponsored by the publishers. The conference will be in San Diego. Do you want to go?" Sterling asked Lynn Jordan, the chair of the school's social studies department. "The conference is scheduled for Thursday and Friday, February 4 and 5. Just the right time to trade the snow and cold of this area for a few days in the warm sun."

"It's very tempting, Grant. But I've already missed a number of school days this year working on the textbook adoption committee. I don't think it would be fair to my students for me to be away much more. Let's think about who else from the department would be a good person to send."

"It's your call, Lynn. Whoever you choose will be okay with me, as long as whoever it is understands that he or she will have the responsibility of sharing conference information with the rest of the department."

"We have a department meeting scheduled for tomorrow," she said. "I'll extend the invitation to the group and let them fight it out. I'll let you know who the lucky person is after the meeting."

Karl Riggins was chosen to attend. Karl was a veteran social studies teacher who had completed 18 years in the district when Sterling was asked to find a place for him at Moundview. Riggins did not have an exemplary record as a teacher, and Sterling was promised two additional teacher aides if he would accept Riggins. Riggins claimed he was being "picked on" by his former principal and had raised a stink trying to get transferred. Riggins had now been at Moundview for 2 years and, although his teaching had improved, he worked with what Sterling called "a union mentality." He had disappointed Sterling often with his refusal to participate in student activities before and after school. "I'm sorry, Grant, but it's not in my contract," he would say when Sterling suggested that his students would really appreciate it if he would attend some of their extracurricular activities.

Although Sterling was not particularly pleased with the department's choice to attend the conference, he made the travel and lodging arrangements for Riggins. Under cold threatening skies, Riggins flew off to sunny San Diego on Wednesday. He was scheduled to fly back on Sunday.

"Maybe a few days in the sun will help bring some warmth to Riggins' disposition," Sterling thought as he made arrangements for a substitute to cover his classes. The substitute was not needed, however. A weather front that threatened to cancel Riggins' flight turned into a nasty snowstorm. The storm prompted the closing of all schools in the district for the Thursday and Friday that Riggins was at the conference.

Sterling was in the hall talking to a group of students when Riggins returned to school on Monday. "Have a good trip, Mr. Riggins?" he hollered as Riggins headed for his classroom.

"Wonderful, Mr. Sterling, the weather was great compared to what you had here. I'll tease you about it later," he laughed.

When Riggins stopped by after school that day, he informed Sterling that since he was officially on duty in San Diego when school was canceled due to weather, the district owed him 2 days of paid leave.

"Let me get this straight," questioned Sterling. "The school district paid your expenses to go to a conference in San Diego while the rest of us froze our butts off here, and you want time off because we had to cancel school?"

"You got it, Grant. I had to be at those meetings while the rest of the district's teachers got to stay home. The district will have to schedule make-up days, but I don't have any days that I'm required to make up. I was on duty those 2 days."

Sterling was flabbergasted. Although he could see the procedural logic in what Riggins was saying, he had a difficult time grasping the fairness of the situation. Where was this man's loyalty?

"Furthermore," Riggins continued, "I will expect some kind of extra duty pay if you want me to train social studies teachers on the methods that I learned in San Diego."

"Karl, help me understand," Sterling leaned toward Riggins. "I understand that what you're telling me is your usual work-to-the-contract way of thinking. However," he leaned even closer to Riggins, "what you're really saying to me is that kids and teachers—your students and colleagues—are not as important to you as your allegiance to your contract, and a substitute teacher can present your lesson plans as well as you can?"

Riggins looked at Sterling for a moment before he answered. "I don't know if I would put it exactly that way, Grant, but, yes, my first allegiance is to me and my contract."

"And you want me to pay you extra to share with your colleagues the teaching methodologies that you got from the conference? The very people who selected you to represent them?"

"Of course," replied Riggins, "Why are you acting so hostile?"

"I find what you're saying appalling . . . no, Karl, just plain crappy. Put your request in writing and I'll consider it."

"I've already given you notice, Grant; I don't need to put anything in writing. Furthermore, I don't appreciate what you just said."

"Karl, I pride myself on controlling my temper, but I'm about to lose it with you. Leave my office now please. You're working overtime according to your damned contract. Next thing you'll be demanding is pay for this meeting." He was shaking as Riggins casually strolled out the door.

"I'm going to nail that man's butt to the wall." He was still angry when he placed a call to Fred Rose, assistant superintendent for personnel.

The very words that he didn't want to hear were the first words that Rose conveyed after Sterling gave him a synopsis of the situation. "Insensitive as it may seem, he's got the ball in his court and we'll go ahead and pay for a substitute to cover for him for the 2 make-up days. I know you don't like it," Rose continued, "and neither do I, but it's not worth the hassle and expense of a formal grievance. You're taking it too personally, Grant. Go find a punching bag, pretend it's Riggins, and beat the hell out of it. You'll feel much better."

Later that week, Sterling met with Riggins during his planning period. "Riggins," he said, "You can have your 2 days off when we schedule the make-up days. I've got to be honest with you though; I don't think it's fair, and I don't like it. Rest assured, however, that I will continue to treat you as a professional even though I don't think you're acting like one."

"That's quite punitive of you, Grant. But you can rest assured that I will never ask you for anything outside of my rights. You really do need to see somebody about that attitude of yours. When do you want to schedule an inservice workshop so I can train the rest of the social studies department in the use of the new textbooks?"

"With or without pay?" Sterling angrily snapped.

"Oh, well," Riggins said, "I'll donate my services this time."

"Forget it, Karl, I wouldn't think of imposing on your peculiar sense of duty in any way. I'll work something else out."

He hoped this confrontation would encourage Riggins to request a transfer so Sterling could say, "You've got to be kidding! I'm not into transferring people that I'd love to fire. Are you sure you don't want to resign?"

Unfortunately, he never got the opportunity to present Riggins with this option. Riggins continued to be a marginal teacher and carefully avoided any violations of his contract. If he had slipped below satisfactory in his teaching, or ignored a contract expectation, Sterling was primed to be unmerciful in his reaction, and Riggins knew it.

Sterling used some of the school's inservice funds to bring a representative of the textbook company to Moundview to provide a special workshop for the rest of the social studies department. He told Riggins that he didn't need to attend.

Don't Spit Into the Wind!

All the district's principals had two telephones on their desks. One was for regular everyday use; the other, called the "crisis phone," was directly connected to the superintendent's office. In emergencies, the superintendent could use this phone to hold a conference call with every outpost in the district. If a building principal was out of the office when a call came through, secretaries were expected to answer the phone and immediately deliver the message to one of the building administrators. The crisis phone was most often used to relay warnings about dangerous weather conditions that could prompt school closings or the cancellation of after-school activities. Although the crisis phone didn't ring often, Sterling was constantly aware of its existence.

It was a Friday afternoon under sunny, clear skies when the phone rang. The superintendent had placed an all-school conference call to alert principals to a police report his office had just received. The message was terse. Before school dismissed that day, each principal was to warn students that a man in a light blue older-model car was attempting to entice younger students to "take a ride with him." The man had been identified by police as an escapee from a local institution who had a history of molesting children. The superintendent also suggested that all principals drive around their school's perimeter as an added precaution.

After acknowledging that he had received the message, Sterling hung up the phone and looked at his watch.

"We still have another class period to go before the dismissal bell for the day," he noted. "Instead of making an announcement over the intercom, I think I'll call all students together for a meeting in the school auditorium." He had some other matters to talk with them about, and he would include the warning at the same time.

He estimated that he'd need about 30 minutes, so he'd announce at the beginning of the final class period of the day, around 2:30, that he was calling an assembly at 3:00 and that students would be dismissed for the day directly from the assembly. He wouldn't require faculty to attend—they deserved a break once in a while, and what better time than on a Friday afternoon.

Sterling made the announcement, and, at the appointed time, students reported to the auditorium for the impromptu meeting. After he dismissed the students, Sterling went to his car and patrolled the neighborhood—something he commonly did anyway. He returned to the office later and reported to his secretaries that everything was okay.

The weekend passed, and Sterling quickly forgot the activities of Friday afternoon. Although it had not been a routine Friday dismissal, it was not what he would call a memorable occurrence. As he approached his desk Monday morning, he noticed a hand-written letter placed squarely in the center of his desk-pad. The date on the letter indicated that it had been written Friday. He read:

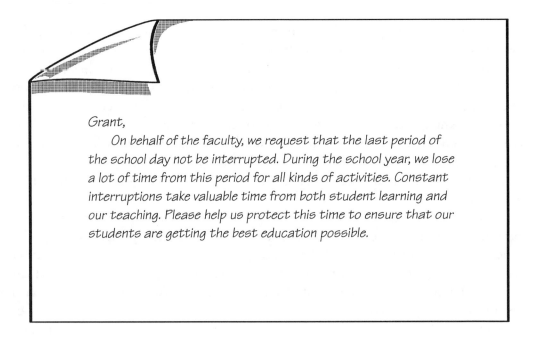

Grant,

On behalf of the faculty, we request that the last period of the school day not be interrupted. During the school year, we lose a lot of time from this period for all kinds of activities. Constant interruptions take valuable time from both student learning and our teaching. Please help us protect this time to ensure that our students are getting the best education possible.

The letter was signed by six members of the faculty. He read the letter a second time and noted that the six signers were all teachers or coaches who sponsored such activities as interschool sports, plays, and concerts. "How ironic," he grumbled. "These are the very teachers and coaches who always ask to have kids dismissed early from afternoon classes to participate in athletics and special rehearsals."

He was flabbergasted at the lack of foresight demonstrated by the signers, and angered by the lack of thanks for giving teachers a break on a Friday afternoon. Even though he hadn't told the faculty the rationale for the assembly, he had assumed that they would see his efforts as a gift. Evidently he was wrong, he thought, as he picked up his phone and summoned his vice principals to his office for an immediate meeting.

He was visibly angry as he confronted his administrative partners. "Alice, Randy . . . read this and tell me what you think!" he said as he thrust the letter in front of them. "Read this and tell me why I shouldn't be livid with this faculty!" Both vice principals sat down and read the letter while Sterling paced and fumed behind them.

"All right," he demanded. "You've read the thing . . . give me one good reason why I shouldn't be angry!"

"Well, Grant," Alice said calmly as Randy nodded in approval, "they didn't understand the importance of the assembly. They didn't understand that you thought you were doing them a favor by not requiring them to attend."

"What was I supposed to do?" Sterling asked. "Announce over the intercom that I needed to have an assembly to warn students about a pervert running around in the community? Then, add, and by the way, faculty, while I'm dealing with this with the kids, feel free to get yourself a cup of coffee, put your feet up, and relax! Yeah. Right! Putting that aside," Sterling continued, "how do you explain the rationale for this request, considering the types of extracurricular activities the signers sponsor?"

Both vice principals reexamined the letter, this time focusing on the signatures. "Well, I guess," Randy said, "these are the ones who picked up the battle flag from a few of the other faculty and decided to carry it to your office."

"I agree with Randy," Alice said.

"So what would happen to their particular programs if I complied?" Sterling shot back.

"Clearly, Grant, the coaches would be very upset. It would play havoc with their schedules and the schedules of other schools if you refused to let athletes out early to travel to or prepare for games. The drama and music teachers always ask for extra rehearsal time before programs. They would be in trouble."

"Right," Sterling interrupted, "the very people who signed this thing on behalf of the faculty! Explain that, if you can."

They had no response. They'd never seen Sterling lose his cool before, and quickly decided that they were not going to be able to respond appropriately to any of his challenges. Although he was extremely angry, his analysis of the situation was all too logical. The signers of the letter were in trouble, and they, the school's vice principals, would be in trouble as well if they didn't recognize two important things. One, it was stupid for these particular faculty members to be the sponsors of this request, and two, Sterling was taking the whole thing personally. They knew how hard he had worked to make Moundview a comfortable, rewarding, and fun place for teachers to teach and kids to learn. And now this. They knew that Sterling was hurt and that they were being used as an outlet for his emotions.

"All right," Sterling said as he looked at their apprehensive expressions, "I'll deal with it. Thanks for listening. I'll let you know what I'm going to do about this later. Have a good day."

He laid the letter aside and proceeded with the normal business of the day. Unfortunately, as the day progressed, his attitude changed from "get mad" to "get even." Although this was an uncommon attitude for Sterling, it continued to fester.

The next regularly scheduled meeting with faculty was Wednesday morning before school. He might want to deal with the letter and its demand at that time, or he could just ignore it and see if the challenge would die.

He made a decision concerning the letter that evening. The next day he called his vice principals back to his office and announced his decision. "Any questions?" he asked when he had finished. Neither Randy or Alice spoke. After witnessing Sterling's anger yesterday, they didn't think anything they said would be right. They sensed the decision he had made was a risky one, one that reflected his need to get even rather than his common sense. Although they could usually be candid with Sterling and make suggestions or debate issues, this time they didn't think he wanted any input from them. There was nothing to do but wait and see how the faculty reacted.

Wednesday morning's faculty meeting had its usual short agenda, and Sterling concluded the meeting by passing out a copy of the letter he had received Monday. He wanted the faculty to have the letter in their hands when he announced his decision.

"I received this letter Monday morning on behalf of the faculty," he explained. "I've read it carefully and considered the problem, and I've decided to comply with your request. Starting today, the last period of the school day will not be interrupted for any reason, except emergencies, for the rest of the year. I recognize what the rewards will be for our academic classes. I also recognize the problems it will cause for our nonacademic activities. But clearly, the signers of this letter," and he purposely emphasized, "on behalf of the faculty, thought long and hard about the consequences of this request and have already figured out how to work around the problem this will obviously create for them. I commend them for their efforts and I'm looking forward to seeing a copy of their revised schedule of events. Thank you for bringing this problem to my attention. Have a good day."

As he left the meeting, he could hear the buzzing sound of teachers swarming around each other to discuss his closing proclamation. He was not surprised to hear a couple of teachers who followed him out say that they had never seen, or even heard of, the alleged faculty-supported letter.

Sterling purposely avoided the teachers' lounge for the rest of the day. He knew from the grapevine that highly charged discussions about the letter were taking place among faculty groups. By the end of the day, without asking, he had a fairly complete picture of the faculty's response. Many were angry at the letter signers for including them in a letter they didn't know about. More important, the academic teachers were unmerciful in teasing the nonacademic ones with the question that Sterling had left in everybody's mind—how are you going to work yourself out of this dilemma?

Alice and Randy reported that a number of coaches had come to them right after the faculty meeting to ask whether Sterling was bluffing and whether he would eventually let them off the hook. The vice principals had told each one that they wouldn't bet on it. Even though they didn't believe he had made the right decision, Alice and Randy were being pulled into Sterling's get-even game. They had no choice.

One by one, the coaches, the drama teacher, and the band and choir directors tried to persuade Sterling to change his mind. At the same time, a large number of math, science, English, and social studies teachers told him it was about time.

Although it was difficult, and schools across the city had to adjust game starting times to accommodate the late arrival of Moundview teams, Sterling held his ground until the school year was completed.

In the end, he knew that he had gotten even with the signers of the letter. He admitted to his vice principals, however, that he had probably been as dumb as the signers were when he made his decision.

"Decisions made in anger," he explained, "are seldom wise decisions. As a result of this fiasco, I am now faced with a faculty that may be afraid to confront me on issues. I need to work hard on getting my image, in their minds, back to a place where they feel free to argue or suggest alternatives to me."

The vice principals agreed with his concern and promised to help him resolve any lingering faculty image problems the next year. And, in the future, they'd try to head off actions that might put Sterling in a similar corner.

Open House, Closed Door

Sterling always scheduled two open houses for parents during the school year. He wanted parents to be able to see their children's teachers in action, in front of the classroom. He wanted parents to feel some of the same excitement that he and his teachers felt toward the education enterprise—and experience firsthand the environment in which teachers and students worked together each school day. Most important, he wanted parents to know teachers by something more than their last names.

His usual open house format began with a brief meeting in the school's auditorium. There, parents received copies of their children's class schedules and were invited to follow them through a shortened day. Each class was 10 minutes long, with the usual 3 minutes between classes. For 2 hours, parents could experience their children's school world.

There was one recurring problem with open houses. Many teachers, although extremely competent working with kids, were scared to death of speaking to a room full of parents. They anticipated open houses nervously. Nevertheless, the open house adventure for parents was always a good exercise in bringing the school and the home closer together. Teachers always pulled it off beautifully in spite of their fears. This is what Sterling was thinking as he welcomed parents to Moundview for the fall open house. His presentation was short, and parents were quickly dispatched to experience the abbreviated version of their children's school day. His job now was to wander the halls giving directions, answering questions, and actively seeking public relations opportunities.

He was visiting with a small group of parents in the hall when another parent suddenly burst out of a classroom. The look of indignation on the man's face caused Grant to excuse himself from the group so that he could catch up with the clearly upset parent and find out what the problem was. He caught the man just as he was leaving the school and heading for his car.

"Sir, excuse me, I'm Grant Sterling. Can I help? You seem to be upset about something." Sterling was close enough to read the man's name tag. "You're Jim Hogan, Lane's father, aren't you?"

"You know, Sterling," Hogan fumbled to unlock his car door. "You've got a real problem with that teacher there, that Miss O'Brian. She's got an attitude problem. I'm too angry to talk about it now. I'll call you tomorrow."

Sterling started to say something, but was cut off as Hogan opened his car door, slid in, and slammed it shut. "Wow," he exclaimed as Hogan gunned his car toward the street. "That guy has got one big burr under his saddle!"

As he went back to his open house hall duty, he planned to chat with Chris O'Brian after the evening activities were over.

"Chris, what's the deal with Mr. Hogan?" Sterling asked her as she got a cup of coffee in the teachers' lounge after open house.

"Beats me, Grant," she said. "I was in the middle of my presentation, when he raised his hand. I could see his name tag and addressed him by his name. I told him there will be time for questions when I finish. Of course, I had already announced that before I even started talking, so I was surprised to see his hand in the air. I started to continue and he began asking me a question. I said to him, 'Mr. Hogan, I'm almost finished.' Then he just got up and left. One of the parents—Mrs. Grey, I think—told me later that she thought maybe he'd been drinking. But, to be honest, Grant, I really don't know what his problem was."

"Well," Sterling said in a comforting voice, "don't worry about it. Maybe he had a fight with his wife or girlfriend before he came here tonight. Who knows! See you tomorrow, Chris."

A week passed, and Sterling had forgotten about the incident between Hogan and Chris O'Brian until he opened his mail on Tuesday of the following week. Hogan had written a letter to the president of the board of education with copies to Superintendent Boughton and Sterling. Hogan felt that he had been "humiliated" by O'Brian and insisted that she be "fired immediately, and if this is not possible, I insist that her teaching contract not be renewed."

Later that day, Sterling discussed the matter with the superintendent. Boughton reminded him that the president of the board routinely responds to constituents who have personnel complaints by simply thanking them for writing and informing them that their concerns have been forwarded to the superintendent's office.

"Has Hogan contacted you directly, other than your encounter as he was leaving the open house?" Boughton asked.

"No sir," Sterling responded.

"I know this guy, Grant. I'm going to call him and tell him that I'm not willing to get involved in the matter until he's talked to you. As you may know, he's the executive secretary of the state school boards association and has always thought that he has power that he doesn't really have. That's a nice way of saying that he's a pain in the butt. I heard through the grapevine that the association is thinking about giving him walking papers. Maybe your situation is an outgrowth of his own frustrations. Anyway, I'll give him a call."

Sterling thought the issue was dead after his discussion with Boughton. He'd wait to see if Hogan called him. He knew that sending a letter to the superintendent or board was usually enough to satisfy a patron's need to vent. He doubted that Hogan would call.

He decided not to share either the letter or his conversation with the superintendent with O'Brian. He and the faculty at Moundview recognized that she was rapidly on the way to becoming an excellent teacher. She didn't need this kind of problem as a first-year teacher. Sharing this with her might interfere with her progress. And she wasn't at fault. He had talked with some other parents who were in O'Brian's room when the open house incident occurred. They all agreed that O'Brian handled Hogan with kid gloves, but that he seemed to have some kind of chip on his shoulder. A couple of parents mentioned that maybe he'd been drinking. Just as Sterling predicted, Hogan never called and, as the school year progressed, Sterling forgot the incident.

Months later, close to the end of the school year, Sterling scheduled his annual meeting with Assistant Superintendent for Personnel Fred Rose. Together, they would negotiate Moundview's staffing for the next school year. Prior to the meeting, Sterling had submitted his projected faculty and staff needs in writing, and now he had the opportunity to defend his requests in person. He and Rose had just about reached an agreement when Rose pulled a copy of the Hogan letter from a folder on his desk.

"Grant, we need to deal with this before I can sign off on your faculty requests for next year. Seems we have a problem here that we need to resolve."

"Wait, wait," Sterling put his hand up as if he was trying to stop traffic. "That's an old issue that I assumed was dead. When the superintendent and I talked, he was not going to do anything until Hogan had dealt with me—which, to this date, he hasn't. What's the problem?"

"Relax," Rose said. "Let me explain what's happened, and what we need to do. First, the superintendent called Hogan. Although he reported to me that it was far from being a cordial conversation, he, just as you had, assumed the issue was dead. Hogan starting calling individual board members with his complaint, however, and although the superintendent has assured them that O'Brian is an excellent teacher and has done nothing wrong, they are tired of his calls and want some kind of action. Now," Rose continued, "I know that Hogan will still have a kid at Moundview for another year and that he's got a sixth grader who will be attending your school year after next. We simply need to move O'Brian to another school."

"Simply?" Sterling was incensed. "Simply move an excellent teacher, who didn't do anything wrong, to some other school so that Hogan will shut up? That's not fair. Let me call Hogan and put this issue to rest once and for all!"

"Grant," Rose looked Sterling straight in the eye, "you're not to contact Hogan. We're going to move O'Brian to another school where she will not have to deal with Hogan. If we leave her at Moundview, he will keep after us until we are forced to fire her. I know that you think we're acting like a bunch of wimps, but do you want to tell her that she's going to be transferred, or do you want me to do it?"

Sterling knew that he had just gotten a direct order. O'Brian was leaving his faculty and he would need to start interviewing prospective candidates for her position. "I'll take care of it, Fred." He would save his indignation for later.

He scheduled a conference with Chris O'Brian after school the next day. Explaining that the politics of the school business can sometimes be unfair was going to be a tough job for him and a difficult concept for a promising first-year teacher to understand, much less accept.

"Grant, you look like you aren't feeling well," O'Brian said as she sat down for her conference. "I hope I haven't done something to upset you."

"No, Chris, you've done absolutely nothing wrong." He would repeat that statement many times before his meeting with O'Brian was concluded.

He gave O'Brian all the facts concerning the Hogan issue, including the politics of the situation. He assured her that a transfer was in her best interest and that Moundview's kids and faculty would miss her. O'Brian was obviously crushed, and he knew that only one of his messages had been received—that she would not be returning to Moundview next school year.

"Chris, I promise you," he concluded, "that after all the Hogan kids have left Moundview, I'm going to invite you back personally." He was not sure she heard his promise as she left school for the day. He was sure, however, that a day that had started out bright and sunny for Chris O'Brian was now overcast, and rain was falling. His faith in the basic fairness of the system was badly shaken that day. He hoped, as he watched raindrops creating designs on the glass of his office window, that the rain would wash away his anger.

O'Brian completed her stay at Moundview with style and continued to demonstrate excellence in her teaching. Hogan never attended another function at Moundview.

A Sterling Moment (IBTC@L)

Bright red T-shirts emblazoned with "IBTC@L" on the back, and worn exclusively by eighth-grade girls, started showing up in the halls and classrooms at Moundview one Monday morning in mid-February.

"Oh, it's a new store opening up in the Landing shopping center," one eighth-grade girl explained when Sterling asked her about it. "They're giving away these T-shirts to advertise," she giggled.

As the week progressed, more and more red T-shirts could be seen in the school.

"Must be some kind of a women's store," Sterling surmised, because only girls were wearing them. "No problem," he thought. "Lots of stores and companies give away promotional items."

Various faculty and staff at Moundview also asked eighth-grade girls about the T-shirts and the "new store," and noted the especially vague, but innocent, answers about what kind of a store this was going to be. None of the eighth-grade boys seemed to know anything about the shirts either.

"No big deal," Sterling told his administrative staff. "Maybe it's some kind of competition for those chain yogurt places—those TCBY shops. Anyway, this too, as does every other adolescent fad, will pass!"

By the next Monday, almost every eighth-grade girl at Moundview was wearing the now well-known red T-shirt. "Interesting," Beverly Watkins, the principal at Lancaster Junior high responded when Sterling shared the "phenomenon" with her that Monday afternoon at a principals' meeting. "*Real* interesting," she continued. "My eighth-grade girls have been wearing green T-shirts with gold-colored letters MVV! I think we may have a problem here, Grant. Your girls are wearing *our* school colors, red and black, and mine are wearing *your* school colors, green and gold. Is there a conspiracy here, or what?" she laughed.

Moundview and Lancaster were located within 5 miles of each other, and the rivalry was strong. Students from the two schools often dated each other, attended the same parties, and competed ferociously during athletic events. A quick comparison of the upcoming athletic schedules for the two schools revealed that a basketball game between the schools' eighth-grade girls was scheduled for the coming Thursday night . . . a long-standing rivalry that always brought out the best in the girls on the court, but the worst of nastiness among spectators.

"Grant, what we have here is some kind of a direct insult being sent back and forth between schools by our eighth-grade girls. I haven't the foggiest what the lettering means, but I think we can assume since yours has an '@L' and mine has an 'MV' that we can assume that part of the message on yours refers to 'at Lancaster' and that the MV in mine refers to 'Moundview.' I think we need to put a stop to this today," she warned.

"You're absolutely right," Sterling agreed.

As soon as they returned to their buildings after the meeting, both principals announced that the T-shirts in question were not to be worn at school or at the game Thursday night. In a telephone conversation the next day, both principals laughed when they compared their discoveries.

"Well," Watkins said, "it was relatively simple to find out. A little detective work on my part revealed that my eighth-grade girls were suggesting that your eighth-grade girls are still virgins, thus the MVV. And even though, I hope that this is true, they consider it to be a profound insult and a severe blow to your girls' adolescent egos. What did you find out?"

"Ah," Sterling responded. "My girls are clearly less caustic and have a much more realistic viewpoint concerning your girls, according to my sources. They were suggesting that all your eighth-grade girls belong to the same club. The IBT club at Lancaster."

He paused.

"All right, Grant, I'll bite," Watkins chuckled. "What does IBT stand for?"

"The itty-bitty-titty club," Sterling announced. "You *do* have one of those over there, don't you?"

Both principals were still laughing as they hung up. They would see each other again Thursday night, as they closely supervised the continuing rivalry between the two schools.

▚▚▚▚ Macho Man

"So what's going on with Ramon Valdez?" Sterling posed the question about the instrumental music teacher to his vice principals at their regular Wednesday morning meeting. "I'm getting an average of three to four kids sent to the office each day by Valdez. He scribbles stuff like insubordination, talking back, or failure to comply. Are you experiencing the same kind of problem?"

"Oh yes," said Alice Grogan, shaking her head in disgust. "In addition, I'm starting to get kids that want out of his classes. Especially band."

"I'm getting that too," Randy Wood echoed. "After that embarrassing band concert 2 weeks ago."

"That was a horrible program, wasn't it?" Sterling agreed. "I felt sorry for the kids. I know that they can play better than that. I talked to Valdez right after the concert to let him know that I thought he could do much better than that. I told him I expected to see some immediate improvement. Maybe this flow of discipline problems we're seeing is a result of his tightening up."

"I don't think so," Grogan said. "I think he had some awfully big shoes to fill when we brought him in to replace Bob Sully. I get the feeling that he treats his students like first graders."

"I get that feeling too," Wood agreed. "The kids tell me that he's always putting them down, and that's why they're starting to smart mouth him. It's a shame that we had to lose Sully."

"I know," Sterling agreed. "But the opportunity came for him to move to a high school band director position. That's what he was waiting for, and he went with my blessing. Anyway, I'll talk to Valdez today or tomorrow. I've been to his classes to observe on a number of occasions, but as usual, when I'm in the room, the kids act like angels, and Valdez puts on the perfect teacher show. Let me see if I can help him."

"Ramon, what's happening in your classes, especially in band?" Sterling asked Valdez later that day. "You've been sending a steady stream of kids to the office for discipline problems. I'm concerned."

"I don't know what started this, Grant . . . I thought we had a better bunch of kids than this at Moundview."

"Started what?" Sterling asked.

"Well," Valdez continued, "I think the kids at this school are prejudiced toward me."

"What do you mean by prejudiced?" Sterling lowered his head and looked at Valdez over the top of his glasses.

"Oh, I hear stuff whispered under their breath when I'm trying to get a point across. Stuff like wetback, taco breath—terms like that."

"First I've heard of it," Sterling said. "You've never written that on the discipline slips you send with students."

"That's because none of them have ever said it to my face," Valdez quickly responded.

"All right, Ramon, I don't like to hear that. I'll talk with students from your classes and put a stop to this nonsense right away."

Sterling met with various students from Valdez's classes the next day. Although none of them would admit that any prejudiced behavior, including name calling, was taking place, they all agreed that they didn't like or respect Mr. Valdez. Sterling thought that by visiting with a number of key students in Valdez's classes, the word would get out that he would not tolerate that kind of nonsense and it needed to stop. Valdez must have also gotten some kind of message from his visit with him. The stream of kids being sent out of his classes for discipline stopped immediately.

A few days later, as Sterling was walking the halls, he was interrupted by his beeper. The prearranged message was a summons to return to the office. He was still softly singing the words of a song by The Village People that he had heard that morning on his way to work. The melody line "Macho, macho man, I want to be a macho man" had stuck in his mind, and he was enjoying repeating it over and over.

"I think we've got a problem, Grant." Sterling was met outside the office by vice principal Grogan. "Valdez has sent his entire band class to the office . . . claims they all called him a derogatory name. He's sitting in your office, and we have about 75 kids crowded into the outer office."

Sterling, followed by Grogan, eased his way through the group of kids silently awaiting the outcome of his visit with their band director.

"Ramon, what's up now?" he asked as he closed his office door. "Is your band about to perform for the office staff or what?"

Valdez was not amused and broke into a tirade. "If you don't put a stop to this immediately, I'm going to report this school and you to the Human Rights Commission."

"Slow down, Ramon. What happened?"

"I told the students to get out the music for an overture we're working on. I raised my baton to start the rehearsal, and when I brought it down for the first beat, instead of playing the assigned music, they all started to sing 'Nacho, nacho man . . . I want to be a nacho man.' "

"Wait," Sterling interrupted. "You mean 'macho man' don't you? I just heard it on the radio this morning."

"No, I don't," Valdez angrily replied. "Nacho, as in Mexican food. Do I need to spell it out for you? N-A-C-H-O . . . they're calling me 'nacho man'!"

Sterling got the picture. "I'll put a stop to this right now," he said. "What kind of punishment do you want me to deal out? You've got the whole band out there in the office."

"I just want it to end . . . this and any other name calling. Can you do that please?" Valdez asked.

Sterling looked at his watch. "Ramon, you go to the teacher's lounge for the rest of this class period, and I'll take your kids back to the band room and talk to them. I promise, you won't have this problem again."

He marched the kids back to the band room as Valdez retired to the lounge. He painstakingly explained to them why their actions were wrong and what would happen if they continued. They agreed that they had misjudged how Mr. Valdez would react to what they perceived as a joke. They thought that he would find it as funny as they did. They promised that it would not happen again. He took them at their word.

Although the situation between Valdez and his students seemed to quiet down, he continued to hear from students and his vice principals that the instrumental music program was doomed if something positive didn't happen soon.

He decided to take the bull by the horns and called Fred Rose, deputy superintendent for personnel. He wanted a meeting with him and District Music Supervisor Ben Ward as soon as possible.

"I'd like to replace Valdez now," Sterling suggested in the hurriedly scheduled meeting. "I accepted Valdez based on both of your recommendations. You told me that he had done an excellent job as an elementary school band director in whatever district he came from. Perhaps that's where he belongs. He's not cutting it at Moundview. He's blaming all his problems on the kids at Moundview, whom he believes are prejudiced."

"Maybe that is the problem," Rose interjected, "Maybe your kids are prejudiced."

"I'll admit that my faculty and I are spending a lot of time working with our kids concerning their relationships with the very few minorities we have at Moundview. We may have a clearly defined case of students demonstrating extreme prejudice toward a teacher. I don't believe it started out that way, however. Valdez's current problems with his students grew out of just plain teacher incompetence, not cultural background or race. I wish I had more time to work with Valdez and his students, but I don't. I'm going to lose the instrumental music program at Moundview if I don't act fast. That's why I asked for this meeting. Can you help me?"

Rose looked at Ward. "Any suggestions Ben?"

"Well, Grant, here's what I can do," Ward said. "We need an additional assistant band director at one of our high schools. I can rotate one of my elementary people through your school to cover Valdez's classes except band. I don't have anyone I trust with that responsibility. In other words, I can move Valdez out and cover most of his classes, but we would have to hire a band director and, as you know, at this time of the year, it's next to impossible to find someone."

"Much less," Rose quickly interrupted, "to find the money in the budget to hire one. Do we have any retired band directors in the area who would volunteer to take over for the rest of the year?"

"None that I know of," both Sterling and Ward agreed.

"Well, Grant, looks like we can help you up to a point. Hey, since you're an old band director, why don't you take the band for the rest of the year? You principals don't do anything anyway," Rose chuckled.

"Yeah, Grant, you could do that. It'd be good for you." Ward exclaimed as both he and Rose looked at each other, nodded in agreement, and laughed.

Sterling abruptly interrupted their merriment. "Done deal," he said. "I'll let Valdez know he is being transferred to the high school, and that he's to report there on Monday. Ben, you need to notify the high school and set up the coverage for the rest of Valdez's classes at Moundview. I'll work on my schedule and free up the time to cover the band for the rest of the year. I'd like to see the names of some prospective replacements for Valdez as soon as possible, however, so we can hire a winner for next year."

"Wait, Grant," Rose said. "I was just kidding. You don't have time to do that."

"I'll have to find the time. You've helped me as far as you could go. I need to chip in too. Just locate some good candidates for me to interview for next year."

"Macho, macho man" was not the tune that was going through Sterling's mind as he drove back to Moundview after the meeting. It was "What kind of fool am I?" from the Broadway musical *Stop the World, I Want to Get Off!*

Valdez was excited about his opportunity to work at the high school level. Sterling, on the other hand, wasn't happy about passing Valdez's problems on to someone else. He was doing this for Moundview kids. To him, they were more important. "Besides," he rationalized, "what damage could a second assistant band director do at a high school?"

Although Sterling found it extremely difficult to block out an hour each day to work with the band, he found the challenge exciting. Although the band kids were apprehensive at first, having their principal as their director, they soon looked forward to presenting their next concert. They knew that he was confident in their ability. He reminded them daily that they had the talent to "bring an audience to its feet." At their next concert, they found what he had been telling them was true. They got a standing ovation from parents and fellow students.

"They just needed someone to believe in them," Sterling told a parent after the spring concert. "They needed someone to tell them that if they practiced and worked hard, they could erase the embarrassment that they felt from their concert earlier in the school year. The kids are really going to like the new instrumental music teacher we've just hired for next year."

Nothing Unusual, Just the Daily In-Basket . . . Again

After 5 minutes on the phone, Sterling knew it was going to be a lost cause to try to change Mr. Greybill's mind, but he knew he had to try, or at least listen. Greybill was angrily denouncing everything he could think of about public schools and Moundview in particular.

"Mr. Greybill, have you ever visited Moundview while school is in session? Perhaps spending a half day here with your daughter, Cindy, might give you a better perspective on public education."

Greybill didn't listen . . . didn't hear a word.

Sterling listened politely for another 10 minutes or so. Then, as cordially as possible, he cut him off in midsentence. "Mr. Greybill, I'm sorry to interrupt, but it's obvious that I'm not going to convince you that you are generalizing about schools, kids, and teachers based on what you read in the newspaper or hear about on TV. You sluffed off my suggestion to come and see Cindy's school firsthand."

"What do you mean, 'sluffed-off'?" he growled.

"Excuse me, but I'm not finished, Mr. Greybill, and I have folks waiting to see me in the outer office. Anyway, I can't seem to influence you, and at this point, I don't even know why I'm trying. If you've decided to place your daughter in a private school . . . more power to you. We'll miss Cindy. Just let us know, and we'll start the paperwork necessary for any transfer you wish to make."

Sterling waited a second for a response, and when none came, he continued, "Now, if you'll excuse me . . ."

Greybill hung up.

"What a turkey," Sterling remarked aloud as he placed the receiver back on the phone, looked at his watch, and then glanced at his daily schedule. "I've got 45 minutes 'til I'm scheduled to make an evaluation visit to Jenson's class. Maybe I can make a dent in this stack of paperwork," he thought.

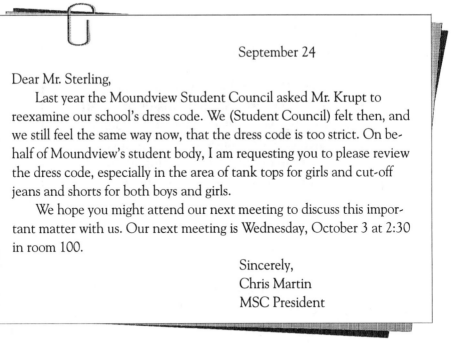

September 24

Dear Mr. Sterling,

Last year the Moundview Student Council asked Mr. Krupt to reexamine our school's dress code. We (Student Council) felt then, and we still feel the same way now, that the dress code is too strict. On behalf of Moundview's student body, I am requesting you to please review the dress code, especially in the area of tank tops for girls and cut-off jeans and shorts for both boys and girls.

We hope you might attend our next meeting to discuss this important matter with us. Our next meeting is Wednesday, October 3 at 2:30 in room 100.

Sincerely,
Chris Martin
MSC President

"How dare Greybill accuse schools of being non-Christian! Who the hell does he think he is?"

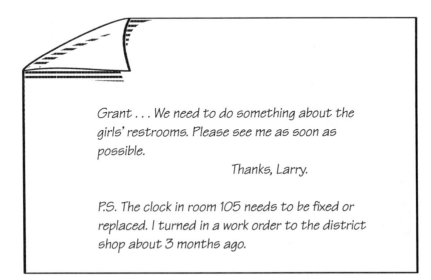

Grant . . . We need to do something about the girls' restrooms. Please see me as soon as possible.

Thanks, Larry.

P.S. The clock in room 105 needs to be fixed or replaced. I turned in a work order to the district shop about 3 months ago.

"I wonder how Cindy feels about her dad's feelings that Moundview kids are possessed by the devil? She seems to be involved in a lot of activities, and every time I see her she looks happy. I'm glad that so and so isn't my old man."

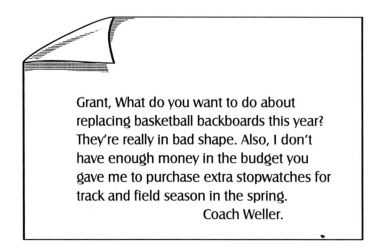

Grant, What do you want to do about replacing basketball backboards this year? They're really in bad shape. Also, I don't have enough money in the budget you gave me to purchase extra stopwatches for track and field season in the spring.
Coach Weller.

"And what's this crap about schools being full of bad kids and incompetent teachers? Ninety-five percent of the kids at Moundview never get into trouble, and on any given day the only incompetent in this school is probably me . . . driven to the brink of insanity by people like Greybill or Greygoose or whatever."

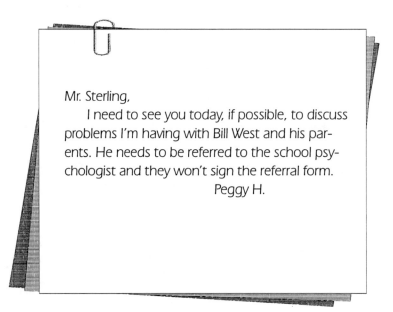

Mr. Sterling,
   I need to see you today, if possible, to discuss problems I'm having with Bill West and his parents. He needs to be referred to the school psychologist and they won't sign the referral form.
Peggy H.

"Dear Peggy, please send me two referral forms: one for Greybill and one for me. We both need to see the school psyc. Maybe we could both go together and sit in a darkened room and babble at each other. Hey, Greybeak, you beakhead . . . did ya see what was in the paper yesterday? Two kids at some school somewhere were actually caught doing something good!"

Grant . . .
Mrs. Clevenger called to remind you that
you promised to speak to the City Women's
Club Thursday at noon.
Shirley

"Thank you for inviting me here today, sweet old ladies of the Women's Club of our fair city. I'm here today to describe in detail the sexual proclivities of teen-age children and the new course we're offering at Moundview this year, Introduction to Whoring and Pimping, which will be taught by a team of our most knowledgeable faculty! Eat that, Greytoad!"

September 24

Grant,

Just a "heads up." The Student Council is going to try to change the dress code again this year. Also they want more school parties with live bands or DJs. We have a good group this year, and I'm pleased to be working with them as their faculty adviser . . . but I feel they may need some direction from you. You might want to attend our next meeting on Oct. 3.

Sam Phillips

"Right . . . more school parties. Dancing. Kids touching each other. Just what Greybutt wants!"

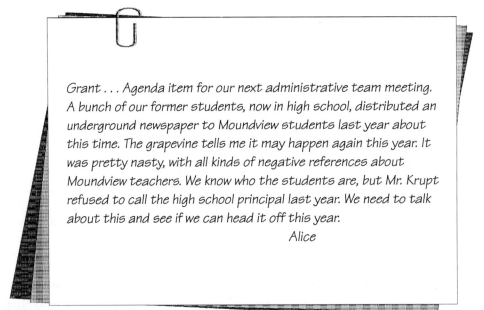

Grant . . . Agenda item for our next administrative team meeting. A bunch of our former students, now in high school, distributed an underground newspaper to Moundview students last year about this time. The grapevine tells me it may happen again this year. It was pretty nasty, with all kinds of negative references about Moundview teachers. We know who the students are, but Mr. Krupt refused to call the high school principal last year. We need to talk about this and see if we can head it off this year.

Alice

"I wonder why Krupt didn't ask for help from the high school's administrative team on the problem? I wonder if Krupt had any problems with Greybill last year?"

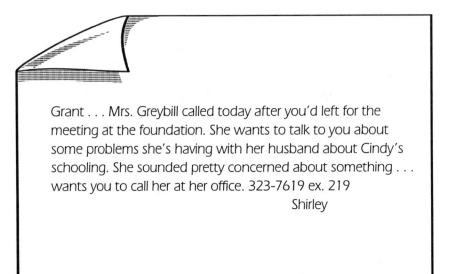

Grant . . . Mrs. Greybill called today after you'd left for the meeting at the foundation. She wants to talk to you about some problems she's having with her husband about Cindy's schooling. She sounded pretty concerned about something . . . wants you to call her at her office. 323-7619 ex. 219

Shirley

"Oh, oh . . . here we go. Ladies and gentlemen, the fun is about to begin. Looks like we have a problem between mom and dad about Cindy's education. Gonna try to get me in the middle. That won't work, but Cindy's caught in a bad place. Better see if I can get mom and dad in here together and talk this out."

Grant . . . Mrs. Green, mother of Billy West, called this morning while you were making rounds. Wants to talk to you about some problem with Peggy Henninger. 323-4491

Shirley

Sterling glanced at his watch. "Time to go," he noted. "Hey, Shirley, wasn't Tarzan—you know, like in *Tarzan of the Apes*—wasn't his ancestral name Greybill?" he asked as he hurried by.

"No, Grant, I think it was Greystoke. Why do you ask?"

"Oh, never mind, Shirley. My mind is wandering today."

Burnout

"He stomped on my foot, Mr. Sterling! Mr. Bowen stomped on my foot for no reason! He's mean, Mr. Sterling! He's a mean person!"

"All right, Gina," Sterling interrupted her outburst. "Settle down and tell me the story from the beginning. What happened?"

Gina was clearly upset as she shared her problem with Sterling that afternoon. "I had just left my locker and had stopped to talk with Shirley and a bunch of other girls," she explained. "Suddenly I felt this hand on my back pushing me. I turned around and it was Mr. Bowen trying to push me out of his way. I said, 'Wait a minute, I'll move, you don't need to push me.' Then he yelled 'Move now,' and stomped on my foot. It hurt, Mr. Sterling!"

"Okay, Gina," Sterling said. "I'll talk to Mr. Bowen about this and get back to you later. Let's have the nurse look at your foot, and then I'll get you a pass to your class." He walked with Gina to the nurse's office. On his way back, he dropped a note in Doug Bowen's mailbox to see him after school that day, "Re: problem with Gina Brown."

"Grant, I screwed up. I really lost my temper with Gina and the other girls she was with. They were blocking the hall, and I was in a hurry," Bowen said as he slumped dejectedly in a chair in Sterling's office. "I caught up with Gina a few minutes ago at her locker and apologized."

Sterling started to acknowledge Bowen's thoughtfulness, but Bowen continued to talk. "Grant, I'm burned out," he said. "I really need to get away from middle school kids. I just don't have the patience to deal with them anymore. The only fun I've had for the last 2 years was at that inservice faculty workshop, when students were not in school and you passed out loaded squirt guns and invited us to use them during the workshop any time we felt frustration. Well, I must have reloaded mine 50 times that day."

Sterling remembered the workshop well. The theme of the workshop was how to avoid teacher burnout. Amid a lot of laughter and mock warfare, much was accomplished that day, even though he became the central target of "burn-out avoidance."

"There's a position open at West High for next year, Grant. Is it all right with you if I apply for that job?"

He could see that Bowen's request wasn't just a cover-up for his mistake with Gina. He was serious. Middle school kids were difficult to work with, and Bowen had been at Moundview for 7 years. He had seen teachers and administrators burn out; Bowen was exhibiting the classic symptoms. He had suffered a number of minor student-teacher relationship problems that year, most of them his fault. Although Sterling hated to lose Bowen, he knew that his answer to Bowen's request would have to be yes.

"Doug, thanks for talking to Gina," Sterling said. "You made a mistake, and maybe by apologizing to her you've helped clear the air. I'm going to call Gina's mother tonight, however, to try to head off what could be potential trouble. Gina has a tendency to blow problems she has at school completely out of proportion when she shares them at home.

"Now," he continued, "as far as the West job is concerned, I don't want to lose you, but maybe you do need a change. You have my best wishes, and I'll write you a recommendation if you decide to apply."

"Thanks. Let me know if you want me to talk to Gina's mother. I'm really sorry about this," Bowen said as he left Sterling's office.

Sterling contacted Gina's mother at home that evening. Although her daughter had never taken a class from Bowen, Mrs. Brown knew through the grapevine that he was well respected by other parents and students. She understood what probably happened. "Mr. Bowen lost his temper. Teachers are human," she said. "I do, however, want to stop by school tomorrow and visit with him about the incident."

"That's fine, Mrs. Brown," Sterling said. "Mr. Bowen's planning period starts at 10:30. Will that be convenient for you?"

He placed a note in Bowen's mailbox the next morning advising him that he had made an appointment for him to visit with Mrs. Brown. "No problem, Doug," the note concluded. "My conversation with her last evening was cordial. She just wants to show support for her daughter by coming in. I'll attend also."

The meeting between Brown, Bowen, and Sterling was as friendly as he predicted. Mrs. Brown simply confirmed what Bowen already knew. Bowen had made a mistake that could have had extreme consequences. As a result of the meeting and Bowen's admission of a mistake, Sterling considered the matter closed and did not file an official reprimand.

Bowen was hired for the high school position, and his career continued to blossom. The change was good for Bowen, and he attacked the challenge of teaching with renewed vitality. Sterling replaced him with another teacher ready and willing to take on the minute-by-minute challenges offered by middle school kids.

Teacher and administrator burnout was an ongoing concern for Sterling. By this time in his career, he had seen the symptoms and the results manifested through resignations, home problems, nervous breakdowns, and, in one case, suicide. Although all these problems weren't necessarily related to job stress, he felt that if he could just convince teachers and others to be tremendously amused by the passing parade of life, they could endure even the most difficult situations. "The world is extremely interesting to a cheerful soul," he believed.

A Typical Day

"And a fine-looking piece of junk it is," Sterling mused as he stood in the lobby of Moundview admiring his sculpture.

Years earlier, he had developed an interest in weaving and metal sculpture. Although his efforts at weaving had gone unnoticed, his metal sculptures could be found in a number of gardens throughout the city. The city newspaper had featured him in an article with a picture spread in its Lifestyles section a few years ago. Now, after a Sunday afternoon of grunting and groaning, with four additional men lifting and shoving, his newest creation had been moved from the school's metal shop to Moundview's lobby.

The sculpture, over 6 feet tall and weighing almost 600 pounds, depicted a clump of sunflowers. It was painstakingly crafted from what artists term "found material," but that Sterling affectionately called "junk." The flowers were supported by stems made of rebar permanently attached to a rusty tractor tire rim. He had purposely placed it in the Moundview lobby to draw attention to his school and entice the local media to do a story. He had contacted the same reporter who had done the earlier feature and advised her of his latest creation. She was due at the school with a photographer at 10:30 that morning, and he was hoping for some posed pictures of students looking at the sculpture.

"Ah yes," he fantasized, "a front-page picture under a headline like 'LOWLY JUNK TRANSFORMED TO ART MAGNIFICENT AT CITY'S PREEMINENT MIDDLE SCHOOL' . . . Scads of dynamite pictures and a highly provocative story on page 2."

His whimsy was abruptly interrupted by the blaring sound of the school's fire alarm. He quickly opened the front doors and kicked the stops down. As he opened the inner doors from the lobby to the main hall, he could see students and teachers quietly filing out of the building. He stepped aside so that he would not be blocking an exit and returned to the main office, where the emergency control panel would tell him the location of the particular alarm unit that had been pulled. The flashing red light told him the unit was located outside the main doors to the science wing. He walked briskly through the halls to ensure that all students and teachers had left the building, and then headed toward the science area. He could smell acrid fumes as he approached the area. As he entered, he saw one of his science teachers and the head custodian with fire extinguishers. They were examining a melted plastic chair they had sprayed with extinguisher foam. The smell was caustic.

"Is this the problem?" he asked.

"Yep," Bob Michaels, the science teacher, answered. "Seems that Doug Andrews decided, for some unknown reason, to see if the plastic material in this chair would melt. As you can see, he got a big surprise. These chairs are really volatile."

"All right, you guys get this mess cleaned up. I'll deal with Doug later. The main control panel also sent an alarm to the area fire station, so I need to tell them we've got everything under control and send them back." He looked at his watch. "10:15," he noted. "I'll need the time for my report." He headed toward the front of the school, cutting quickly through the main office, stopping just long enough to ring the bell that would signal the all clear for students and teachers to return to their classrooms. As he turned toward the office door that would lead him to the front entrance, he noticed Doug Andrews, his gourmet plastics chef, sitting in a chair, crying. He purposely ignored Andrews and hurried to the front door. As the last crowd of students followed their teachers into the building, he was met by the local fire station's assistant chief and a city fire marshal. Standing behind them were the reporter and photographer from the newspaper, as well as Richard Kealy, the district's food services supervisor.

"Did I come at a bad time?" Kealy asked.

"Not if you like fried plastic chair! Can you come back in about an hour?"

"Well, I did have an appointment with you at 11:00. I'll come back then. We have a problem with one of your cooks."

"Whatever, Richard. Better make it about 11:30—I should be free by then." Sterling turned to talk to the reporter and photographer. "Give me a couple of minutes, will ya?"

He proceeded to explain the alarm and fire situation to the assistant chief and marshal and took them to the badly damaged chair. He promised to file a report later that day and drop a copy off at the neighborhood fire station. He made a mental note to notify Doug Andrews's parents concerning Doug's actions, and that Doug would have to be suspended from school.

Sterling was now free to meet with the press. He looked at his watch. "11:15 . . . jeez, I hope they're still waiting!"

"Can you tell me about the fire?" Sue Kent, the reporter asked as Sterling escorted the assistant chief and marshal through the school's lobby.

"Sure, Sue," he answered. "Seems that one of our students decided to see if a plastic chair in the science lab would melt if he held his Bunsen burner next to it . . . no big deal. I don't have any more information on the situation. I haven't had time to talk to the kid yet. So anyway, what do you think of our newest addition to Moundview?" He pointed to the sculpture.

"It's, uh . . . quite big, Grant," Kent said in a hesitant voice. "Can we get some kids out here so my photographer can get some pictures? Then you can give me some background on this . . . what do you call it?"

" 'Sunflowers Rising.' It's a clump of sunflowers, Sue. Excuse me for a minute, I'll hustle up some kids."

He returned a few minutes later with a group of students, and, while they examined the sculpture in various poses choreographed by the photographer, he gave Kent the background she needed to develop her story.

"Finally," he thought, "things are almost back to normal."

After sending the kids back to class and thanking Sue Kent and the photographer, Sterling returned to the office. Doug Andrews had been moved to the school's clinic.

"He threw up, Grant," one of the office secretaries said. "He's in the clinic lying down. He's really upset."

"He should be," Sterling said.

"Richard, I can see you now. What time is it? 11:45 . . . sorry I'm late. What's up?" Richard Kealy was responsible for the operations of the cafeterias throughout the school district. Although he was well respected for his cafeteria management skills, he often ran into problems with principals. He couldn't seem to understand that schools didn't revolve around food services.

"Grant, your cafeteria manager called me yesterday and told me that she was having problems with one of her bakers. She told me that you were aware of the problem and that she would like to replace the lady. Is this all right with you?"

"Richard, hold on a minute would you please? My secretary needs to say something to me." Shirley Brown had stuck her head around the corner to catch his attention.

"Yes, Shirley. What is it?"

"Grant, Mr. and Mrs. Andrews—Doug's parents—are here. Seems that Doug called them from the phone in the clinic. They're very upset. I've got them in with Doug at the moment. Thought you better know."

"Thanks, Shirley. I'll be right there!"

"Richard, I've got to tend to this fire problem. Can you come back later, or call me this afternoon?"

"Well, Grant, this is a pretty important problem too, you know!"

"Will lunch be served today, Richard?"

"Of course."

"Then we don't have a problem, at least until tomorrow. I'll get with the cafeteria manager this afternoon and the problem will be solved. Fair enough?"

"Okay, you handle it. I was just going to help."

"I appreciate that, Richard, I really do. I'll talk to you later."

He walked over to the clinic. "Mr. and Mrs. Andrews, let's go to my office. Doug, you come too. Let's find out what happened this morning in the science lab. Shirley, I need a fire incident report form, and both a 1020 and a 1030." Shirley recognized "1020" as a short term suspension form and "1030" as an expulsion form. She hoped that he wouldn't have to expel Doug.

As Sterling escorted Doug and his parents to his office, he could hear a bell ringing. He glanced at his watch. 12:00, the bell for lunch.

"Doug, tell us what happened."

Doug tearfully recounted the events leading up to and causing the fire. His parents were devastated. Doug was a straight A student, a gifted athlete, and a quiet, polite young man. "How could this have happened?" was the unspoken question of the three adults listening to Doug.

"So, Doug," Sterling recapped, "you had this sudden attack of dumbness caused by simple curiosity. Is that correct?"

"Yes sir," Andrews quietly said.

"And you understand the problem you caused for the school?"

"Yes, sir."

"And you understand the problem you've caused for your parents and me?"

"Yes, sir."

"Doug, go back to the clinic for a few minutes while I visit with your folks. Okay?"

"Yes sir . . . I'm really sorry this happened."

After Doug left, Sterling explained to Mr. and Mrs. Andrews what he would have to do to comply with the city's fire code and school district policy. Because he believed that Doug didn't really anticipate the dangerous nature of his action and didn't do it to harm others, he would file the mandatory report with the fire marshal, but would suggest that no further action be taken. In addition, he would not expel Doug from school, but issue a short-term suspension. Doug would be barred from school for the next 10 days. Although Mr. and Mrs. Andrews were still visibly upset, they accepted what he needed to do, and thanked him for his understanding. He walked Doug and his parents to the front door.

"Interesting sculpture," Mr. Andrews commented as he left the building.

"Yes it is," Sterling thought as he closed the door and headed for the cafeteria. "And if the building had burned to the ground, my sunflowers would still be standing!"

He entered the cafeteria just as the bell rang summoning the last group of students back to classes. 1:00. Lunch period was over for another day.

Mary Singleton, Moundview's cafeteria manager, was in her office as he walked through the kitchen.

"Mary, Richard Kealy was here to see me this morning. We still have a problem with one of your cooks or bakers or somebody?"

"I'm sorry, Grant," Singleton said. "I've tried everything. Ellen Greenway just can't get the knack of it. I have to throw away half the rolls she bakes each day. She can't seem to follow a simple recipe. Some of her rolls are too hard, and the rest don't even rise. Kealy's on my back about food waste and costs. Can I let her go and get a substitute until I find someone else?"

"Sure, Mary. I know you've worked with her as best you can. Give her her walking papers this afternoon if you want."

"Grant, I've never done this before. I . . . well, could you help me?"

"You want to do it now, Mary?"

"Yes, please. Let's get this over with."

Greenway was called into the cafeteria office. "You mean you're firing me because my buns are too hard or won't rise?" she sputtered.

"Yes, Ellen," he responded in a quiet voice. "It's just that simple."

"Well, we'll see what my union has to say about this," she exclaimed as she went to her locker, got her coat, and left.

"I know that was hard for you, Mary. It's never easy to let someone go. Forget about it," he said as Singleton wiped her eyes with a tissue.

"Let's see," Sterling pondered as he walked back to his office. "What did we learn so far today? We learned that newspaper reporters are on time, my sculpture is 'quite big' and 'interesting,' that plastic doesn't just melt, it burns and stinks. The fire alarm works, and our practice drills paid off. Richard Kealy is a turkey. Doug Andrews was dumb today, but is sorry. And Ellen Greenway's buns won't rise."

His analysis of the morning's activities was quickly forgotten as he plunged into the paperwork that had accumulated on his desk. He finished the report for the fire marshal and put it in his briefcase to deliver on his way home that evening. He was still working his way through a stack of papers when the final bell rang, signaling the close of the school day. He could hear kids' locker doors banging closed. "3:30 . . . another day in the record book," he laughed.

"Grant, Linda sent a dozen cinnamon rolls over from the home ec department. The directions for preparing these for breakfast are taped on the lid. It's after 4:00—why don't you call it a day?"

"Thanks, Shirley, and I'll thank Linda tomorrow. I'll take these home with me tonight."

As he continued to work on a report, the smell of cinnamon began working on him, and he couldn't resist lifting a corner of the tinfoil cover.

"Boy, those look good. So what if they're cold. I missed lunch today and I'm hungry!"

He carefully lifted one of the rolls from the pan.

"Awfully small and doughy, kinda chewey—but good," he observed and gently pulled out another one. Before he finished his report, he had devoured six cinnamon rolls.

"Shirley," he shouted. "If you want one of these rolls you better get it now! I've eaten a half dozen already!"

Shirley came rushing in the door.

"Didn't you read the directions Linda taped to the tinfoil? Those haven't been cooked yet, Grant. They're going to start rising in your tummy. Don't eat any more!"

"Oh. Okay," he said sheepishly.

Within 10 minutes, he started to feel the effect that internal body heat and moisture have on active yeast. The cinnamon rolls were rising in his stomach.

"Shirley, what should I do? I've got stomach cramps like you won't believe!"

"This too shall pass, Grant," she grinned unsympathetically. "By the way, you've got a call on line one from some gentleman representing the food worker's union. Said he wants to talk to you about firing a cafeteria worker whose buns wouldn't rise. Do you want to talk to him? Maybe he can help you!"

"Put him through," he groaned. "I'm still on a steep learning curve!"

One Block at a Time

I'm trying out masks
Of people I know
And if what I am
Discourages me,
I'll leave it and go
To one that others
Accept and know.

Greg Glover, eighth-grade student

"I'm reminded that Thomas Jefferson said, 'That government is best which governs the least.' That statement, however, as commonly cited, is incomplete, and as a result its essence is distorted. What Jefferson said was, 'That government is best which governs the least, *because its people discipline themselves.*' Would Jefferson still believe that in today's environment? I believe he would," Sterling said as he sat down at the table. He had called a meeting of some senior faculty at Moundview to discuss how discipline might be handled under a middle school profile rather than the junior high concept. "Students need to understand," he continued, "that their actions have consequences—that rules have meaning, are reasonable, and not everything can be explained away, eventually worked out, or made whole again. Rules, regulations, policies, and procedures need to be presented and explained in such a way that they can be easily understood by adolescents. And, finally—and I really believe this—the best discipline for middle school kids is that controlled by peer pressure. The same pressure that causes students to do 'wrong things' can be used to ensure that most students do 'right things.' "

"Whoa, that's certainly deep philosophical thinking for this early in the morning, Grant," Larry Mathews, a seventh-grade math teacher, said with a laugh.

"One step above deep doodoo, I think," Glenn Johnson, an eighth-grade social studies teacher, joined in the laughter.

"Grant, get serious . . these are middle school kids you're talking about!" Betty Nash, one of the school's home economics teachers, added. "Kids that don't deal with reality."

"Betty," Mathews quickly noted, "it's strictly hormones."

"Hormones mixed with idealistic disillusionment," Johnson said, joining in the fray.

"Now who's getting philosophical?" Sterling asked as he joined in the laughter.

"No . . ." Sandra Bostitch, open education coordinator, announced, as if to end a debate. "It's hormones combined with idealism, disillusionment, a need for independence, extreme self-consciousness, and a fragile ego. These kids are constantly asking the question 'Where do I fit in?' And," she added, "they define 'fitting in' as being part of a group."

"Well, I have to agree with all of you," Sterling said as he looked around the table. "But you're also agreeing with what I said at the beginning of the meeting. *If* the most important thing in an adolescent child's life is peer relations, then peer pressure may be *one* of the answers to effective discipline. The kids at Moundview need to feel that they are an integral part of the school's programs, including discipline. If we provide the right kind of guidance and advising for our students—on a level that's just as important as academic prowess—then the kids will take care of themselves."

"Right," Bostitch agreed. "Our new adviser base program will be a place where teachers and students work together to overcome kids' self-consciousness and to work at improving their relationships with peers and adults. If a strong adviser-advisee relationship is developed, then advisers can help the kids clarify their changing and conflicting values, and also improve their views of themselves, their peers, and their adult relationships."

"So what are you saying?" Mathews asked with a tinge of frustration in his voice. "That we let kids run the show here? Develop some sort of student court system? I can't see where we're going with this discussion. These kids need constant supervision. It's like the devil has taken over their bodies, souls, and minds sometime during the sixth-grade year and remains a part of them until they 'mature' . . . whatever that means."

"Yeah," Johnson quickly added. "I've been teaching these kids for 15 years and I've been fighting back the 'devil' in them at every turn. They expect us—the kids do—to hold them in place . . . otherwise this school would explode. You'd have kids trying to fly off the roof, while others are filling the basement with water so they could have nude swimming parties. Wait a minute," he hesitated, "maybe that's exactly what Grant wants!" The room erupted in laughter. "Yes," he continued, "I can see the headlines in the paper now—'Grant Sterling Fired as Principal at Moundview: Diabolical Programs Uncovered Throughout the School.' "

"Larry, Glenn," Sterling said as the laughter subsided. "As much as I appreciate what you've just said as an understandable, although highly exaggerated, description of middle school kids, I hasten to point out that you *still* seem to be agreeing with me. Flying off the top of a building, flooding the basement, and nude swimming are all examples of things that adolescent kids *might* do if pressured hard enough by their peers."

"You know, folks," Nash declared, "we're all heading in the same direction with this conversation." She had been taking notes . . . carefully avoiding the whimsical banter of the group. "When we really take a close look at middle school kids, we know that until now, their world has been controlled by parents. Under parental guidance, they've remained fairly naive and lived in a comfortable environment. As they enter adolescence, their comfortable world starts to fall apart as the 'real' world emerges with its challenges, difficulties, and problems. It's a tough world for them to relate to, and they look to their peers for support and guidance. It seems to me that self-control, fitting in, and being pointed in the right direction are things that *can* be controlled and directed through peer pressure, within, of course, guidelines that clearly define the limits of what you have jokingly labeled as 'diabolical' behavior. Don't you agree?"

"Oh, I think we all agree with that, Betty." Sterling looked at each faculty member. "Let me suggest this . . . at least for a start," he continued. "The committee working on the adviser-advisee concept has already decided that the adviser base should be a supportive "home environment" to help kids deal effectively with their changing world. That's where discipline can be discussed, foundations laid, and students held accountable in some way for their individual actions. With the exception of district rules and some general school rules, each adviser base should be allowed to set its own expectations for how its students will behave. When a student is sent to the office for some discipline problem—say, refusing to quiet down in class—a copy of that referral can be sent to the student's adviser."

"That's good," Mathews piped up. "That's like a double whammy. No, like a triple whammy. First, the kid's in trouble with the office, then with his or her peers for making the group look bad, and then with his or her adviser. And . . . if the adviser decides to call the kid's parents, we've got a triple whammy and a half! I like that idea. We put the adviser in a mentoring position as far as academics and attendance go, and we add the power of peer-group-supported discipline."

"You know," Johnson added, "this makes sense. The adviser base committee is recommending that we be responsible for our own advisees from day one. If we're going to be held responsible for a kid's grades and attendance, we've got to have some of the same discipline leverage that the principal's office has. Would you agree, Grant?"

"Within reason, Glenn. Let's try this on for size. Suppose Jimmy . . . uh . . . Jones is sent to the office for failure to comply with some teacher request . . . like 'sit down and pay attention.' I need to make a record of that in case he continues to be a discipline problem and might need to be looked at later for possible suspension or expulsion. But there's no reason why a copy of the discipline referral form can't be placed in his adviser's box for additional action. Ninety-nine percent of the stuff that kids do that gets them sent to the office calls for a simple warning and/or advising, not a suspension or expulsion. As far as the 1% goes, however, although the adviser will be notified, my office will act quickly and decisively."

"Let's tell the adviser base committee to sell this concept of discipline to the faculty," Bostitch suggested. "Betty has been taking notes. Betty, can you put this discussion into a recommendation and forward it to the chair of that committee . . . and provide each of us with a copy?"

"I can do that, Sandra. Okay with you, Grant?"

"Yep. I think we can adjourn the meeting," Sterling smiled.

As he walked back to his office, he visualized a cinder-block foundation being built by a number of skilled professionals. "One block at a time," he thought, "with each block being laid by the people who have to make the final structure livable." Faculty and staff "buy-in" was going to be the mortar that held the foundation of the middle school he envisioned together.

"You're looking awfully smug, Sterling!"

"I'm feeling good, you offensive little troll. Hand me what you're waving in your hand, and get back under the desk," Sterling barked.

"You're going to love this," the troll snapped back. "It's a call slip," he said in a sing-song voice, "for you to call Mr. Samuel Block. He's an attorney who's been contacted by the parents of Sidney Collins. You remember Sidney, don't you?" The troll snickered. "He's the kid you suspended for 5 days, yesterday, for mooning a teacher's aide in the library. His parents and attorney think you were too rough on the kid . . . think you've ruined his ego for life by suspending him. Probably want you and the taxpayers to provide him with therapy to 'overcome' the damage you have done to his self-esteem. You're a bad man, Grant Sterling . . . a really, really bad person."

"Mr. Block, this is Grant Sterling, principal at Moundview. How can I help you? . . .

"Yes sir," Sterling responded to the voice on the phone. "I fully realize that not all kids are angels. However . . ."

As he explained the school's position, he reread a note the Collins kid had left for him.

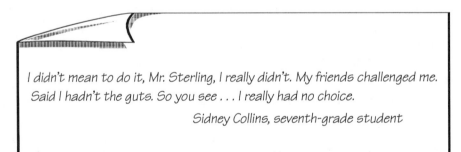

I didn't mean to do it, Mr. Sterling, I really didn't. My friends challenged me. Said I hadn't the guts. So you see . . . I really had no choice.

Sidney Collins, seventh-grade student

▬▬▬ E Pluribus Unum

Sterling hadn't turned on the lights in his office when he came in. He just wanted to sit quietly in the natural light provided by his window and think for a while. He'd been burning the candle at both ends, negotiating with various faculty groups and committees as more of the building blocks of the new middle school he envisioned were slowly being laid. It was 6:00 on Monday morning, and a critical week in his middle school preparation lay ahead. Thursday was a scheduled inservice day for

Moundview teachers, and although students had the day off, he and his staff would put the final stamp of approval, he hoped, on the school's transition plan. Although he was tired of meetings and somewhat wary of Thursday's debates, discussions, and committee reports, he looked forward to definitive agreements and closure.

He sat behind his desk and felt protected by the office, its sound, its morning gray, its morning chill. He touched the desk, and it was cold. "The boilers must have been shut down over the weekend," he guessed. "By the time faculty and students start arriving the building will be warm. You know," he grinned, "if I order the boilers shut down at the close of classes on Wednesday . . . keep them off on Thursday . . . the cold of the building might 'chill' some of the usual pontifical pondering out of various factions of the faculty. Naw . . . those few may have cold hearts and cold feet, but the temperature won't have any effect at all on their vocal cords."

He slid open the deep file drawer of his desk and looked at an accumulation of jam-packed folders. "Model Philosophy and Rationale, Community Support." His eyes skipped randomly from folder to folder. "Instruction in the Middle School," "Assertive Discipline," "Adviser Base," "Standard Curriculum," "Exploratory Curriculum," "Elimination of the Star System," "Job Descriptions," "Differentiated Staffing." "Well, the pieces of our new middle school are all here. They've been created, borrowed, and conjured up from effective schools around the country. They've been cussed, discussed, and marketed. It's damn well time to get these pieces together. Jelled. Connected. Get the show on the road."

He stretched, yawned, and listened to the increasing traffic of people in the outer office. "Time to step into my principal's act and inspire the troops," he declared as he closed the desk drawer, stood up, forced a smile, and stretched again. He turned on the lights and opened his office door.

"Good morning, Phyllis!"

She looked up, slightly startled. "Well, good morning to you, Grant! I . . . I didn't know you were in there."

"I feel like I've been in there all weekend. Tell me this week's going to go fast . . . I'm tired already."

"Well," she grinned, "there's no school on Thursday, if that helps. Just think, Grant . . . no kids on Thursday . . . you get to spend the whole day with faculty and staff. That'll be exciting!"

"That reminds me, Phyllis. Would you call Richard Kealy, my favorite food mogul, and have his department provide us with box lunches for Thursday? Oh, and donuts or cinnamon rolls and coffee at 8:30 too. He'll moan and groan; just tell him to bill it to Moundview's activity fund."

"Will do, Grant. Do you want those cinnamon rolls cooked or uncooked this time?" she laughed.

Just as Sterling had wished, the week was moving along at high speed. He'd been busy doing what he liked to do best—"just takin' names and kickin' butts—that's my primary job," as he often announced. It was late on Wednesday afternoon when he finally had an opportunity to sit down for a moment with his administrative team.

"So, tell me what you predict for tomorrow's meeting. I've scheduled coffee and donuts for 8:30, with committee meetings from 9:00 to 10:30. That should give them enough time to put the finishing touches on their reports. I've scheduled an hour for each report and any discussion that follows."

"Well," Alice noted. "The faculty and staff have already approved the model philosophy and rationale that Jenny's committee drafted. Tom's community support committee finished its work early and presented it to the faculty before the holiday break. You know, I think we only have to hear and adopt the reports from the committees on the adviser base program, exploratory curriculum, and elimination of the star system."

"Yep, that's what my notes tell me," he agreed, "and I've placed those committee reports on the agenda in that order. 10:30-11:30, adviser base . . . 11:30-12:30, lunch . . . 12:30-1:30, exploratory curriculum, and we'll finish out the day with the star system stuff. But my original question was, what do you predict for tomorrow's meeting? How do you see tomorrow going . . . what kinds of last-minute tirades can I expect from some of our hard-liners?"

"You *know* these three reports are going to be the most contentious." Randy looked squarely at Sterling. "Every discussion the faculty has had about middle school development has identified these areas as problematic. I don't expect these committee reports to be accepted without some debate."

"We're lucky, however. We've got strong-willed and thoroughly dedicated folks on those committees. They're not about to take a whole lot of crap from naysayers. We'll let them handle whatever comes up. I want us, if possible, to take a back seat during discussions. I want as much faculty buy-in as possible . . . I don't want any part of this program to look like it came from administration. Anything else for the good of the cause today?" Sterling looked at each team member. "Okay, then . . . see ya tomorrow."

"These folks either forgot to eat breakfast this morning or they've laid aside any diet plans for the day," Sterling thought as he watched his colleagues devour the donuts and cinnamon rolls Kealy had provided. "All right, folks . . . time to pick up any last crumbs and head for your committee meetings. We'll reconvene at 10:30 sharp for Dave's committee's report on the adviser base concept. As I reminded you in yesterday's bulletin, I ordered box lunches and soft drinks for all of us . . . however, the way we attacked the 'continental breakfast,' I don't know how hungry we're going to be," he laughed. "See you at 10:30 . . . let's have fun today, and at the same time, let's get this middle school transition completed!"

"Grant, may I talk to you for a minute?" Milt Jackson, an English teacher, asked.

"Sure, Milt," he replied as he sat down at one of the tables in the meeting room.

"I don't know how to say this, Grant . . . but I really don't want to teach and work under this middle school thing. Seems to me that you're changing the whole concept of what a junior high school is all about . . . changing the whole atmosphere from one of mastering academics to one that seems to be focused on adolescent growth and development. Now, I will admit that junior highs . . . this one included . . . have become what you call 'miniature high schools,' but I gotta tell you, I like teaching in the high school style. I like the lecture structure rather than your so-called participatory method. Would it be okay with you if I request a transfer to a high school? I know that Keith and Sharon are going to talk to you about this same thing, if they haven't already."

"Milt, I know how difficult this decision must have been for you, and if you recall . . . when I first announced that I wanted the faculty to look at the possibility of changing Moundview from a junior high to a middle school, I said that some of you will not feel comfortable changing to middle school concepts. Remember? I also said that if we, as a faculty, decide to change, and anyone feels they can't go along, then I would honor any requests for transfers. You're a good teacher, Milt. I will hate to see you go . . . but you gotta do what feels right."

"Thanks Grant. You know, I've been thinking about this ever since that particular faculty meeting. I guessed you were dead-set against keeping the junior high school intact. I think it's interesting how you've formed all these committees to disguise the fact that you're really behind the scene calling the shots."

Sterling leaned back in his chair and scratched his head. "You think so, huh, Milt? Well, you'll pardon me . . . but I need to get back to the office and do some chores. See ya at 10:30!"

He would not be unhappy to see Milt's transfer request. He and a few other teachers, including Keith Dunlap and Sharon Waters, needed to move to a high school environment. Milt had simply beaten him to the punch.

"Grant." Phyllis peeked around the corner of Sterling's office. "It's almost 10:30, you'd better head for the meeting."

"Oops . . . thanks Phyllis . . . almost forgot what time it was," he said as he stepped into the main office and picked up the microphone attached to the school's intercom. "LADIES AND GENTLEMEN . . . MEMBERS OF THE FAMOUS, AND OCCASIONALLY INFAMOUS, MOUNDVIEW FACULTY AND STAFF. JUST A REMINDER THAT WE NEED TO RECONVENE IN ROOM 115 AT 10:30 SHARP . . . AND THAT WOULD BE NOW. THANK YOU."

It was almost 4:30 when Sterling returned to his office and closed the door. He sank into the chair behind his desk and let out a deep sigh. June Hazel's mobile caught his attention as it slowly rotated . . . blown by the air flow from the heat vent on the ceiling. June had died a few years ago, but her memory, and the memory of his first year as a principal, lived on with each turn of her colorful creation. He quickly scanned the notes he had taken during the day's meetings.

Adviser base: Report by Dave's committee seemed to be well received. A few questions raised . . . will need to be resolved before we start building the activity schedule. Concept approved.

Exploratory curriculum: Excellent report by Monica for her committee. Much interaction among faculty, and many questions remain. Committee has promised to meet individually with each faculty member to solicit additional input and ideas. Even so . . . concept approved.

Elimination of the star system: Although this concept raised the most eyebrows at first, Harold and his committee have done an excellent job of selling the importance of the concept to faculty and staff. We still have to do some work with the community, however. Concept approved.

The entire faculty agreed that continuing meetings with the community and students will be absolutely necessary to the success of the program. Meetings should be scheduled during March, April, and May, and a meeting should be held before school starts in the fall. Faculty agreed that a faculty-staff public relations-marketing team should be selected by me to assist in this process.

Box lunch was terrible. Kealy continues to be an impostor!!!

"Come on, Phyllis . . . let's call it a day!"

"Was it a good day, Grant?"

"It was a great day, Phyllis . . . and tomorrow's Friday!"

The middle school model developed and implemented by Moundview faculty and staff would soon be adopted by the board of education for every junior high school in the district. Years later, Sterling would discover that the Moundview prototype was the model for many successful middle school programs across the country.

For Discussion ▨▨▨▨

General Questions

Using the Sterling paradigm (http://www.corwinpress.com/dunklee.htm) as a model, and speaking from the perspective of a principal, evaluate each episode as follows:

What are the dominant behaviors exhibited by Sterling in this episode?

Is there consensus about this in the class? If not, explain the different viewpoints.

What were the primary actors' individual motives?

How effective was Sterling's behavior in this situation and why?

Can you identify other avenues or approaches that might lead to the same, or a better, conclusion?

If Sterling was a woman,

▨ As a female reader, can you identify methodology or behavior that you would change to bring the episode to the same, or similar, closure?

▨ As a male reader, what differences in methodology or behavior would you expect to see?

Specific Questions for Each Episode

When Lip Gloss Becomes Lip Glow

1. Your school district has a specific policy regarding students' use of alcohol on school property. Do you know what the policy is? Can you think of any occasion when you might bend the rules a little as Sterling does in this case? If so, what mitigating circumstances would encourage you to take a calculated risk that could be considered insubordination?

2. Sterling says to the Moundview counselors, "How do you want to handle this? Any suggestions?" What role, if any, should counselors play in suggesting what to do in situations like the lip gloss incident?

What if . . . another student brought alcohol to school in the future, and Sterling suspended that student for the full 10 days mandated by district policy?

Good Intentions, Good Results, Bad Choice

3. How important is it to check the background of people you invite in to work with students? Do you have a legal responsibility? Moral responsibility?

4. This episode illustrates the value of developing a personal support network both in and outside of the school. How do you go about developing this kind of network?

What if . . . Green had sexually abused a Moundview student during his tenure there?

What if . . . Sterling hadn't previously developed a strong rapport with the chief of school security?

Title Censored

5. Do school districts have a tendency to practice *ex post facto* crisis management? If so, why?

What if . . . Sterling had refused to meet with Mr. and Mrs. Curtis?

What if . . . Sterling had notified teachers of the Curtises' demands and concerns?

A Classic Snow Job

(No specific questions)

Don't Spit Into the Wind!

6. What do you think might happen in your school district if the independent action of one principal upset the interschool athletic schedule for a major portion of a school year?

7. What would effectively stop the possibility of backfire as a result of Sterling actions? School climate? Fear of administrative reprisal?

8. What role does autonomy play in managing an individual school within a multiple-school district?

What if . . . the other schools had refused to adjust their activity schedules in response to Sterling's request?

What if . . . as a result of this confrontation, the teachers were no longer comfortable exchanging ideas with Sterling?

Open House, Closed Door

9. What does the word *fair* mean when dealing with political power? Clearly, Sterling's values are being compromised in this episode, specifically right versus wrong. How adaptable should effective principals be with their personal values?

A Sterling Moment: IBTC@L

(No specific questions)

Macho Man

10. Sterling has other marginal teachers in his schools and hasn't demanded that they be transferred out during the school year. How would you explain his quick action to remove Valdez?

What if . . . personnel had refused to transfer Valdez?

Nothing Unusual, Just the Daily In-Basket . . . Again

(No specific questions)

Burnout

11. Suppose that you had an especially talented teacher who filled a unique role in your school. If that teacher showed significant signs of burnout, would you be more concerned about the teacher's welfare or maintaining the opportunities the teacher provided students in your school? Explain.

A Typical Day

12. In the introduction to this book, there is a reference to the nonlinear nature of events in a typical school and the need for an effective principal to maintain a linear focus. In this episode, what skills or abilities does Sterling demonstrate that make it possible for him to maintain a linear focus?

One Block at a Time

13. Who had control of this meeting?

14. You have been introduced to the troll in several episodes. What does the troll represent?

What if . . . Sterling hadn't "seeded" the meeting by introducing, and then reinforcing, peer pressure as a motivating factor in adolescent behavior. Would the group have come to the same conclusion?

E Pluribus Unum

15. Why doesn't Sterling react to Milt's remark insinuating that Sterling is calling the shots—managing the outcomes of committees—behind the scenes?

16. How much influence, if any, should a principal or leader have on the outcomes of empowered committees?

What if . . . Sterling had refused to support Milt's, or any other faculty member's, requests for transfer?

7

A Transition

An Invitation to Intrigue, Corruption, ▨ Cheap Romance, and a PhD

"Why a Saturday meeting?" Sterling wondered as he hung up the phone after talking with Superintendent Boughton. "Why does Boughton want to talk to me in 'an environment where we won't be interrupted'?" Sterling's mind engaged like a computer searching for a "what did I do wrong now?" file. He wondered if the problem was something that might have happened at Moundview. Sterling didn't like meetings with superiors when he didn't have at least some knowledge of the agenda.

Two days later, the mystery of the Saturday meeting was still bothering Sterling as he parked his car in front of the district's administration building and quickly walked to the superintendent's office.

"Come in, Grant. Sorry about having you come in on a Saturday. My schedule has been horrible the past couple of weeks, and it doesn't seem to be letting up. Anyway, I wanted to talk to you as soon as possible about a problem that I'm hoping you'll be able to help me with. I've got a real tricky administrative dilemma at City High."

Sterling relaxed.

"You told me a few months ago that you wanted to start work on a doctorate," Boughton continued. "And you suggested that if you were accepted into a doctoral program that you might need some release time. Are you still thinking along those lines . . . about getting an advanced degree?"

"I was accepted into the program at State University about 2 weeks ago, Dr. Boughton. I still haven't decided, however, whether I have the time, money, or guts to proceed."

"I'd like to see you get your doctorate, Grant, and I think I can work out an interesting assignment for you that will allow you the kind of time you're going to need. As I mentioned, we have administrative problems at City High. Specifically, with the principal, Jim Wakefield. I'd like for you to accept the position of associate principal next year and then acting principal the following year. Because there are five other administrators at City High, you would be able to use them to cover your office whenever you had to leave early for classes. This assignment would at least carry you through your doctoral classwork. Then, unless you choose to stay in the position longer, we could assign you temporarily to one that would allow you the time and energy to finish the research for your dissertation. I know this sounds rather patch-work, but it might help solve a problem for the district and, at the same time, provide an opportunity for you to secure your PhD. What's your thinking?"

"Well," Sterling leaned back in his chair. "I appreciate your vote of confidence concerning my efforts if I decide to move forward on a PhD. I guess I'm out of the loop, however, as far as the administrative problems you mentioned at City High. Can you fill me in?"

City High was not the high school that Sterling's students at either Arthur or Moundview attended. It was, however, the high school that Center kids attended. Since Sterling had left the Center community, City High had retired one principal and two others had resigned.

"I've never had any direct dealings with Jim Wakefield," Sterling told Boughton. "As a matter of fact, I've only been in the building a half-dozen times."

"It's probably good that you haven't had contact with Wakefield. Listen, Grant, I'm not telling you anything today that Wakefield doesn't already know. He knows he's in hot water and that his role at City High next year is strictly as a lame duck principal. I've told him, and the board supports me, that he can remain in that position for 1 more year while we decide what to do about the lawsuit. He's been told that we're bringing in an associate principal to run the building and, regardless of the outcome of the suit, he's out of there at the end of next year. That's when we'll name you acting principal until you decide what you want to do—stay or leave."

"I still seem to be missing a big part of this puzzle, Dr. Boughton. What's with the lawsuit?"

"I'm going to give you a complete set of documents outlining the situation at City High, including all the information concerning the lawsuit. I wanted Larry Frost, City High's area assistant superintendent, to be here today to help me convince you to make this move, but Larry called me this morning . . . the flu bug caught up with him. He really wanted to be here though. He said, and I quote, 'I've never seen Grant sweat.' He'll come out and meet with you at Moundview next week. He'll be able to answer any questions you still might have after reading the stuff I'm giving you this morning."

"Dr. Boughton," Sterling leaned forward in his chair. "You and I both have the reputation of being bottom-line thinkers. Let me ask you this. Are you ordering me to go to City High, or are you asking me? If you're asking me, how much time do I have to consider this, as well as make a decision on whether or not to pursue a doctorate? And finally, maybe a stupid question, but the real bottom line for me is, do I really want this assignment?"

Boughton laughed. "I'm asking. I can't think of anyone more qualified to go over there and clean up the mess Wakefield has made. I'd like to know your decision before the next board meeting in 2 weeks. As far as enjoying the job—I don't think you're going to like it one bit! I think you're going to be asking me 2 years from now to find something else for you. But, remember, it will give you the opportunity to start your doctorate."

Before Sterling left, Boughton handed him a cardboard box. "Your reading materials, Grant. Knowing how you like creative problem solving, I think you'll find the City High stuff in here reads like a dime novel full of intrigue, corruption, and cheap romance. Have a great weekend, and keep up the good work at Moundview."

"Creative problem solving is another phrase for 'Grant, we need a clean-up job done again,' " Sterling reasoned as he put the box in the trunk of his car.

Sterling was finishing his sixth year at Moundview, and had his middle school program solidly in place. Other junior highs in the district were well under way in their transformation to middle schools using the Moundview model.

"I'm not excited about leaving middle school kids and teachers," he thought as he drove away from the administration building. "I'm excited about the prospect of starting my doctorate, however, and Boughton certainly seemed more than eager to help."

Instead of going home, Sterling drove to his office. He wanted some uninterrupted time to go through the pile of documents that Boughton had given him. "I wonder what Boughton meant when he said the box contains stuff that reads like a dime novel?" Sterling's curiosity would soon be replaced by outright disgust.

"My God," Sterling thought as he carefully placed the City High materials back in the cardboard box and locked it in his office closet. "Jim Wakefield is one perverted cookie. Teacher morale at City High must be one step from hell. I need Larry Frost to fill in some blanks before I decide whether I want to risk potential professional suicide by accepting this assignment!"

Frost was sitting in his car waiting for Sterling to arrive at Moundview on Monday morning. Sterling and Frost had been friends ever since Sterling helped the elementary principals by getting Greta Thompson to resign from her position as a traveling music teacher 12 years ago. At that time, Frost had recently retired from the Army and was an elementary principal.

"Colonel Frost, sir. You're up early this morning." Sterling gave him a half-hearted salute. "Sorry you missed the party Saturday morning."

"I haven't talked to the superintendent yet," Frost said. "How'd the meeting go? You told him you'd accept the position, didn't you?"

"Larry, I told him that I thought that you were the best administrator for that position and that I should replace you as area assistant superintendent. I think he kind of liked my suggestion!"

"Right," Frost responded in a deadpan voice. "You got time to talk with me this morning?"

"For you, I'll make time, if you don't mind drinking coffee for a few minutes while I hustle up a vice principal to cover for me in the main office."

Frost retired to the teachers' lounge while Sterling got things ready to go for the school day.

"All right, Larry," Sterling said as he closed his office door. "I've looked over all the materials Boughton gave me. What did I miss?"

"I have to tell you, Grant, this is one of the messiest situations I've ever seen. Before this is over, we're going to lose a whole bunch of administrators, Associate Superintendent O'Brian being one of them. Me too, possibly, along with Assistant Superintendent Rose. And, of course, Jim Wakefield—what an asshole! I've requested a transfer to another area job, but I'll stay, if the board wants me, and if you accept the associate principal position. The superintendent's neck is in a noose on this one, and if he can't solve the problem, he'll be gone too."

"That last bit of news really doesn't give me impetus to accept this job," Sterling interrupted. "The superintendent made me some promises that he wouldn't be able to keep if he wasn't here."

"Oh, I think you're going to pull this out of the bag for him, and both of you will be here long after I retire," Frost said, quickly covering his tracks.

"Look, Larry . . . enough doomsday anticipation! Please start from the beginning and give me your perspective to help me fill in some blanks I have from reading legal stuff. I need to get a big enough handle on the situation to make an intelligent decision."

As Frost started speaking, Sterling could sense from his voice and body language how angry he was. He painted a picture so bizarre that Sterling would have thought he was fabricating most of it if he hadn't seen the documentation in the box Boughton had given him.

"It all started with a tape recording that had been presented to Assistant Superintendent O'Brian by Peggy Overling, City High's media specialist," Frost recalled. "It seems that she and Wakefield had been having an affair for about 2 years. The affair became well known to the faculty, and she was afraid that her husband or Wakefield's wife was going to find out about it. She went to him to tell him she was going to stop seeing him. He got quite angry and threatened to transfer her to another school if she didn't continue. She walked out of his office and returned later in the day with a tape recorder in her purse. He flew off the handle again and repeated his transfer threat, adding some statement about getting her fired. Then he cried and begged her to stay with him. What a jerk! Can I have some more coffee?"

Sterling left, walked down the hall to the lounge, and returned with Frost's refill. "You're really angry about this," Sterling said as Frost continued.

"So she gets scared and takes this tape down and plays it for O'Brian. He tells her that he'll take care of the whole situation and for her not to worry. He goes over and gives Wakefield the 'good ole boy' treatment. You know, the 'shame on you' scenario . . . 'You better cool it for a while' game. Well, Wakefield made life miserable for Overling, and no matter how hard she tried to get O'Brian to do something, he sat on his hands. She finally resigned and, as you know, is now suing the school district for sexual harassment and demanding big bucks. And I think she's got a good case! In addition, and this just blew my mind, her attorney put out a search for any other women who have had similar experiences in the district, and six other former employees have joined her in the suit!"

"Okay, I've got that information figured out, Larry. What's with the store and gas station out on Highway 9?" Sterling asked.

"Well, wait . . . that's coming. What you don't know is that Wakefield was also having affairs with two other faculty members at City High. He had three affairs going at the same time. One of the teachers left the district to get away from him, but the third one, Kathy Newman, is still at the school. In fact, she handles the books for his Highway 9 enterprise."

"Now you're pulling my leg," Sterling interrupted. "Wakefield is not that much of a charmer!"

"No, it's a power thing . . . They're afraid of him. I told you this whole thing is bizarre!" Frost took a gulp of coffee and continued. "So, anyway, Wakefield bought this old country store and gas station out near Star City. He had City High custodians out there doing repair work and building counters and cabinets on school district time. He had his head custodian, Jerry Rand, contracted to be the foreman on the job, and was paying him a salary out of City High activity funds. He pays Kathy Newman, and three other employees too, but out of business profits. He was also using the school's activity van to haul supplies and materials out to the store."

"Wait, hold on Larry, it sounds like the district has sufficient grounds to fire Wakefield right now. Misuse of funds, personnel, equipment, maybe materials, possible sexual harassment. Why is he still at City High?"

"Politics, Grant. Wakefield's brother is a highly placed state official. He and some other top dogs here in the city have really put the screws to board members to ease Wakefield out without criminal charges. They've also put a muzzle on the media. All the activities I've mentioned have stopped, although Wakefield still has the store, and Newman and Rand still work for him outside of the school day. He's been told that if he keeps his nose clean, he can stay at City High for next year, and then, I guess, he'll be placed in some obscure office counting paper clips or something. Bottom line, Grant, the board won't let Boughton fire him."

"So, Larry . . . what do think I should do?"

"I'll tell ya, Grant . . . I don't know how to advise you in this case. How important is a PhD to you? What do you want to do with it if you get one?"

"It's fairly important to me, Larry. It's kind of a life goal, I guess. I don't have any plans for the future that are different from what I'm doing now. School administration is still fun. I don't know, maybe I'll apply for your job when you retire."

"You better hurry," Frost laughed. "Listen, I don't know where you'll end up with the City High situation. It won't be fun, I'll guarantee you that. I think you ought to go for it, however, and use the deal Boughton is offering to get your degree. You can always back out later."

"Let me think about it, Larry. I told Boughton I'd let him know in the next couple of weeks. You know, it'd be a lot easier if he just ordered me to go."

"Probably, Grant. But in this highly volatile situation, he wants you to be a part of that decision. He knows he's asking you to risk 2 years of your professional career to help him get the situation under control. But he's willing to reward you up front by giving you a chance to get that doctorate."

"Bust one bun for City High, bust the other working on a PhD. Since I only have two buns, Larry, what would I have left to sit on when I'm finished?"

"Your PhD and a letter of thanks from the school board. What more could you ask for? I gotta go, Grant. Talk to you later."

That night, Sterling agonized over the decision he had to make. As he reviewed his years in public education, he reconfirmed his belief that although they should be "above it all," school districts are no different than any other enterprise. School districts are, after all, microcosms of society, and exhibit the same kinds of contamination that can infect any population. Nevertheless, Sterling had a difficult time thinking of educators as anything but a group of highly trained professionals who, because of their work with children, should be exemplary—the last people one would ever think of as committing any kind of indiscretion. Although Sterling knew full well that he and his fellow educators were not perfect, he practiced the philosophy that, while educators had a right to a private life, they had an obligation to keep their private life just that—private. Corruption or impropriety should never be associated with school people. He had, however, witnessed the firing of teachers and administrators for immoral conduct, misuse of school funds, and other miscellaneous indiscretions. And, although it was difficult, he acknowledged that people, even school people, are not perfect.

"You know," he thought, "except for the individuals directly involved in this fiasco . . . a few years from now, people outside this school district will never believe that this kind of thing can take place in education. What a mess—what a challenge."

A few days later, Sterling sent Boughton a note. "Pencil me in for City High next year. I'll do the best I can."

The Moundview Finale

"Now, in closing . . . before I officially thank you all for another successful year, and we race to see who can get out of the parking lot the fastest . . . over the past 6 years, we, the faculty, staff, and administration of Moundview, have made this school one of the most exemplary middle schools in the country. The school is now solidly built on a foundation of education, not just schooling. We have taken the ideals of how to educate adolescent kids and put the ideals into practice, and we have served as the developmental as well as the implementation model for two thirds of the district's junior highs as they converted to middle schools."

A smattering of applause broke out. "All right, Grant . . . enough speechmaking. The sun is shining and the beach is calling for me," a laughing voice from the back of the room interrupted.

"Oh, yeah? Whataya mean, the beach . . . you promised me you were going to help me paint my house!" someone jokingly responded.

"Maybe he thought you were talking about a beach house!" a third party interjected, and the room exploded in laughter.

"I know, you troublemakers . . . I know, I've said some of these same things in previous end-of-the-year faculty meetings, but this year it takes on a very special meaning for me to share, for the last time, my feelings about this school and this faculty."

The room was suddenly frozen in silence.

"Last time, Grant? Did you say last time?"

Sterling took a deep breath. "Folks, I don't know any easy way for me to say this, so just let me give it to you straight," he said as he took another even deeper breath. "As you have undoubtedly heard through the grapevine, and lately in the press, there've been some problems within the administration at City High. I've been asked by the superintendent to assume the position of associate principal at City until some of the problems are resolved. It's not a position that I applied for, nor is it a position that I particularly want. After studying the difficult situation City is facing, however, I decided to accept the position, at least temporarily, to see if I can help. How does this change affect Moundview? Well, you're going to have a new principal . . . but the finest and best leaders at Moundview will still be here next year. You built this program . . . *you* are the finest and best leaders. I'm confident that Moundview will continue to provide its kids and parents with the best program in our city. I . . ." Sterling stopped, removed a handkerchief from his back pocket, and took a quick swipe at his eyes. "I'm sorry . . . I . . . I can't talk anymore, folks, it's time for us to leave."

The faculty were stunned and speechless. The only sound came from a hamster cage in the corner of the room. One of the creatures had stepped on the revolving wheel, making a slow, metallic whirring noise. Sterling left the room . . . he couldn't look back.

For Discussion

General Questions

Using the Sterling paradigm (http://www.corwinpress.com/dunklee.htm) as a model, and speaking from the perspective of a principal, evaluate each episode as follows:

What are the dominant behaviors exhibited by Sterling in this episode?

Is there consensus about this in the class? If not, explain the different viewpoints.

What were the primary actors' individual motives?

How effective was Sterling's behavior in this situation and why?

Can you identify other avenues or approaches that might lead to the same, or a better, conclusion?

If Sterling was a woman,

- As a female reader, can you identify methodology or behavior that you would change to bring the episode to the same, or similar, closure?

- As a male reader, what differences in methodology or behavior would you expect to see?

Specific Questions for Each Episode

An Invitation to Intrigue, Corruption, Cheap Romance, and a PhD

1. What organizational failure would make it possible for the principal at City High to act in such a manner?

2. Is there anything about this episode that you find disturbing? If so, list your concerns and rank them according to priority.

3. Your district has policies regarding sexual harassment and misuse of school funds, materials, equipment, personnel, and the like. What questions do you have concerning the procedures called for in such policies, that is, investigation, reporting, and so on?

The Moundview Finale

(No specific questions)

8

The City High Years

Reestablishing a Power Base Within a Power Base: I Agreed to This?

"You know, Grant, I didn't ask for you to be transferred here. I didn't have any input in that decision. If I had, Rob Simmons would have been my first choice. I just want to put that information right up front," Jim Wakefield, the principal at City High announced.

"Look, I hear you, Jim," Sterling retorted. "You know all too well I wasn't transferred here. And, in spite of the fact that I wasn't your choice, we'd better be able to work together. If not, it's going to be a long year for one of us. We've got 2,300 kids out there, 250 teachers, and God knows how many staff members . . . all waiting to see if we can get the school year started without problems."

"So, we've got a meeting with Area Superintendent Frost this afternoon. Any idea what it's about?" Wakefield asked, his voice tinged with contempt.

"I think," Sterling replied, "that he's got new job descriptions for both of us."

"Well," Wakefield slowly leaned back in his chair, "I'm guessing that this is the day that I get the word that I'm supposed to play 'lame duck' this year while they fight with my attorneys over some alleged crap. I'm sure they've filled you in on all that stuff."

Sterling avoided responding to Wakefield's comment. He didn't want to become party to Wakefield's legal dilemma. "I'll see you at 1 o'clock then, Jim. In the meantime, I need to get moved into my office. Any chance you can take me on a tour of this place after that?"

"We'll see," Wakefield said in a resentful tone.

Sterling returned to Wakefield's office promptly at 1 for the meeting with Larry Frost. There were three people already seated around the table—Wakefield, Frost, and a third man Sterling didn't immediately recognize.

"Sit down, Grant," Wakefield said. "This is my attorney, Fred Border."

Sterling leaned across the table to shake hands with Border as Wakefield explained that he'd asked Border to be present at the meeting. Larry Frost was on the telephone making arrangements for the school district's attorney to be present also. Sterling gathered from Frost's conversation that he hadn't known that Wakefield would have his attorney here today.

"Our attorney will be here in about 15 minutes," Frost said as he hung up the phone. "In the meantime, Grant, why don't you and I take a walk?"

As he followed Frost out of Wakefield's office, he could sense Frost's anger at the situation. It was clear that Wakefield wasn't going to have any meetings with his superiors without his attorney at his side. An act, Sterling thought, that could cause some acute communication problems until the legal matters were settled. His exact role as associate principal, already hazy, was becoming cloudier by the minute. "I hope Boughton and his staff have all their ducks in a row," he thought to himself.

"That S.O.B.," Frost muttered as he and Sterling walked from the main office to the hallway. "All right, Sterling, here's the game plan. When our attorney gets here, I'm simply going to hand both you and Wakefield a document that outlines each of your job descriptions for this contract year. Wakefield isn't going to be happy, and his attorney will 'throw a hissy.' His job description requires him to report to work each day, but he has been stripped of all authority to run the school. That includes the supervision and evaluation of personnel, curriculum management, budget access, and disbursement. His job, believe it or not," Frost said disgustedly, "is to be in his office . . . nothing more, nothing less . . . until our attorneys give us the green light to terminate his contract. Welcome to City High, Grant," Frost said sarcastically. "You had fair warning, and you took the job anyway. You may, however, have signed a pact with the devil," he laughed.

The meeting lasted all of 10 minutes, and predictably ended with the attorneys barking at each other across the table. Frost and Sterling left the battlefield quickly; their presence wasn't necessary. Assignments had been given, and both Sterling and Frost felt they had better things to do than listen to verbose legal posturing. Frost returned to the safety of his office at the district's administration building, and Sterling, closing his door behind him, sat down at his desk to study the document he'd just been handed.

Anxious to get a feel for the City High environment, during the next few days, Sterling introduced himself to the custodial staff; spent a few minutes at the desk of each of the school's secretaries; set up a meeting with the counseling staff; and asked each of the four vice principals to meet him Friday morning at 8 o'clock at the district administration building, where he'd reserved a small meeting room. He wanted a private discussion with them . . . away from City High . . . away from the dour influence of Wakefield. He needed to build an administrative team loyal to him, regardless of how Sterling felt about Jim Wakefield and his problems.

As Sterling pulled his car into the district building's parking lot, he was met by Wakefield.

"Good morning, Jim. Got a meeting here too?"

"You're not having a meeting with my vice principals without me present," Wakefield said angrily.

"As a matter of fact, I am. Let's not have a scene here in the parking lot, Jim. I'll be glad to fill you in when I get back to the building this afternoon. In the meantime, please excuse me. I have people waiting."

Wakefield was livid. Fortunately, he went back to his car and left.

"What have I gotten into?" Sterling sighed as he entered the building.

Harlow Bartlett, Rob Simmons, Gloria Robertson, and Maury Gilbert, the vice principals in charge of City High's four divisions, were waiting for him as he entered the room and closed the door.

"Good morning, folks . . . thanks for being prompt. I won't waste time telling you that my role here is a difficult one. I think you know that already. So that we don't have any misunderstandings today or the rest of the year, I made each of you a copy of my district-mandated job description. It's self-explanatory, I believe. I have a rather lengthy agenda for us this morning, but before I start, which of you, or which of your secretaries, notified Jim Wakefield that we were meeting here this morning?"

There was a long moment of intense silence. "Okay, never mind." The first nail had been driven to build a new power base. He would not tolerate dual allegiance. "Now, what do I need to do to ensure the safe and orderly start of the new school year?" he asked as he pulled a notepad from his briefcase.

"Nothing really, Grant," Rob Simmons said as he looked around the table at his colleagues. "The master schedule has been built; students have been placed in classes; all faculty and staff vacancies have been filled . . . we're ready to go!"

"All right then, how do you think I should approach the teachers and staff concerning my role and Wakefield's? You've got to admit this is an extremely unusual situation."

"I think," Gloria Robertson said pensively, "that you ought to avoid any mention of Jim's problems, or any mention of problems you might have with him, and simply do the same thing you've done here. Pass out a copy of your job description, which clearly puts you in charge of the school, and say to them, just as you said to us, this is an extremely unusual situation. Then reassure them that school goes on, regardless of that situation, and that it will not have any effect on them or their students."

The others' silence signaled their tacit approval of Gloria's statement, and Sterling moved on to discuss the budget and student discipline procedures and briefly review each vice principal's extracurricular duties. The meeting ended at 11:30, and although most of the discussions had been tense, the group was laughing and shook hands with him as they left the room.

"Grant, see ya for a moment?" Larry Frost had stepped out of his office just as Sterling was about to leave the building. "So now you've met Wakefield's cronies," Frost laughed as he escorted Sterling into his office. "Not one of them . . . not *one* of them," he emphasized, "is principalship material. Wakefield hired all of them because he felt they would follow him blindly. He was right! What a bunch of wimps! Anyway, how'd your meeting go?"

"We're going to have a good year, Larry. Does your job description include keeping Wakefield off my back? If not, please add it to your list. He's probably going to try to sabotage my every move. And if he succeeds . . . and if City High has problems as a result of his actions, then, my friend . . . well, City High is your responsibility too. Maybe Larry, just maybe," Sterling grinned, "we've both signed a pact with the devil." It was his turn to laugh this time, as he could readily see that Frost had not thought about the possibility of Wakefield getting revenge.

"Have a good rest of the day and a great weekend," he said airily as he left Frost's office.

First Friday

Whenever he had a break, Sterling's first priority was to get away from his office. It had been a busy day, and he'd been "landlocked" behind his desk. This Friday, the end of the first week of school, was no different, and he needed to get a feel for how school was going. Most school administrators and teachers who have spent a few years in the school business develop a kind of sixth sense that permits them to "read" the general environment of a school simply by walking the halls.

Sterling finished his walk just in time for the final dismissal bell and stepped outside to watch the gleeful exit of students clearly anxious to start their weekend activities. A few minutes later, a refreshed Sterling returned to his office and opened a folder marked "Monday Morning Administrative Team Meeting." He started to jot down some of the things he wanted to discuss with various team members when his interoffice phone rang. He could tell from the extension light on the receiver that it was Betty, his secretary.

"Yes, Betty?" he answered.

"Mr. Sterling," she said in a voice that told him that someone was in the outer office and could hear her talking. "Mr. O'Brien, father of James O'Brien, is here to see you."

Sterling smiled. "From the sound of your very formal voice, I take it you know Mr. O'Brien, Betty?" he asked quietly.

"Yes."

"Problem parent?"

"Yes, sir," Betty responded.

"Anything I already know about?"

"No sir, I don't think so."

"Okay, Betty. Help me prepare for this meeting by answering yes or no to some quick questions. About a student problem?"

"No. Well, perhaps."

"Sports?"

"Yes." Betty sounded surprised.

"It's usually one or the other when a father wants to talk about something related to his son. Unhappy because his son was cut from a squad?"

"Not that I'm aware of."

"Hates a coach?"

"Yes, I think so."

"Wants him fired?"

"Oh, yes."

"Football?"

"No."

"Basketball?"

"Yes."

"Thanks, Betty. Show Mr. O'Brien in."

The meeting with O'Brien was short and to the point. O'Brien wanted his son's basketball coach fired. Sterling listened carefully and assured Mr. O'Brien that he would look into the matter. As he escorted O'Brien out, he noticed that a teacher, Mark Prince, was visiting with Betty.

"Mr. Sterling, can I visit with you for a moment?"

"Sure Mark, bring your coffee and come in."

"I'm sorry I haven't had time to get to meet you earlier, but I was so busy this summer . . . right up to the start of school . . . that I didn't get the chance to take you up on your invitation to stop by before school started. But I feel that I know you quite well after hearing what you had to say during our preschool orientation meetings. I just wanted to stop by and welcome you to City High. We certainly need your leadership. Well," Prince continued. "That's all. Thanks for seeing me. Let me know if there's anything I can do to help you. It's a killer job."

"Thanks, Mark," Sterling smiled. "Please call me Grant. You know, since I have you here, I could use your help on a problem. I was going to talk to you sometime next week about this, but now is as good a time as ever, if . . . if you've got a few minutes."

"Sure, Grant," Prince eagerly responded.

"I'd like to take a couple of minutes and review with you . . ." he stopped for a minute, swung around in his chair, and removed Prince's personnel file from the cabinet behind him. "I've read your file and jotted down some notes. They're clipped to the front. Would you take a moment to look over my notes and talk with me about them?"

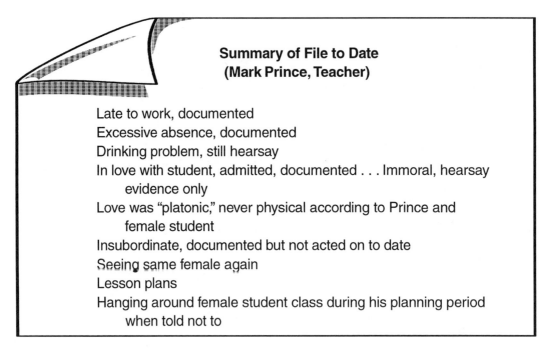

**Summary of File to Date
(Mark Prince, Teacher)**

Late to work, documented
Excessive absence, documented
Drinking problem, still hearsay
In love with student, admitted, documented . . . Immoral, hearsay
    evidence only
Love was "platonic," never physical according to Prince and
    female student
Insubordinate, documented but not acted on to date
Seeing same female again
Lesson plans
Hanging around female student class during his planning period
    when told not to

Sterling could see that Prince was suddenly uncomfortable as he quickly scanned the notes and flipped through the folder.

"I think I've seen all of this, Grant," Prince said, his voice unsteady. He wanted another cup of coffee.

"Get some coffee, and let's talk," Sterling said in a benign voice.

"Okay, look, Mark, we both know that there are a number of problems here. We need to talk about them so that you and I are both working from the same foundation. Do you want me to talk, or do you want to discuss anything in your folder or in my notes?"

"That's not what I came in here for," Prince said, noticeably annoyed.

"I know," Sterling calmly responded. "But let's review this stuff anyway. First, it looks to me like you're guilty of being really dumb. Second, it looks like you're about one step away from being terminated for insubordination. Mark, it's like this. I don't want to prejudge you before I've seen you in action, as a teacher. But I've studied your file so I can help you plan some strategies that might be beneficial. I can forget about the past, but your folder is a little unforgiving. So, let's let the folder lie dormant for a while and let your record with me be the thing you and I have to worry about. From today, Mark, I'll judge you by what you do, not what you did. I'll put my notes in a formal letter to you to remind you what I expect from you this year. Fair enough?"

"Yes, I guess so," Prince looked at the floor.

"All right. You and I are starting with a clean slate. Understand, however, that the problems summarized in my upcoming memo to you are yours to resolve. You don't have a whole lot of wiggle room. The things you see in my notes, soon to be covered in a memo, are things that could cause you to lose your job if you don't take them seriously. I'm not going to chase you around. I don't have the time to harass you, and neither do any of my vice principals. But if you repeat any of the problems documented in your file, well . . . you know where I stand."

Prince sat silently.

"Okay, Mark. Thanks for stopping by. Let's both have a great year."

"Yes, sir," Prince said quietly as he left Sterling's office. "Thanks for visiting with me. Again, welcome to City High."

"Betty," Sterling said after Prince left, "I'm going to write a brief memo to Mr. Prince before I leave today. Would you type it up first thing Monday morning . . . send it to Prince and put a copy in his personnel file?"

"Will do, Grant. I'm leaving now. Have a good weekend."

"Same to you, Betty. Oh . . . before you leave, what time is that band booster club picnic this evening?"

"7:00, Grant. Have fun."

Letterhead

Date: September 15, 19XX
Memo to: Mark Prince   DRAFT
From: Grant Sterling
Subject: Summary of Conference held Friday, September 12, 19XX

As mentioned to you in our conference on September 12, I am writing this memo as a summary of the matters we discussed.

In addition to reviewing the contents of your personnel file, we discussed specific matters relating to your conduct as a member of the faculty at City High and your overall role as a professional. Specifically, I advised you that:

1. You are required to turn in lesson plans each week to your department chair.
2. Excessive tardiness could lead to suspension and/or termination.
3. In the event of excessive absences, you will be required to provide your supervising vice principal with verification of need from a medical doctor.
4. Any improper conduct with any student may lead to immediate suspension and/or termination. You are expected to maintain a professional relationship with your students.
5. If for any reason you have problems, personal or professional, seek immediate assistance.

Thanks for your attention and cooperation in the matters outlined above. I'm looking forward to your having a very successful year. Please feel free to contact me directly if you have any problems.

    cc: Personnel File
        Supervising Vice Principal

▬▬▬ Monday's ~~Milieu~~ Menu

Monday:	
7:30	CHS Business Manager
8:00	CHS Activities Director
8:30	CHS Athletic Director
9:00	CHS Head Custodian
9:30	CHS Counselors
10:00	CHS Vice Principals
11:00	↓ ↓

"We 13 are the administrative team," Sterling decreed. "Ultimately, all major problems are to be solved through the insight and actions of this team. Although we will all continue to make and implement decisions independently within our individual job responsibilities, major problems—those that may affect the school at large—should be resolved in our Monday morning scheduled meetings.

"Now, I know," he continued, "that you're thinking that shared decision making has become an overused expression, but I know it works. I think that the days when an authoritarian principal sat in his or her office and made all the decisions are gone. You folks have ability and talent that should not be overlooked in the management of this school. And I know that you were not consulted concerning major decisions under the previous principal. That changes today." After a moment of silence, the room came alive with conversation of agreement. Sterling glanced around the table, and it seemed to him a comfortable feeling was growing among his new team. The Monday morning meetings were scheduled and convened from that day on.

First up . . . (7:30): Sterling's uncompromising business manager who always seemed to be short of temper, short of money, and short of personality. "But," he thought, "she doesn't need a charismatic disposition for her job . . . just a steady hand on the computation side of her computer's well-worn keyboard." Edith Hanover had been the bookkeeper/business manager at City High for 31 years. She had manipulated the keyboards of as many different calculating machines as the school had had principals. The only difference . . . her old machines were prudently squirreled in a closet while her former bosses were discreetly stashed in pastures (as in "out to") or some cemetery. Sterling would allot 30 minutes for her report, thank her, and then see her out in time for his meeting with the school's activity director. She always left his office shaking her head and mumbling, "I don't know how we're going to do it, Mr. Sterling . . . I just don't know!" Sterling always gave her a pat on the shoulder while reassuring her that only she could keep City High afloat.

Dave Milton was the school's activity director and loved the prestige of his position. He enjoyed controlling students and teachers with the illusory power of his magic calendar. However, for his Monday morning presentations for Sterling (8:00), he insisted, in lieu of presenting Sterling with an updated copy of the master activities calendar, on setting up an easel with a giant poster board carefully depicting all the school's nonathletic activities for the next month. He would then proceed to give Sterling a rapid-fire, sales-type explanation of each activity and how difficult it had been for him to adjust the schedule to accommodate various personnel. Sterling would listen thoughtfully to his presentation while jotting down dates and times in his calendar.

"As usual, Dave . . . good work. I'm sure you'll be able to resolve that conflict . . . you know, the one on the 15th, after talking with the stage-craft teacher." Sterling often wondered whether this guy had any personal life. Not only did he schedule all the school's activities, he also attended them to make sure everything was just right.

"I know you're a busy man, Grant . . . but I hope you'll be able to stop by as many of these as possible."

"I'll be at all of them, Dave. Thanks for the invitation and your presentation this morning."

8:30: Like many men who spend much of their lives involved in sports, Skeet Goodlove, City High's athletic director, was heavyset but in solid shape for a man in his mid-50s. He played tennis at every opportunity and worked out regularly in the school's weight room. An all-conference football player in high school and college, Goodlove had been a physical education teacher and the head football coach at City High before assuming the position as the school's athletic director.

"No problems, boss," Goodlove usually proclaimed, immediately followed by the announcement that "all practices and games are set, game officials have been contacted . . . we're ready to kick some butt."

He could not ask for a better athletic director. Any problems that might arise concerning athletics Goodlove solved quickly and quietly. That's why he was usually able to start the Monday morning meeting with statements like "No problems . . . we're ready to go . . . we're gonna win." The only exception this Monday was that Sterling had a concern he wanted to share with Goodlove. As the new principal at City High, he needed Goodlove's background experience.

"Skeet, I'd like to visit with you about Phil Hollister. Does he have some problem with the community that I need to be aware of?"

"Phil Hollister's one of the best varsity basketball coaches I've ever worked with," Goodlove quickly remarked. "Why do you ask . . . what are you hearing?" Sterling could hear the defensiveness building in Goodlove's voice.

"Well, I . . ." Before he could answer Goodlove's questions, Goodlove continued.

"I don't know how anybody can be on his case. Pardon my anger, Grant, but what you are probably hearing is coming from the O'Brien family, and they're full of it and themselves. They decided 2 years ago that Hollister should've won the state basketball championship, and he didn't. So they wanted him fired then, and they're still whipping a dead horse today. Well, he hasn't been fired, and now it's just an ego trip for them and a few of their sick friends."

"It's that simple, Skeet?" Sterling asked.

Goodlove thought for a moment. "Basically yes. Oh, he's made a few mistakes . . . but nothing of consequence. The O'Brien family and some of their cronies just like to stir up the community."

"What part of the community?" he prodded.

"Whata ya mean, Grant?"

"Does the O'Brien family and their following have any power in the overall City High community or is their power limited to their neighborhood or something?"

"I don't know how to answer that, Grant."

"Fair enough, Skeet . . . let me try it this way. Do you think I need to do anything other than wait and see what happens during the school year? The basketball season? Do you think I ought to be seriously considering action against Hollister? Bottom line now—do I need to be looking for another basketball coach this year?"

Goodlove looked down at the conference table and shook his head from side to side. "Grant, we may have some problems, I don't know. I don't really think there's anything you or I should do right now. You said it best. It's a wait-and-see situation."

"All right, then," Sterling said nonchalantly. "We'll look on the bright side and see what happens. You need to share with Hollister the fact that I'm aware of the situation, whatever it is. Okay? And, Skeet, in the future, before you say 'no problems boss,' make sure. I don't like surprises."

"No problem, boss."

9:00: Sterling didn't look forward to any meeting with Jerry Rand, City High's head custodian, but he knew that very soon he was going to replace him with Ned Garcia, Rand's chief assistant. In the meantime, he would quietly listen to Rand outline building maintenance priorities and custodial personnel problems, and his incessant bitching about how "slovenly" students and teachers were. Sterling knew that when Garcia took over, students' and teachers' comfort would be the top priority. He saw Garcia in much the same light as he did Goodlove. The City High custodial work force had 63 full- and part-time employees responsible for keeping the building heated and cooled, handling minor plumbing and electrical repairs, repairing equipment, and keeping the grounds in pristine condition, along with general cleaning. Although Rand had done an admirable job as head custodian, he, under the tutelage and protection of Wakefield, had expanded his job from "custodian" for the school to "manager" of the school. His influence on the day-to-day operations of the school had adversely affected almost every activity, both academic and extracurricular. Rand knew that Sterling was watching him closely.

The meeting with City High's counselors (9:30) was always a difficult one. Although Sterling was vitally interested in their activities, they preferred to meet with him one on one instead of in a group. He had convinced them that the Monday meeting was important to him and that they could still meet with him individually anytime. They refused to be involved in any group decision-making process, however—even when it directly affected their department. They insisted that he guide them by calling the shots. They didn't think that counselors should be involved in any type of administrative matter, but were often the first ones to grumble when changes were made without their explicit input.

Although all the meetings were important, the meeting with the vice principals (10:00) was the most important and often had to be adjourned and reconvened after lunch or in the evening due to inherently difficult agenda items. Sterling's administrative meetings generally proceeded at a good pace. The agenda usually included general communications, attendance, student functions and activities, curriculum development and revision procedures, and any other items brought to the table either by him or by the VPs. Faculty and staff personnel problems were left for last. "Sometimes," he thought, "the adults I work with are far less mature than the kids." A typical Monday morning agenda might look like this:

Agenda—Monday, September, 15, 10:00 a.m.

General communications:	Sterling *et al.*
Overview of homecoming week:	Simmons
Attendance policy concerns:	Bartlett
Truancy data	
Analysis of problem	
Proposals for consideration	
New policy	
Eliminate option periods for open campus	
Noon hour	
Curriculum considerations:	Robertson
Senior seminars	
School-within-a-school concept	
Classroom utilization and master schedule:	Gilbert
Administrivia:	Sterling
Chapter VI initiatives	
State aid formula	
Enhancement of field trip procedures and policy refinement	
Personnel:	Sterling *et al.*
Evaluation deadlines	
Problems	

"Let me start this part of our meeting by saying that I spoke to Skeet this morning about Phil Hollister," Sterling announced. "Skeet and I agreed that we should take a wait-and-see attitude about Phil's tenure as head basketball coach. I questioned Skeet about Phil based on the fact that I'm getting a little pressure from one segment of our community . . . namely, the O'Brien family."

Without much discussion, wait and see was the consensus of the group.

"Grant, what are you going to do about Mark Prince?" Harlow Bartlett questioned. "The case we were building against him for ongoing insubordination was blown because of the problems Wakefield's having. We need to get this guy out of the classroom as soon as possible."

"Harlow, I'm still studying the record. I'm thinking about giving this guy a fresh start, but with a very short leash. Here's a summary of what I have on him, and what I've done."

Summary of File to Date (Mark Prince, Teacher)

Late to work, documented

Excessive absence, documented

Drinking problem, still hearsay

In love with student, admitted, documented . . . Immoral, hearsay evidence only

Love was "platonic," never physical according to Prince and female student

Insubordinate, documented but not acted on to date

Seeing same female student again

Lesson plans

Hanging around female subject class during his planning period when told not to

---

Action to Date (Mark Prince, Teacher)

Summary memo written to Prince outlining possible insubordination charge based on above.

1. Advised about work ethics and requested
2. To provide M.D. statement on any absences above sick leave allotment
3. Advised to seek assistance (no cost to him—district provided) if he has drinking problem
4. Ordered, again, to stay away from female student
5. Lesson plans are to be submitted each week to department chair
6. Department chair advised to review and document

"I'll either reform him . . . or get him," he continued. "You all can place your bets with my secretary today as you leave. How much was your raise this year?" They all laughed. "Now," he continued, "let me bring you up to date on this Bill Groften matter."

"Yes, please do," Maury Gilbert remarked. "Who'd you piss off to get stuck with that loser? Don't the folks at central office know you have enough problems without being stuck with that . . ."

"Relax, Maury," Sterling interrupted. "I'm going to stick him in the media center and put him in charge of checking out equipment to faculty. He's not going to come in contact with students. In other words, I'm not going to let him teach. I'm hoping he'll resign, and if he doesn't, we've gained some personnel in a critical area. Who knows, he may like it. On the other hand, if he screws up, it would be the last straw, and he will be dismissed. He knows that. I haven't had time to pull together the stuff on him that was sent over from personnel, however; I can assure you that his file is substantial. Well, on that cheerful note, and remembering that agenda items are due by Friday noon for next Monday's meeting, let's adjourn. It's time for us to gear up to manage another 3,000 student feeding frenzy—oh excuse me—lunch hour."

As Sterling started to leave the office with his VPs, his secretary gently escorted him back.

"What's the problem, Betty?"

"A group of students in the outer office is asking to see you. They're upset and insistent that they talk to you about Mr. Prince. I think you ought to see them before you go to supervise lunch."

"But, Betty . . . I may miss the corn-dog-on-a-stick-with-mashed-potatoes special the cafeteria is advertising today!"

"I'll see that they save one for you, Grant. Should I show these kids in?"

Betty ushered in 12 students. They'd been talking as they entered his office, but now were silent.

"I'm told that you wanted to see me about a teacher," Sterling said. "Who wants to start? It will be confusing for me if you all talk at once."

The students looked at each other and finally fixed their attention on one boy.

"I guess I can explain why we're here, Mr. Sterling."

"Good. What's your name?"

"Larry Browning, sir."

"Go for it, Larry."

"Well, sir," Larry started. "Everyone here has a problem with Mr. Prince, and they're all different, but they're kinda about the same thing." Larry paused and flipped his head to shake back his long hair. "It's that we can't stand Mr. Prince. He's unfair, he's critical, he's crude, he picks on us, and we think something needs to be done."

For the next 30 to 40 minutes, Sterling listened to an outpouring of complaints from each of the students. As the impromptu meeting neared its end, he had written 2 pages of notes.

"All right gang," he stood up, "do I have all your concerns? Anyone have anything else?"

For a moment the room was quiet.

"Well, Mr. Sterling," a young lady stepped forward. She introduced herself as Kathie Williams. "I'm really embarrassed to tell this, but . . ." she hesitated and looked at the floor. "But when I said I wanted to go with the group to see you, he said . . . uh, Prince said, 'What's the matter Kathie, did you miss your monthly period and want to go talk to God about getting an abortion?' "

"I'm really sorry about that comment, Kathie," Sterling said with a grimace. Kathie didn't know it, but she had just hammered the last nail in Prince's coffin. "Thanks for sharing with me, folks. I'll get on your concerns right away."

He closed his door as the students left. He sat down in his chair, leaned back, and closed his eyes for a moment. Later that day, after school was dismissed, he would suspend Prince pending a due process hearing. He knew he now had enough to terminate Prince. He called for a substitute to replace Prince effective the next morning.

"The cafeteria is closed, Grant," Betty said as she pushed the office door open with her shoulder. "But as I promised, here's your corn-dog-on-a-stick-with-mashed-potatoes special. I tried to keep it warm under my desk lamp for you."

"Thanks, Betty. Tell me. Do you believe everything I tell you?"

"Of course, Grant. Shouldn't I?"

For Discussion

General Questions

Using the Sterling paradigm (http://www.corwinpress.com/dunklee.htm) as a model, and speaking from the perspective of a principal, evaluate each episode as follows:

What are the dominant behaviors exhibited by Sterling in this episode?

Is there consensus about this in the class? If not, explain the different viewpoints.

What were the primary actors' individual motives?

How effective was Sterling's behavior in this situation and why?

Can you identify other avenues or approaches that might lead to the same, or a better, conclusion?

If Sterling was a woman,

■ As a female reader, can you identify methodology or behavior that you would change to bring the episode to the same, or similar, closure?

■ As a male reader, what differences in methodology or behavior would you expect to see?

Specific Questions for Each Episode

Reestablishing a Power Base Within a Power Base: I Agreed to This?

1. What could Wakefield do to sabotage Sterling's efforts to fulfill his job description?

What if . . . Wakefield had insisted on attending Sterling's meeting with the vice principals?

First Friday

2. What different kinds of information-gathering techniques does Sterling use to stay on top of things?
3. What is the purpose of Sterling's memo to Prince?
4. What would you do regarding Prince after reading his personnel file?

Monday's ~~Milieu~~ Menu

(No specific questions)

It's Simple, But Timing Is Everything

"So, whadja find, Grant?" Larry Frost asked as Sterling entered Frost's office.

"Well," he said as he sat down and opened a folder of papers. "It's not good. Since arriving at City High, Wakefield has given Jerry Rand nothing but excellent performance evaluations. There's nothing negative in his personnel file at the high school, and nothing in the personnel files here at the central office. In other words, I can request a transfer based only on my early observations and opinions, rather than on anything concrete. I think there's probably enough information somewhere to build a case for termination, but I can't get a handle on it yet."

"But in the meantime you want him out of there and replaced."

"Oh, there's no question about that, Larry. He's been a part of the declining morale problem at City High for a long time. I agree with the documentation that you folks gave me about Rand's alleged involvement in some of the stuff Wakefield has been doing with the store and gas station he bought, but I can't find a way to relate it to his job performance yet."

"Okay, then," Frost leaned back in his chair, "we'll simply notify Rand that he's being transferred because you want a head custodian who fits your ideal rather than one who was selected by someone else. We'll make it as simple as that. And, if he files a grievance with the union, we'll just stick to that story. Agreed?"

"Pretty weak, Larry . . . but the district's done it before . . . and it's important that we remove him, so I'm willing to take the heat, if any, to get him out of the picture."

"I thought you might say that," Frost agreed as he leaned toward Sterling. "So, I've made arrangements for Rand to report to the service center as soon as you meet with him and give him the news."

"Okay, Larry—done deal. Thanks for your support on this. I'll be talking to Rand Tuesday of next week. I'm not going to have time to see him today, and I'm going to be out of town all day and into the evening on Monday to attend a statewide conference on accreditation . . . yeah, it'll be Tuesday midmorning before I can meet with him. Oh, and by the way, I won't be at the board of education meeting Monday night."

"No problem, Grant . . . however, you're going to miss some fun. The board will be announcing that Wakefield is being transferred to the Adult Education Center until the outcome of his harassment suit. I expect that some of his loyal followers will be vocally unhappy. Wait 'til we fire his philandering butt," Frost sneered. "Anyway, I know you don't care about that . . . you'll just be glad to get him out of your hair. Concerning the Rand transfer . . . I'll notify Beatrice at the service center to expect him first thing Wednesday morning,"

"Sorry to miss that particular board meeting, Larry," Sterling said sarcastically as he stood up to leave. "I hate to run, but we've got a home football game tonight. And, you never know, the coaches might want me to 'suit up.' "

"That'll be the day, Grant," Frost laughed as Sterling hurriedly left his office.

Tuesday morning, as he started to turn into the parking lot at City High, Sterling noticed Rand and Wakefield putting boxes in Wakefield's car. To avoid a probable confrontation, he drove past the lot and parked his car on the other side of the school. "Looks like Wakefield got the word at last night's board meeting and he's not wasting any time moving out. It's going to be a good day at City High. And, to make things even better, though he doesn't know it yet, Rand will also be leaving today. No, more than good, it's going to be a great day today!"

As soon as he reached his office, Sterling called his vice principals to inform each of them that Jerry Rand was going to be officially notified that he was being transferred from City High to the service center, and that today would be his final day at City High. The faculty and staff would be notified by memo early Wednesday morning that Rand was gone and that Sterling had appointed Ned Garcia, currently serving as assistant head custodian, to the position of acting head custodian until further notice.

Sterling waited until he was sure Rand had finished helping Wakefield move. He picked up his two-way radio and called Rand.

"Yes sir, Mr. Sterling. 11 o'clock in your office. I'll be there."

"What can I do for you, Mr. Sterling?" Rand asked as he entered the office.

"Please sit down, Jerry. I need to speak with you about a new opportunity for . . ."

"You're going to transfer me out of here, aren't you?" Rand interrupted. "I've been warned—I've been expecting this. What are your grounds?" he said in a challenging voice.

"Why do you think that's what happening?" Sterling asked calmly. "What do mean, you've 'been warned'?"

"That's my business," Rand sharply retorted. "I asked you what your grounds are."

"Well, Jerry . . . let's make this as simple as possible. In the first place, you're right. I am going to transfer you . . . to the service center, effective 8:00 tomorrow morning. Please remove any personal belongings from the building by 5:00 today and give your keys to Jack Carson in the school's security office. He'll be expecting you. Now, as far as grounds go, I think your contract states that you serve the district wherever it needs you. You've never had an exclusive contract with City High. But, if you really feel like you need grounds, let's simply say that I want somebody in your position who fits my personal image of a head custodian, and that's not you, Jerry. Bottom line: I don't want to work with you, and I know that you probably didn't want to work with me from day one. You can't be loyal to two bosses, Jerry . . . and your loyalty packed up and left early this morning. Do you have any other questions?"

"Nope," Rand said with a "get-even" sneer on his face.

"Thank you for your service, Jerry. If you feel like you can't work today, you may leave as soon as you turn in your keys."

"We'll see," Rand said in a disturbingly quiet voice as he left.

Three weeks later, to the day, Sterling was summoned to the superintendent's office to meet with one of the school district's attorneys.

"Mr. Sterling, may I call you Grant?" Steven Goldsmith, an attorney Sterling knew from some of the legal seminars that principals were required to attend, said, closing the office door.

"Certainly, Steve. How can I help you?"

"It involves an employee by the name of Jerry Rand. Let me just ask you a few questions, if you don't mind, and then I'll bring you up to date on what Rand is doing. Fair enough?"

"Fire away."

"All right, Grant. Do you know a person named Jerry Rand?"

"Yes, of course. He was . . ."

Goldsmith interrupted. "Where do you know Jerry Rand from?"

"He was the head custodian at City High."

"Do you know where he's assigned now?"

"My best knowledge, the district's service center."

"Do you know how he got from his assignment at your school to his current assignment at the service center?"

"He was transferred."

"Who asked that he be transferred?"

"I did."

"Why? Just generally for now. Okay?"

"I identified him as a part of a morale problem at the high school."

"When did you, to use your words, identify him as a morale problem?"

"Prior to my assuming the position of principal at City High."

"When did you formulate this opinion? Spring of last school year?"

"Yes. But wait a minute, please. You're taking me down a path with your questions, and I don't know where you're going or what this is all about. May I ask you a question before we continue?"

"Go ahead, Grant." Goldsmith leaned back in his chair.

"I can only assume from your line of questioning that Rand is threatening some kind of grievance or lawsuit. If that's true, then I need to know whether you are representing me at this point."

"Grant," Goldsmith leaned forward. "I represent the school district, and I represent you and anybody else that Mr. Rand and his attorney might challenge. May I proceed?" Goldsmith glanced at his notepad. "I think my last question had to do with when you formulated your opinion that Rand was a problem . . . and I suggested spring of last year, and you said 'yes.' "

"Sometime during the spring semester of last year is correct; I reported to City High for duty on July 15."

"So, you made this assumption quite a while before you actually reported to the high school. How did you get sufficient information to make this determination?"

"Basically, talking to people who had an inside track to what was going on."

"Fair enough for now, Grant. But you waited almost 4 months after you assumed your new position before you actually transferred Rand. Why?"

"I notified my immediate superiors that I wanted Rand transferred as soon as possible. I talked to them shortly after July 15."

"Did they suggest waiting for some reason?"

"No, I suggested that I would review Rand's performance evaluations and see what else I could find that might make the transfer process less of a personal thing and more of a performance-based thing."

"So, how did it end up? Rand claims you were out to get him from the start."

"To be honest with you, I was. I, and others, had identified him, for a number of reasons, as part of the continuing morale problem at City High. He had to go."

"Why did you select Tuesday, the 24th of October, to notify Rand?"

"I met with my immediate superior the previous Friday. Arrangements had been made to transfer Rand to another assignment. I could have done it on Monday; however, I was out of town on school business and didn't return until late Monday night. Tuesday the 24th was the first opportunity I would have to see Rand."

"You didn't attend the board meeting on Monday night, the 23rd?"

"As I said, I was out of town."

"Did you know, or did anyone tell you, that Rand spoke publicly at the board meeting . . . addressed the board concerning the transfer of former City High Principal Wakefield? Said stuff like the school would collapse without his leadership, and so forth?"

"Yes, I heard that."

"Now this is important, Grant. Did you hear that before or after your meeting with Rand? The meeting where you notified him of his transfer?"

"Oh, I didn't hear anything about that until after school was out on Tuesday. I think I heard it from a parent or somebody who was at the board meeting."

"Do you remember that person's name?"

"No, sorry, I don't."

"So, Grant, would I be correct in saying that you didn't transfer Rand as a result of something he said or anything he did at the board of education meeting on Monday night, the 23rd of October? Would I be correct if I said that the reason you transferred Rand on the 24th of October was that you felt it was in the best interest of City High?"

"Yes, and yes. I was not aware at the time I talked to Rand about anything that went on at the board meeting the prior evening, and his transfer *was* in the best interest of City High."

"Okay, Grant, you can relax now. Let me take a minute and tell you what's going on."

"Thanks, Steve. I'd like to know."

"Well, Grant, Rand is claiming, through his attorney, that you and the folks here in central office transferred him Tuesday morning as a direct result of his speech supporting Wakefield at the board meeting on that Monday night. He's claiming you all have violated his constitutional right, his First Amendment right, to free speech. They've filed a writ in federal district court that we must respond to. I'll keep you informed. Any questions?"

"Do you have any answers at this point?" Sterling asked, in part facetiously, and in part out of shock.

"Go back to work, Grant . . . you've got nothing to worry about. I wish this transfer had taken place on Monday. The timing sure stinks. However, anytime, even a year or more after Rand spoke at the board meeting, he could still claim that he was being punished for his ineffectual plea in support of Mr. Wakefield."

"You know, Steve . . . the interesting part about this, now that I know what's going on, is that even if I knew about the board thing and the possibility of being sued . . . I still would have transferred Rand. It needed to be done. It was the right thing, and as a result, City High faculty, staff, and students are working in a lot friendlier place."

Listen With Your Heart

The room—usually filled with the sounds of principals teasing each other about such things as last week's football games, whose "assertive discipline" programs are working best, and who's doing this or that—suddenly became deathly silent.

"Ladies and gentlemen, I'm sorry and deeply distressed to announce that Darrell Gingrich, son of our colleague Rick Gingrich, died late last night. Darrell, a sophomore at City High, committed suicide in the basement of the Gingrich home. Arrangements have not yet been made . . . I'll have my secretary contact you with more information as it becomes available."

The superintendent, visibly shaken, completed his announcement by adjourning the meeting—a meeting that had been called to discuss budget matters. "School business is just not very important today," he said slowly. "Please go back to your buildings and listen closely to your kids, not with your minds, today . . . not with rules, regulations, policies, or procedures . . . but with your hearts."

The room remained silent. No one moved, no one spoke, as the superintendent quickly left. Finally, a voice somewhere in the room angrily expressed the innermost, suppressed feelings of the group. "Dammit, dammit, DAMMIT!" It was immediately interpreted by the group as a sign to leave. Sterling remained behind . . . Darrell was a student at his school. His father was not only a professional colleague, but also a very close personal friend. He knew Darrell well.

He was still shaking his head in disbelief as he opened the note the superintendent had handed him just before he made his announcement. "Grant, please see me for minute before you leave."

"Betty, the Supe wanted to see me."

"I know, Grant . . . go on in . . . he's expecting you. I'm sorry about the Gingrich boy," she said quietly.

"Grant," Superintendent Boughton spoke in a distraught tone, "here's the deal. I talked to Rick. He called me about 3 o'clock this morning. There's no blame here, but he found a packet of material, dated yesterday, about suicide that had been passed out in your sophomore psychology classes at City High. He said that his son was in one of the sections of the class, and he thought the teacher's name was Levy. He's not connecting his son's death with the class, but rather thought you might want to know that others may see some connection.

"I think, assuming that the other students don't know about Darrell yet, that you need to meet with the kids in that particular class. The word on this—this coincidence, I hope—will spread like wildfire. Be prepared to deal with some concerned parents and, of course, the press. You can bet that I'll be getting some calls too. Let's keep this as low key as possible, for the Gingrich family's sake. Call me if I can help."

The drive back to City High from the central administration building was a short one, but seemed very long this particular day. As soon as he arrived, Sterling pulled Darrell's schedule card from the attendance secretary's file and told her not to call his parents, even though he would be reported absent by his teachers today. A glance at the card immediately confirmed that Julie Levy was his psychology teacher. He quickly called an emergency meeting of the school's four counselors, informed them of the situation, and told them what he planned to do.

"I want one of you to go to Julie Levy's class as soon as we've finished here and tell her that I need to see her in my office now. Cover the class until I can get a sub for the rest of the day. I'm going to send her home . . . I think she'll need that. I think this is going to be difficult for her, even though it's certainly not her fault. I want the rest of you to inform your secretaries to cancel your appointments for the rest of the week and to accept only emergencies. As soon as you've finished, hustle to the auditorium. When I've finished talking with Julie, I'm going to call Darrell's psychology class to the auditorium, and we're—underline "we're"—going to talk with them. Finally, I'm going to call in the entire sophomore class, and again we're going to talk with them. This incident calls for crisis intervention on the part of this office, but most important, your department."

With the simple proclamation "let's do it," Sterling dismissed the group and closed the door behind them. He needed a moment alone. A gentle knock on his office door quickly brought him back to his official self.

"Grant, you wanted to see me?" Julie Levy said in an upbeat voice.

An Adjunct Lecture: Tools of the Trade

Sterling looked at his watch as he slowed for a traffic light. 7:15, he noted as he pulled to a stop and waited. The sun was just setting on the horizon, and he was tired. Although he had been busy all day, he wondered just what he had really accomplished. It had been one of those days, he thought, when his plan for productivity had been replaced with the tasks of resolving insignificant and, for the most part, petty personnel problems—the kind of work that keeps a school stable, but really doesn't help it move forward. He didn't like being trapped behind his desk, even for a day. "School is not a proper place for those who are prone to mediocrity, the status quo, or monuments to the past," he had unloaded on Betty as he left his office for the day. "This is a place for thinkers, for professional educators, for people who have the energy and the attitude to move the education enterprise forward . . . not just stand around and nit-pick."

Betty had simply smiled, winked, and gently reassured him that "tomorrow will be a better day, Grant. I promise I'll line up a whole new cast of characters and situations for you."

Finally, the light changed, and he hurried to his last appointment of the day. He'd promised David Horn that he would lecture the education leadership class at Central University that evening. Horn had asked him to share common personnel problems his students might run into working with faculty and staff. Although Sterling believed he had an obligation to promote the development of future school administrators and regularly took his turn as a guest lecturer in a number of the universities in the area, he really didn't want to lecture this evening. "If I lecture," he thought, "after today's schedule, and the crappy mood I'm in, I'm liable to give these students a pretty distorted view of personnel administration."

After the usual introduction and presentation of Sterling's resume, Dr. Horn turned toward Sterling and motioned. "The class is yours." Sterling hesitated for a moment, walked to the front of the room, and glanced at his audience—a classroom full of teachers working toward the master's degree and state certification that would qualify them to apply for positions as school administrators.

"How 'bout I start this evening off with three very distinct questions for us to consider and debate? One question will deal with why you're here, in this room, at this time tonight, and the other two will deal with why I'm here, in this room with you, in such a lousy mood. Oh," he quickly continued, "you didn't know that I'm in a bad mood. Well, trust me . . . my smile masks a lot of frustration. Maybe, just maybe, by debating these three inquiries, you'll have a better picture of why you're here and what you can learn from this class that will help you succeed in spite of the kinds of frustrations that seem to be inherent in school administration."

The class was silent, and Horn had a questioning look on his face as he slowly moved to the back of the room.

"Okay then . . . can I take your lack of immediate response as tacit approval for me to proceed? Here's question number one. Is there anything you learn in graduate school about education leadership and management that has any application to the real world?" He waited a moment for his question to sink in. The sea of faces previously looking at him were now focused on pages on which the class hastily scribbled notes.

"Okay," he continued, "question number two. Of the following groups of people—students, parents, faculty, or staff—which group is likely to cause the most problems for a school administrator? Which group do you think you, as school administrators, will be the most glad to see depart at the end of the school year?"

"And the third question," Sterling paused for a moment to make sure everyone was listening. "If the position you're hoping to assume some day has its share of undesirable moments like I've had today, how do you plan to succeed?"

"Well, I can answer your second question easily," a young man in the back of the room spoke up. "With all the problems we have with students and their parents these days, as a teacher, I'm glad to send students off for the summer to terrorize their parents—the same parents who tell us over and over again that their kids can do no wrong. We bust our butts for their kids, and the kids don't appreciate it, and neither do their parents. So, it's kids first, parents second in response to your question."

"Thank you, Mr. . . . . I'm sorry, I don't know your name, but I'll bet you feel better after getting that off your chest," Sterling grinned and the class laughed.

"But he's right," a student in the front row quickly added. "Just look at the kinds of problems we have with our students—poor discipline, lousy attitudes about school and learning, drugs, sex, fighting, weapons—you name it, we deal with it every day!" she exclaimed.

"Yes," another student agreed, "and when we contact their parents, they tell us stuff like 'we're picking on their child,' or, 'so, what do you want *us* to do?' or—my favorite one—'well, we can't handle them at home either!' Oh, wait," the student continued, "that's *not* my favorite one. My real favorite is the parent who says that 'when so and so is at school, it's your problem . . . that's what you get paid for.' I love that one!"

"So," Sterling interrupted, "what I'm hearing is that students and their parents are the ones you would be the happiest seeing depart at the end of the school year. Now, imagine for the moment that you're the principal of a school. Would you still feel the same?"

"Sure," one student responded and the class agreed. "Principals have to deal with those same kids and parents all the time."

"All right," Sterling interrupted a room full of agreement. "Give me two lists. I'm going to record them on the overhead. Give me a list of student problems and a list of parent problems. Then we'll assign the entries on both lists into two categories— serious and petty."

After about 10 minutes, the class seemed satisfied that it had given him a fairly comprehensive list in each area, and that it had separated serious offenses from petty everyday kinds of problems. Students were shouting items that they wanted included. Sterling could hear the tension in their voices diminish as they unloaded their anger.

"Now," he said as he placed a fresh transparency on the overhead, "I want you to think like a principal, the person in charge of keeping the school running and keeping all personnel—students, parents, teachers, support staff—heading in the right direction. Again, give me a list. I'm going to write these on the overhead too. Give me a list of adult employee problems. You know, faculty and staff. And then we'll categorize these problems as either serious or petty."

As students started to suggest items for this particular list, the room became full of laughter. "Oh, yeah . . . that too," someone remarked in response to another's statement.

"Remember that situation over at Sunnyside Elementary School?" somebody asked another student across the room.

"Oh, jeez," another student added, "we've got a bunch of people at our school who whine and bitch all the time. You know," she continued, "I've come to the conclusion, after 11 years as a teacher, that whining and bitching are contagious. Our whole school is infected. Except me," she hastily added with a twinkle in her eyes.

Again, after about 10 minutes, the list seemed complete to the students. "Now," Sterling commented, "you've given me a list of school- based problems concerning faculty and staff. What about personal problems . . . home or life-based problems that often end up in the principal's office?"

"You mean like divorce, or death in the family?" somebody asked.

"Yes, or money problems, or a new teacher trying to find a place to live, or buy a new car on time with no credit record."

The room and the list came alive again, as Sterling's facial expressions alternated back and forth from grin to grimace.

"All right," he smiled, getting their attention. "I just have to go back for a moment to the young lady who regaled us with the infected school syndrome. She's piqued my interest."

"That's me, sir. I hope I didn't upset anybody."

"No, of course not. All of us in this room have listened to a fair amount of whining among our colleagues. I just want you to expand your thoughts, if you would, so that all of us have a clear picture of what whining and, to use your term, bitching, is."

"Well," the young lady continued, "maybe I should use the word 'complaining.' Or maybe the word 'hypocrisy.' I've taught in two schools—6 years in this school district and 5 in another. It's the same. We're supposed to support our kids and their activities, but some teachers find reasons not to. Like, 'hey, we're besieged with requests to sponsor this or attend that, or support this. We've got to be careful, the students are *doing* things. They're thinking for themselves. Stop them!' And then there are the teachers who take out their anger by resisting—not turning in lesson plans or information sheets for substitute teachers. These are the ones who carry grudges over petty problems as long as possible . . . it doesn't even matter whether the problems are real. They seem to believe that if you must work hard, work at being negative. Don't expend your energies planning curriculum or teaching strategies. That sort of thing occupies valuable time and diverts your attention from thinking up things to complain about. In adversity, don't pull together, pull apart. Take joy in the division of camps. Then, when the chips are down, be a chameleon. Switch sides. Keep things stirred up. Does that paint a clear enough picture, Mr. Sterling?"

"Oh, yes, very clear. Thanks for expanding on your earlier comment," he grinned. "So, guys, before we take a break—which list, student/parent or faculty/staff, has the most entries on the 'serious' side? Which list has the most entries on the 'petty' side? You know the answer, and the proof is on these overheads. The group principals are the happiest to see go home at the end of the school year is not the students and their parents, but rather, *you*! After the break, if you haven't killed the messenger, we'll tackle the other questions, which you will find, in reality, are unequivocally tied to the question we just resolved."

During the break, Horn took Sterling aside. "I had no idea where you were going with those questions, Grant. But I have to admit you've got them thinking about personnel issues in a different light than their textbook suggests. I think I know now where you're going with the next question. This is a great approach! When do you find time to develop your presentations?"

Sterling sighed. "I don't develop my presentations, David. They develop themselves every day, every hour . . . whether I want them to or not."

After the break, the students wanted to continue their discussion of personnel problems and principal involvement. Sterling was able to interject his own frustrations—the problems he had dealt with all day that had put him in a sour mood. He shared with students his feelings as he left his office—that his plan for productivity today had been replaced with the tedium of resolving insignificant and mostly petty personnel problems—and what he had said to his secretary about nit-picking and professionalism.

"Now," Sterling quickly shifted topics. "We could talk about personnel issues forever, but let me go back to question number one for a few minutes. It's important, and it's a question I'll bet everyone in this room has asked themselves sometime in the program. The question is: Is there anything you learn in graduate school concerning education leadership and management that has any application to the real world? The answer is yes. Your graduate coursework covers the fundamentals—the basic tools you'll need in your 'toolkit' to do the job in school administration. You need to start sharpening those tools now. You can do that by applying your readings and class lectures to the things you see and experience in your own school. Study your own principal; learn about how the school really works and your school's relationship to the district. Talk to your principal—ask questions! Don't just see your own classroom, look around. Listen and learn the politics of change . . . the politics of endurance. You're gonna need sharp tools, and a lot of them, if you plan to succeed in administration. Start adding to your basic university toolkit right now. When you're on the job, it will be too late. Someone may nail a 2 × 10 across your door, and you'd better have a saw handy. When things start coming apart, you'll need the right hammer or screwdriver. And when you try to initiate change, a good pry bar and a set of chisels will come in handy. Oops, sorry, I seem to be getting carried away with my toolkit metaphor. Anyway, I can see by the smiles on your faces that—excuse the pun—I've hit the nail on the head.

"Finally," he said as he looked at the classroom clock, "the last question I posed was: If the position you're hoping to assume some day has frequent undesirable moments, how do you plan to succeed? Let me quickly give you my insight on personal survival and success, as I see we're about to run out of time. This is something that you must develop for yourself. It's not something you're going to learn in any university classroom. This is a skill that is very personalized. Let me tell you how I deal with my frustration. First, I have always been enormously amused by the passing parade of life. My curiosity about life is as insatiable as my constant need to seek out and find the humorous side of everyday events, especially problems that cross my desk. In other words, I laugh away a lot of my day-to-day frustration. Second, and I believe most important, is that you have a life outside of your profession. You have interests, favorite pursuits, people, and places that are not related to your work, but rather to your avocations. I try very hard not to take my job home with me. I leave it at the office. My time is up. It's late. I hope I've given you some things to think about, and maybe, just maybe, a tool or two for your toolkit. Thanks for inviting me."

A Sterling Moment (When Logic Fails)

"So, what are you saying here, William? That you're appealing a short-term suspension from school . . . which, by the way, you have a right to do, I won't argue about that. You're appealing because you believe that your division vice principal is 'out to get you' because of some incident that happened last year? He's holding a grudge? Is that what I'm hearing? I'm not supposed to hear anything about the current incident . . . like I should overlook the fact that you were referred to your division VP because you climbed up on a basketball hoop, stood on the rim, and attempted a somersault into the waiting hands of your buddies below? I should overlook the fact that the glass backboard shattered into hundreds of shards raining down on people, and now I'm faced with finding money in the school's budget to replace it? That you could easily have been hurt . . . that other people could have been badly hurt. Is that what you're saying? Am I confusing you with too many questions?" Sterling looked intently at William and then leaned slowly back in his chair and sighed.

"Your turn, William. Please feel free to continue."

"Ah, come on, Mr. Sterling . . . I explained what Simmons did to me last year just 'cause I lost my cool with Mrs. Little."

"You mean Mr. Simmons, don't you? Let's see," he casually leafed through William's folder. "Was that the incident where you called Mrs. Little a 'two-bit whore,' or something like that, when she jumped your case in class for not shutting up?"

"Man, she dissed me . . . right in front of the class," William exclaimed, his forehead wrinkled.

"And you were suspended from school for 10 days. Right?"

"Yeah, but . . . she deserved it. You don't do that to another human being. Not in front of their friends. Man, that sucks."

"And you think that Mr. Simmons still remembers that and is out to get you?"

"Right," William responded, believing Sterling had finally gotten the picture.

"Tell me, William, how many times before this current incident in the gym have you hung on any basketball hoop in this school? Be honest . . . if you say never, you know, and I know, that would be a lie. Come on, talk to me, how many times?"

"Well, you know, we all do it, except in a regular game."

"And how many people do you know who have climbed up on the hoop and attempted a somersault?"

"Come on, Mr. Sterling, I was just horsing around."

"Of course, you were, William, I understand that." William's eyes lit up. For a moment he believed that Sterling was actually human and that he had convinced him that he shouldn't be suspended.

"Be careful, William." William's facade had changed from defensive to relaxed. "You know, false security can lead to letting one's guard down."

"Huh?" William looked at him.

"William, let me tell you something that you probably don't know. First, Mr. Simmons has more important things to do than think about, much less remember, your incident with Mrs. Little last . . . whenever. He's not out to get you. But . . . listen carefully now, this is important . . ." Sterling lowered his voice as if he didn't want anyone else to hear what he was about to say.

"What you don't know . . . is that late at night, when the building's empty, all the basketball hoops in the school get together and plan revenge on students who abuse them. They compare notes, write down names, and plan their attack. So you see, Mr. Simmons wasn't out to get you. You were had, man. You were on the list. The hoop you somersaulted from broke its own backboard just to get you in trouble. Man, don't ya just hate it when that happens . . . when somebody or something holds a grudge?"

William was now staring at him as if he had lost his mind.

"So William," Sterling leaned forward in his chair, "What are you going to do with this 5-day vacation that the hoop has graciously given you because you were targeted to be had? Never mind, William, see you in 5 days. You're a good kid for a high school junior. You are a junior, aren't you?"

"Mr. Sterling," William said in a pleading voice.

"Good-bye, William."

"Mr. . . ."

"On your way out, would you please close the door?"

"But . . ."

"Thanks, William," Sterling said as he closed William's folder and placed it gently in his out-basket.

Soliloquy ▬▬▬

"I gotta tell ya, this place is the pits. How the school district has allowed what's happened here to evolve is beyond rationality. Some people on the faculty and staff have told me that I'm too idealistic. That I want too much too fast. That I want to resolve the negative climate here and change the 'this is the way it's always been' attitudes that have taken years to develop, overnight. I'm not too idealistic. You are not idealistic enough. Yes, I believe in a positive, proactive approach to everything. I'm tired of being challenged with nothing but narrow-minded negativism. Now, you evil little troll, if you've missed my point, what I'm trying to say, loud and clear, is that

I find this whole attitude toward mediocrity unacceptable! Perhaps it's time you came out of your hiding place under my desk and offered some real, constructive advice. Why am I always stuck making decisions by myself? You could help, you know!"

"Take two aspirin, Sterling . . . call me in the morning."

"Right . . . like that will help. You're despicable, you know that? I'm stuck in a place with a staff that believes that the name of this institution should be changed to Status Quo High, Home of the Withering Wimps . . . and you're suggesting I take two aspirin!"

"Okay, then . . . go buy a sports car, a bright red one. That old Caddy you're driving now really sucks for air!"

"You suck for air, and your attitude is no better than that of most of the people I'm forced to work with. I think it's high time this school faced up to the issues of dedication, hard work, commitment, and the challenge of positive leadership."

"Sterling . . . is this some kind of 'State of the Union' speech I'm being forced to listen to?"

"Maybe it is, dammit! I'm angry. I'm depressed. I'm tired of being expected to accept crap cheerfully from all sides. I need a positive commitment from the people in this school who call themselves professionals. Now, do you, or do you not, have any advice for me before I walk down the hall, step up to the microphone, and convene this month's faculty meeting?"

"Oh, Sterling, it's all in your mind. Things are going fine out there. Let well enough alone. You don't need to rock the boat. You could become a wimp too! On the other hand," the troll continued, "why don't you just grab the mike, turn the volume up as high as it will go, and after you've pierced everyone's brains with massive screeching feedback from the amplifier, announce that you're going to fire everyone who doesn't match your idealistic outlook on life, liberty, and the pursuit of whatever? That might work!"

Sterling picked up his notes for the meeting and started toward the door. "Thanks, troll. As usual you've been a great comfort for my distressed soul. Go back to whatever you do when you're not trying to destroy my self-confidence."

"Oh, no, wait, Sterling! I've got one more suggestion. This will really work . . . trust me! Give them these lines from Steinbeck. It works for me every time," he proclaimed as he jumped from the floor to the top of the desk, straightened his suit coat, cleared his throat, and started. "Ladies and gentlemen of the City High faculty, 'there is a crime here that goes beyond denunciation. There is a sorrow here that weeping cannot symbolize. There is a failure here that topples all our success.' And then, Sterling, hit 'em hard with this final line and run quickly from the room. Leave them either in shock or in a state of profound revelation. Why are you laughing, Sterling . . . you asked for my help. Here's your final Steinbeck shot. Are you ready for this?" he said as he spread his arms out as wide as possible, his palms to the ceiling . . . " 'And in the souls of the people the grapes of wrath are filling and growing heavy, growing heavy for the vintage.' "

Sterling was still laughing to himself as he entered the meeting room and approached the microphone. "Good morning, ladies and gentlemen. I just have a few agenda items for us today and then . . ."

Nothing Unusual, Just the Daily In-Basket— One at a Time

"My God," Sterling exclaimed as he searched for the usual heavy stack of notes, memos, and letters that Betty always placed in the center of his desk each day. "Only three items this morning. Looks like I'm going to have some time today to cause problems, ask questions, hassle folks," he grinned. "All right, let's see if I can earn my salary today."

October 5

Dear Principal Sterling,

My name is Roger Thompson. I live at 4201 W. Central and my phone number is 323-4405. Directly across the street from my house is a large parking lot for two stores. Occasionally I see drivers' education cars from your school practicing parking in the back area of the lot. Usually there are two or three students in the car, along with an instructor. During the past few weeks, however, one of your cars has been parking back by the grove of trees at the northwest corner of the lot. Two people are in the car and seem to be more involved with each other than learning to drive. The car's license plate number is DFG 23219, and I usually see the car at about 9:30 a.m. on Monday and Thursday. I'd rather not get involved, so I thought I should just send you a letter.

Sincerely,
Roger Thompson

Sterling quickly located his list of administrative assignments and identified Rob Simmons as the vice principal in charge of driver education. He picked up his phone and punched Simmons' extension. His secretary answered—Simmons was in conference with a parent.

"Sandra, please ask Rob if he would get a copy of current drivers' ed. car assignments and a recent schedule of off-campus training times and routes. As soon as he has this information, tell him I need to meet with him."

"I hope it's not what I'm thinking," he shook his head.

Date: October 7
Memo to: Grant Sterling
From: Loretta Greenwood, Division IV Counselor
Subject: Student, Larry Robert Hemingway

Grant . . . as you know, Larry Hemingway, a student assigned to Division IV, was shot and killed in a gang fight last weekend.

Larry's brother, Gary, is also a student assigned to Division IV. I have met with Gary and our student government president, Angela Kent, and we would like to have a memorial service for Larry this Friday, October 10. I need some guidance from you. This is what we'd like to do.

- The service would be in the auditorium during the final period on Friday.

- You need to decide how to excuse students to attend.

- Of course, Larry's family would be invited. What about opening it up to other friends and people from the neighborhood where the family lives?

- Would you be willing to say a few words about Larry and gang violence?

Clearly, we must be responsive to this matter. Please contact me about this as soon as possible.

"Betty," he said as he picked up his phone while opening the right drawer of his desk. "I need to see Loretta Greenwood and Harlow Bartlett right away, if possible. Tell them it's in regard to Larry Hemingway."

"Aspirin—there's a bottle in here somewhere," he thought as he scuffled objects around in the drawer.

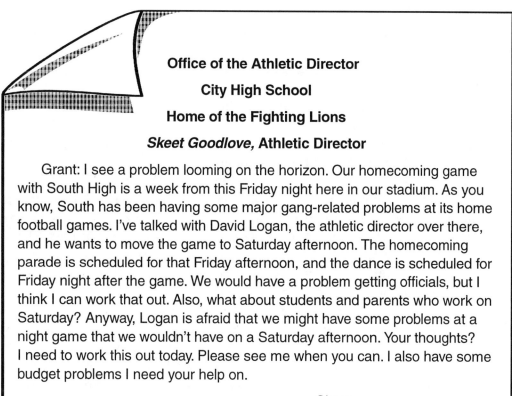

Office of the Athletic Director

City High School

Home of the Fighting Lions

Skeet Goodlove, **Athletic Director**

Grant: I see a problem looming on the horizon. Our homecoming game with South High is a week from this Friday night here in our stadium. As you know, South has been having some major gang-related problems at its home football games. I've talked with David Logan, the athletic director over there, and he wants to move the game to Saturday afternoon. The homecoming parade is scheduled for that Friday afternoon, and the dance is scheduled for Friday night after the game. We would have a problem getting officials, but I think I can work that out. Also, what about students and parents who work on Saturday? Anyway, Logan is afraid that we might have some problems at a night game that we wouldn't have on a Saturday afternoon. Your thoughts? I need to work this out today. Please see me when you can. I also have some budget problems I need your help on.

Skeet.

"Where is that bottle of aspirin?"

"Betty," Sterling yelled out the door. "Do you have any aspirin?"

"Sorry, Grant. I don't. Loretta and Harlow are here. Do you want to see them now?"

"Yes, thank you, I do . . . send them in please."

"I have some aspirin in my purse, Grant," Loretta announced as she entered his office. "It's upstairs. Do you want me to run up and get it?"

"Never mind, Loretta, I'll live. Sit down, please. Harlow, you're looking tanned today. Play some golf over the weekend?"

"Yep, looks like you could use some outdoor activity yourself, Grant. I don't get headaches since I took up walkin' the front nine."

"Well, Harlow, I may be about to give you one, I'm afraid. Loretta, thank you for the memo concerning Larry Hemingway. Let me ask you this. What would the ramifications be—if any—if we, the school, didn't do anything about this matter, other than what's already being done? I understand the school's newspaper is doing quite a feature about Larry and a separate story about the incident."

"What memo?" Bartlett interrupted.

"Oh, I'm sorry, Harlow. I thought you had probably seen it. Take a moment to get up to speed on Loretta's plan."

He waited until Bartlett finished reading.

"Hey, this is real nice, Loretta," Bartlett commented.

"Right," Sterling thought to himself. "And this is why, Harlow Bartlett, you're still a vice principal at this school."

"Okay," he looked at Loretta and Harlow. "Answer these questions for me. First, my question about ramifications if we do nothing other than the school newspaper stuff. Second, if I put out an announcement that students can be excused from 6th-hour class to attend the memorial, how many will attend, and how many will just skip out the door? How would we notify parents that their child may have left school early? Maybe even to look for revenge . . . the cops haven't identified the shooter yet. I'll bet some of our kids know who did it. How do you know if the very people who put Larry in a casket wouldn't find out about the memorial service and decide to carry on their war right here at school . . . maybe even during the service?"

"Grant," Betty interrupted. "Rob Simmons is here to see you . . . you called him about something concerning driver education?"

"Thanks, Betty. Hold on to him for a minute. I need to talk to him."

"Look, folks," he continued. "This isn't going to work unless you can answer my questions. Why don't the both of you go back upstairs and think about this whole thing. Harlow, I want your input . . . no, I want your recommendation on this matter later today. Fair enough? Loretta, we'll have a decision for you today, I promise."

"Betty, I can see Rob now. Thanks for meeting with me, Loretta, Harlow. You're right, Harlow, I need to take up golf. I work much better when I'm tanned."

"Rob, thanks for jumping on my request. Let me look at your material while I share this letter from a concerned patron with you."

Both men studied the documents they had traded for a moment.

"Rob," Sterling looked up and noted that Simmons had finished reading. "Do you want to investigate this, or do you want me to handle it?"

"I'll get on this right now, Grant. I'm afraid we may have a problem here. I'll let you know what I find out. If it's the teacher I'm thinking about, well . . . we've had some rumors before."

"Skeet, you got any aspirin?" Sterling asked as he slipped into Goodlove's office, moved a bunch of gym shorts off a chair, and sat down.

"Nope, never use medicines, Grant. Just lift weights when I feel one comin' on. Does the trick every time. Come out here and let me show you."

"Not today, Skeet, thanks anyway. Listen, I've been thinking about this home-coming problem. Let's move ahead with our original schedule. I'll hire some additional security for all the events scheduled for that date. I'm not about to let South's problems change our plans. Moving from a night game to an afternoon game isn't going to stop somebody from causing trouble. Larry Hemingway was shot and killed last Saturday afternoon at the mall. Move ahead, Skeet. Okay?"

"No problem, Boss."

On the way back to his office, he realized that his headache had disappeared. "I wonder where I left it," he mused.

Option or Opportunity?

"I'm pooped," Sterling grumbled as he closed the door to his office and headed home. "11:15, and I'm due back here for a meeting at 7 o'clock tomorrow morning. This is the pits!"

He knew he needed to set some new priorities in his professional career. He'd been accepted into the PhD program at State University and had been traveling back and forth to the university, some 30 miles away, 2 nights a week for nearly 2 years. Between his university obligations and City High's rigorous extracurricular activities schedule, Sterling was seldom home before midnight, and spent most weekends studying. During the next 12 months, while continuing to be the chief administrator at City High, he was scheduled to take his final comprehensive examinations, defend the examinations in orals, and start the intensive research necessary to write his dissertation. "There's no way I can do that with my present assignment," he groused, "and I've come too far to abandon my efforts toward my degree now. I could finish 2 years from now, if I could get some release time. You'd think, after accepting the kinds of assignments I've had over the past 15 years, that I should be able to march into the superintendent's office and demand a leave of absence. Most principals have at least a 'honeymoon' year their first year in a new school. I've spent my so-called honeymoon years cleaning up other people's messes. In fact, I've never had an easy first year. I guess, when you've been typecast as the district's troubleshooter, your first year is kinda like a lover's first quarrel rather than the proverbial honeymoon. But," he laughed, "making up was sorta fun."

He called the superintendent's office the next morning to make an appointment. A few days later, as he entered the superintendent's office, Boughton said, "Grant, you look tired!"

"I am tired, Dr. Boughton. Thanks for seeing me today. I need a favor."

"I can guess what it is, Grant. You're going to ask for some kind of release time so you can finish your work at State. Am I right?"

"As usual, you've got me pegged, sir. Why did you think . . . how did you . . ."

"Been there, done that, Grant," Boughton laughed. "You're hitting the final stretch in your program, and there are no longer enough hours in the day. Well, you can forget a leave of absence unless, of course, you're wealthy enough to survive for a year or so without salary. The board eliminated paid leaves for administrators quite a while ago. You've forgotten. But I anticipated that you might need some help soon . . . and Lord knows I owe you a favor or two. Been thinking . . . how would you like to have an elementary principalship for the next couple of years? Still hard work, but minimal evening and night activities. Then," he continued, "after you finish your degree, you can see what might be available if you want a change. Who knows, you might fall in love with elementary school kids. Anyway, how's that sound to you? Are you interested?"

"Do you have somebody in mind to replace me at City High?"

"Remember Doug Neiswanger? He left the district about 3 years ago to take a job in Montana. Well, seems his wife hates it out there and wants to come home. Her parents live here. I think he's ready for a high school principalship. What d'ya think?"

"Doug Neiswanger would make an excellent high school principal, Dr. Boughton. But can Grant Sterling run an elementary school?"

"Hey, for a couple of years while you're hammering out that dissertation . . . I'm willing to bet on it."

"Yeah, but would elementary teachers and parents accept a principal who's been working at the secondary level for this many years? I'm kinda concerned about that."

"Grant, the question is not whether they will accept a secondary principal, but rather, will they accept *you*. That's been the central question with every administrative assignment you've had since day one, Grant," he laughed. "You'd be accepted with open arms . . . trust me!"

"Talk about catchin' a guy off balance," Sterling laughed. "Can I think about this for a few days?"

"Actually, take a few weeks if you want. No hurry. Just think, Grant . . . you could go from being the shortest guy at the high school to the tallest kid in an elementary school!" They both laughed.

As he started to leave, Boughton stopped him at the door.

"Grant," he said quietly. "The board's going to announce my retirement at the next meeting. I can't make any promises about what kind of an assignment you might get when you finish your degree. Just so you understand."

"I heard the rumor about your possible retirement. Is this something you want?"

"I'm looking forward to it. I've been here too long, and I'll be 65 in May. I'm ready."

"We'll miss you, sir."

"I'll miss most of you folks too."

As Sterling headed toward the parking lot, he couldn't help thinking . . ."Is this a way to get at least a part of my life back and maintain sanity, or would I be asking for trouble if I accept Boughton's offer? Where would I end up if I didn't like elementary school administration? With Boughton leaving, I might not have as strong a political mentor in the front office."

"Sterling! Whatcha been up to? I haven't seen you since the administrative workshops last August. How's City's basketball team going to be this year? Is this the year for the state championship?"

"Bob . . . nice to see you. How's it goin' with you?" Sterling responded as he stopped and waited for Bob Spencer to catch up. Spencer was principal at Madison Elementary School. Before that, he was the principal at Rocky Run, an elementary school whose students attended Moundview after they completed the sixth grade.

"So, Grant . . . state championship this year? I hear you've got the talent. I also hear you've really been kicking butt at City since you took over from Wakefield. Wasn't that a mess?"

"You have *no* idea, Bob. It was more than a mess. Hey, help me for a moment, and then I promise I'll give you the scoop on our basketball team. Bob, what's the difference between your job and mine, other than all the after-hours stuff?"

"That's a strange question, Grant. You doing some research on that in your doctoral program?"

"No, not . . . not really," Sterling hesitated. "Let me . . . let me rephrase the question. Do you think I could make it as an elementary principal?"

"I liked your first question better, Grant. The only difference, other than the one you've mentioned, is the size of the kids. Teacher problems are the same, parent problems are the same, although they're more active in their kid's education. I would imagine, and I've never been a secondary school principal, that it's a much slower, quieter environment. Not as many major problems, you know. As far as your second question goes . . . yeah, you could make it. In fact you'd make a damn good elementary principal. The kids are much more fun than what you're used to. I wouldn't trade my job for yours in a million years. You're not thinking about . . ."

"Bob, you can put your money on City High to take the state championship this year. With Gary Simmons at center, Jimmy Washington at guard, it's a done deal! Gotta run, now . . . gotta get back in time for the daily food fight in the cafeteria. We're serving spaghetti and meatballs today."

"Hey, that sounds like a Kodak moment to me," Spencer laughed as Sterling headed for his car.

The Diogenes Factor

Greenwood Public Schools
Unified School District # 620
City High School
Home of the Fighting Lions
Office of the Principal

Date:	February 25
Memo to:	Sarah Comstock, Director of Public Relations
	Greenwood Public Schools
From:	Grant Sterling, Principal
	City High School
Subject:	Newspaper Article—*City Journal,* February 25

Sarah: I read with great interest the article on City High's standardized test scores in this morning's City Journal by reporter J. J. Jackson. I appreciate the "spin" you provided for Jackson explaining the differences between City High's scores and the scores of our suburban high schools. However, I hasten to point out that attributing our lower scores to lack of parental guidance in our inner-city community is rather "old hat."

Recognizing that board members and the taxpayers who elected them to office also read the Journal, why not just tell the truth? In spite of my efforts, the superintendent's efforts, and the efforts of the good people of the City High community, this school remains understaffed (I realize that our pupil-teacher ratio is the same as the other high schools), materially underequipped, and financially strapped by our inability to generate the kinds of personal donations of money available in the higher-income areas of our city.

You suggested to Jackson, and you're quoted as stating, that "City High's parents should do more to provide students with a home environment that is conducive to wanting to learn and succeed in life." That's an insult to the majority of City High's parents and to the faculty and administration of this school. Comparing this school to other schools in the city, I realize, is an issue forced on us by the press; however, who will benefit from the conclusion you have provided to the paper? We are doing the best we can at City High with the staff and materials available to us.

According to ancient Athenian lore, Diogenes searched, with lighted lantern, through daytime Athens for honesty, and in his search easily found selective evidence and misleading comparisons that favored one class of people and the things they did over others. This is what is happening here as those who view City High from the outside consistently promote misleading underestimates of program effectiveness.

Sarah . . . these kinds of statements from your office and in the press are worse than saying nothing. They obscure the problem and delay productive solutions.

At your earliest convenience, I would like to sit down with you and J. J. Jackson to explore this issue further and see if we can't generate some press that will help City High rather than disguise the problem.

cc: Superintendent Boughton

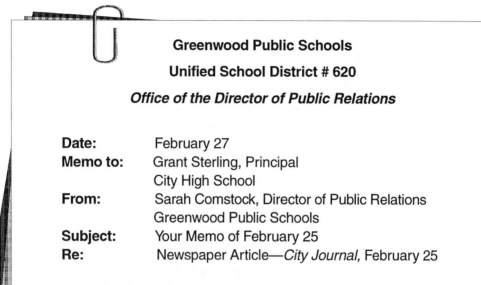

Greenwood Public Schools

Unified School District # 620

Office of the Director of Public Relations

Date:	February 27
Memo to:	Grant Sterling, Principal
	City High School
From:	Sarah Comstock, Director of Public Relations
	Greenwood Public Schools
Subject:	Your Memo of February 25
Re:	Newspaper Article—*City Journal,* February 25

Grant: Thank you for your memo of February 25. I have forwarded your memo to the superintendent's office for his consideration. Rest assured that I have every intention of supporting your efforts at City High in every way possible. By the way, congratulations on the winning streak that's being accumulated by your basketball team. What wonderful public relations it is to have such talented sports teams at your school. I've attended two games this season, and I must also compliment your school on its half-time shows.

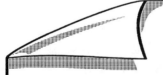

Greenwood Public Schools

Unified School District # 620

Office of the Superintendent of Schools

Date:	March 3
Memo to:	Grant Sterling, Principal, City High School
From:	Dr. Everett Boughton, Superintendent of
	Schools, Greenwood Public Schools
Subject:	Your Memo of February 25 to
	Sarah Comstock, Director of Public Relations
Re:	Newspaper Article—*City Journal,* February 25

Grant: Cool it on this matter.

WHILE YOU WERE OUT

TO: Grant
FROM: Betty
SUBJECT: Mr. Henry from the Neighborhood Coalition for Better Schools called about our test scores and the newspaper article in the *Journal.* He would like to visit with you about this. You can reach him at 252-7104.

Greenwood Public Schools
Unified School District # 620
City High School
Home of the Fighting Lions
Office of the Principal

March 3

To the Parents of the City High School Community:

I read, as many of you also did, the article in the February 25 edition of the City Journal titled "Test Scores Differ among Greenwood High Schools." The article was written by J. J. Jackson, a reporter for the Journal.

I just wanted you to know that the faculty and administration at your high school take strong exception to the reasons given in the article about City High's test scores being lower than other schools in the district. The truth of the matter does not lie in City High's community support for learning, but rather in the school district's inability to provide our school with the proper support we need to raise our students' abilities to perform better on standardized tests. It's as simple as that. I know from the phone calls I've received, and the notes you have sent me, that you are concerned about the article's implication that you, as parents, are not doing your best to prepare your children for school. The comment in the article that states, "City High's parents should do more to provide students with a home environment that is conducive to wanting to learn and suc-ceed in life" is an insult to City High's parents and to the faculty and administration of this school. I urge you to send your views on this comment directly to J. J. Jackson at City Journal, 115 W. 16th Street, Greenwood City.

Sincerely,
Grant Sterling, Principal
City High School

cc: Superintendent Boughton

Greenwood Public Schools

Unified School District # 620

Office of the Director of Public Relations

Date:	March 5
Memo to:	Grant Sterling, Principal, City High School
From:	Sarah Comstock, Director of Public Relations, Greenwood Public Schools
Subject:	Your Letter to Parents, Dated March 3
Re:	Newspaper Article—*City Journal,* February 25

Grant: Thanks for sending me a copy of your letter to parents concerning the *Journal* article of February 25. I'm sure your parents appreciate your support in this matter. I have forwarded a copy of the letter to the superintendent's office for his information. I'm sure he'll be pleased. Keep up the good work. Looks like your basketball team is headed for the play-offs this year!

Greenwood Public Schools

Unified School District # 620

Office of the Superintendent of Schools

Date:	March 7
Memo to:	Grant Sterling, Principal, City High School
From:	Dr. Everett Boughton, Superintendent of Schools, Greenwood Public Schools
Subject:	Your Parent Letter, March 3
Re:	Newspaper Article—*City Journal,* February 25

Grant: Excellent letter to parents . . . keep up the good work!

cc: Sarah Comstock

WHILE YOU WERE OUT

TO: Grant
FROM: Betty
SUBJECT: Mr. Jackson from the *City Journal* called this afternoon at 4:00.
Would like you to return his call at 252-6648, ASAP.

War of Words

"Look, Gary . . . all I said was . . . here, let me get a copy of the bulletin with my exact words in it. All I said was . . . here look at it! All I said was 'Faculty . . . I'm well aware of the frustrations you must be feeling as your contracts for next year are being bantered around in the press. I urge all of you to read the BOE salary and fringe benefit offers and compare them with the union's counterproposals. In the meantime, as difficult as the collective bargaining process is, please don't let it interfere with the quality of teaching our students at City High deserve.' Now what's wrong with that? Did I split an infinitive or something? Why are you so uptight about my wanting to ensure that these often silly . . . mostly nasty annual negotiating processes don't adversely affect teaching and learning at my school?"

"It's simple, Sterling. You're attempting to stifle union members at this school from freely discussing what this stupid board is trying to do to teachers. It's even simpler than that, Sterling, although I doubt that you as an administrator can fully understand where I'm coming from. This board and its agents, including you, are attempting to bully teachers into accepting a salary package that is clearly an insult! As executive director of the local, I'm not about to stand for that from you or any of your counterparts."

"That's monumental bullshit, Gary, and you know it! I could give a rat's ass about what's going on between your organization and the board. I've got a school to run here. If I had my way, and if the money was there, I'd give teachers triple their current salary, and I'd at least double mine and throw in a sports car. The point is—don't waltz into this building and tell me what I can or cannot do."

"You know Sterling, I've heard that you can be pretty hard-nosed . . . but a pompous little son-of-a bitch?"

"Gary," Sterling bit his lip as he stood up from behind his desk. "Gary, I object to, and I find totally offensive, your allegation that I'm . . . I'm . . . little. Now, you've had your last words in this discussion. My last words are, and I'll make this as simple as possible so that you can understand . . . remove your butt from this building now, and if for any reason you feel you need to set foot in here again, you will have to call this 'bully,' 'agent,' 'hard-nosed,' *big* 'pompous S.O.B.' in person, on the phone, in advance, so you can hear me say NO! You are persona non grata at City High. Test me, please . . . I'd love to see you escorted out of here in handcuffs. Eat that on your way out, Gary!"

Sterling slammed the door behind Gary Sutherland and picked up his two-way radio. "100 to 106, 107, 108. I have advised Gary Sutherland, an adult, white male, 40ish, in a gray suit, carrying a briefcase, to leave the building immediately. I imagine he's walking down the main hall west to the parking lot. If you see him, introduce yourself and hold the door open for him, please."

"10-4, 100," came the businesslike responses.

"Damn," Sterling declared, "I'm late for my meeting with the English department chair. Settle down, Grant," he said to himself as he left his office for the second floor conference room. "Settle down."

Later that day, Jesse Mills, the union's teacher representative at City High, called to make an appointment to see Sterling. Mills, a veteran teacher with 16 years under his belt, was one of City High's best math teachers.

"Ask him if now would be all right, Betty, I'm free," Sterling said as he looked at his appointment book. Within 15 minutes, Mills was sitting in Sterling's office.

"Grant, you and I seem to have developed a good rapport. I like what you've done here, and I support your efforts to continue to drag this place," he laughed, "into the modern world. But," he continued, "I agree with Gary Sutherland. You need to stay out of this negotiations thing. You're trying to serve two masters . . . the board and your teachers. You can't do both. Whether you like it or not, you represent the board when negotiations are the subject at hand . . . and, for all practical purposes, I represent the teachers at City High. Sutherland called me a while ago and told me about the confrontation—actually he called it a 'pissing contest'—the two of you had this morning. I'm sorry about that . . . hope it won't happen again. As far as your squib in the daily bulletin yesterday, I agree with your efforts. Let's cut a deal. If you feel that you need to say anything about teacher morale or quality as it relates to the collective bargaining problem, let me say it for you. Just call me, tell me what you're seeing, and let me act as your spokesperson. I feel just as strongly as you do about keeping City High going in the right direction."

"Jesse, you've got a deal," Sterling reached across the table and shook Mills's hand. "I wish I had thought about talking to you before I put that statement in the bulletin. I just thought . . . well . . . I didn't think. Thank you, Jesse. I don't always do the right things!"

"So far you've done the 'right' things here. This one was just a little less right! I'll get Sutherland calmed down; he's a bit of a fanatic about his job . . . but then, so are you. I understand from him that he got a personal escort all the way out to his car this morning. Is this a new service you've introduced for visitors to City High?" he laughed.

"No, not really. But I'm guessing Sutherland got my message!"

"Oh, he did, Grant. He did! But you can forget about asking him for any favors!"

Within 5 minutes after Mills left, Sterling had cleared off his desk, stuck some papers in his briefcase, and was headed out the door.

"Another day, another 50 cents, Betty. Have a good evening. See ya tomorrow!"

"Grant," she responded in her usual unemotional voice. "Tomorrow's Saturday!"

"Oops, two mistakes in 2 days, Betty. I'm clearly cracking up!"

Sterling wheeled his car to the right and then to the left and headed up the drive from the parking lot to the street. He glanced back at the prominent facade of the school as he pulled onto Main Street. "Pissing contest? Is that what he called it? Hmmm, if that's the case, he never had a chance!"

■ For Discussion

General Questions

Using the Sterling paradigm (http://www.corwinpress.com/dunklee.htm) as a model, and speaking from the perspective of a principal, evaluate each episode as follows:

What are the dominant behaviors exhibited by Sterling in this episode?

Is there consensus about this in the class? If not, explain the different viewpoints.

What were the primary actors' individual motives?

How effective was Sterling's behavior in this situation and why?

Can you identify other avenues or approaches that might lead to the same, or a better, conclusion?

If Sterling was a woman,

- As a female reader, can you identify methodology or behavior that you would change to bring the episode to the same, or similar, closure?

- As a male reader, what differences in methodology or behavior would you expect to see?

Specific Questions for Each Episode

It's Simple, But Timing Is Everything

1. Is the overall welfare of a school more important than a potential lawsuit?

2. Rand is claiming a violation of his First Amendment right to freedom of speech. Do you agree? Why or why not?

3. Why didn't any of Sterling's superiors call him first thing Tuesday morning either to warn him about a potential violation of Rand's rights or to order Sterling to wait?

4. What are Rand's chances of winning this case in court? Rand will claim he was being punished for his speech, and will produce copies of all his previous excellent evaluations. Sterling and his superiors will simply claim that it was done in the best interest of the school district and that they had the right to transfer any employee at any time. Sterling will be the only one who can claim that because he was not at the board meeting, he couldn't possibly have known about Rand's speech. And, even though his superiors were in attendance at the board meeting, no one told him about Rand's actions.

Listen With Your Heart

5. Do you have a working knowledge of your school's or district's crisis intervention program and procedures? What are they? What is the role of the principal in crisis intervention?

What if . . . some members of the community contended that there was a connection between the boy's death and the curriculum in the school's psychology classes?

An Adjunct Lecture: Tools of the Trade

6. If you were a member of the class in this episode, what would you list under the headings student problems, parent problems, and faculty and staff problems?

7. Which of those items you listed would you categorize as serious and which as petty?

8. Sterling suggests several ways to "sharpen your management tools." Can you list some other ways?

A Sterling Moment (When Logic Fails)

(No specific questions)

Soliloquy

What if . . . Sterling had vented his frustration, in much the way he did to his troll, to the faculty and staff?

Nothing Unusual, Just the Daily In-Basket— One at a Time

9. In the driver education investigation, Simmons could find a number of different explanations for the Thompson letter and for the incident he's describing. What are some of those explanations, and what actions might you take to resolve each one?

10. In the Hemingway matter, Sterling presents two general questions for consideration. Both questions can be answered only through the development of both positive and negative scenarios. After thinking about such scenarios, would you approve, disapprove, or modify the original request?

11. In the homecoming matter, a number of positive and negative scenarios can also be developed. After thinking about such scenarios, would you have approved, disapproved, or modified the original request? Regardless of your decision, if a serious incident took place, how would you defend your decision?

12. Is the development of hypothetical scenarios (mental forecasting) a positive tool in decision making? Why or why not? When, if ever, could it be considered a negative tool?

Option or Opportunity?

13. What do you think are the major differences between the secondary and elementary principalships?

The Diogenes Factor

14. As you read through this episode, were you able to predict what might occur next?

15. What is happening? Explain from the viewpoint of each document's writer, including guessing what the call slip from Mr. Henry would reveal when Sterling returned his call.

16. Why does Sterling decide not to "cool it," as directed by the superintendent?

17. Develop some alternative scenarios concerning why J. J. Jackson wants Sterling to call him. How would you handle each of these scenarios?

18. Can you explain the actions of the director of public relations in this matter?

What if . . . Sterling had ignored the *Journal* article and just dealt with parental phone calls and notes?

War of Words

19. What is a middle manager's role during teacher contract negotiations (or meet and confer objectives)?

9 ☺))

A Transition

Playing the Odds

There was little traffic at 6:10 in the morning as Sterling wheeled his car into the parking lot of the Medical Building. He'd lost a filling the day before, and his dentist had agreed to see him at 6:30. The dentist knew that Sterling didn't like to be away from the school and could usually accommodate him before or after regular hours. The door to the office was still locked, so Sterling sat in the lobby and waited. The cover on a recent *Adult Ventures* magazine caught his attention. "How to Live the Good Life After 40" was the lead article. Sterling looked at his watch and started reading. ". . . plenty of exercise . . . healthy diet . . . don't smoke . . . limit alcoholic beverages . . . well, I got one out of four. . . . learn to relax . . . plan time for yourself . . . enjoy your job . . . start a hobby . . . now, I'm one in eight!"

"Good morning, Grant. Let's get you in the chair and see how much damage I can do to your checkbook with this visit. I looked at a Mercedes yesterday, and I can still hear it calling my name. How you doing?"

"Well, Ken, I was fine until I read this article in the current *Adult Ventures*. I think we can just let this tooth go; I may be dead before the end of the day, according to this. Have you read it?"

"Yep, I'm going to make 70, according to my interpretation of what the author is saying!"

"The way I interpret it, you may make 70, but it looks like you're going to have to do it without my contribution to your Mercedes fund."

"All right, sit down, relax, and let me take a look at your problem. Yep, you've lost a filling on the occlusal of number 29. Everything else looks okay, when's your next regular appointment?"

"Nex onth, I ink."

"Good, you're about ready for a cleaning. It looks to me like the reason you lost this particular filling is that you're grinding your teeth. Have you been under a lot of stress lately?"

"O ore an usul!"

"Huh?"

"O ore an usul!"

"Well, something's causing you to grind your teeth. Better watch that . . . I don't want to be fitting you for false teeth! Just a little pin-prick now, and we'll have you out of here in no time."

"Don't grind your teeth? Now I'm one out of nine! The odds are really stacked against me," Sterling thought to himself as the dentist carefully refilled his tooth.

When Sterling arrived at his office that morning, still a bit Novocain-frozen, he was met by Maury Gilbert, one of his vice principals. "Good morning, Maury, I was about to call you. Bring me up to date on the situation with Diane Brewster. I understand she's got some kind of a bone to pick with her physics teacher, Lillian Brazeale. Have I got my characters right?"

Gilbert carefully explained the situation to Sterling.

"So, how are you going to handle the problem?" Sterling asked.

"I don't know what we should do, Grant."

"That wasn't the question, Maury. I don't remember the word *we* in my question!"

"Are you suggesting that the decision on this is up to me?" Gilbert asked. "Don't you think we ought to discuss it in Monday's administrative team meeting?"

"Maury, refresh my memory . . ." The Novocain was starting to wear off, and Sterling was beginning to feel some discomfort. ". . . didn't you apply for the principal's job here when we dumped Wakefield?"

"You know I did, Grant. What's that got to . . ."

"Well, this is a perfect example of why you weren't selected. This is not a decision you need help on. This is a decision *you* need to make. Now go and do it, whatever . . . just do it! This is one time I'm not going to hold your hand. I'd rather cover for your decisions, right or wrong, than to be continually plagued by your indecisiveness!"

"Geez, Grant . . . I didn't mean to . . ."

"Let me know what you decide, Maury. I've got an appointment waiting," Sterling barked as he picked up the phone.

"Betty? Is Mr. Forsom here yet? Thank you."

"Mr. Forsom, come in please," Sterling said as he met his visitor at the door. "Have a seat, sir. How can I help you?"

"Mr. Sterling, you'll recall that my son Chris was expelled early this semester for alleged drug possession. Well, he's been home for almost 5 months now, and I think it's time for you folks to reconsider and let him come back to school. I talked to Mr. Simmons, Chris's vice principal, and he told me it was out of his hands and that I should talk to you. So . . . here I am."

"Mr. Forsom . . . I think this was explained to you at the time of Chris' expulsion. School district policy clearly states that any student caught possessing drugs will—not might, or may—but will be expelled from school for the remainder of the school year. Even if it wasn't board of education policy, I would have expelled him for that length of time anyway. The answer is no. Chris can't return to school until next semester. That's first semester of next school year. I'm sorry for you and your family, especially Chris, but if I recall the case, he was caught red-handed, and we also had some suspicion that he was dealing."

"So, what am I supposed to do with him in the meantime?"

"I think we suggested counseling?"

"Who's gonna pay for that?"

"Mr. Forsom, I can't help you with this problem. Bottom line . . . Chris will be welcome back next school year, and if he stays clean we shouldn't have to worry again."

"So, why did Simmons tell me to talk to you? Why didn't he just tell me no? Why did he suggest I should see you? Is there some loophole that he knows that you know about that would allow Chris to come back?"

"I don't know why Mr. Simmons told you to talk to me . . . and no, there's no loophole."

"You people are idiots! You know that. You ought to get your stories together!"

"Thanks for stopping by, Mr. Forsom. Have a good day!"

"Who do you think you are, dismissing me in that way?"

"Have a good day, Mr. Forsom."

"You're an asshole, Sterling," Forsom bellowed as he stomped out of the office.

"Add that title to my list, Betty, if it's not already there," Sterling said quietly as he picked up his mail from her desk. "And, when you get a chance, call Simmons, please, and tell him I need to talk to him today, in my office, when he has a free moment."

"Will do, Grant. Here's a call slip from Superintendent Boughton. I told him you were with a parent when he called. He asked that you call sometime this morning. How's your tooth?"

"Sore, but getting better . . . thanks for asking."

"Thanks for returning my call, Grant," Boughton said when Sterling returned his call. "Doug Neiswanger called me yesterday, and he does want to come back, if we have a job for him. Have you given any thought to my suggestion about taking an elementary principalship for the next couple of years while you finish your doctorate? I need to make a decision pretty soon and take it to the board."

"Would you throw in a Mercedes on the deal?"

"No. Why?" Boughton laughed.

"Could you guarantee I will live longer if I accept this elementary school assignment?"

"That I can guarantee . . . without hesitation!"

"Done deal, boss! Give me a few days 'heads up' before it's announced."

"Maybe this will shift the odds more in my favor," Sterling thought as he hung up the telephone. "And I won't need to meet with my attorney just yet. I won't be needing to draw up a will right away!"

For Discussion

General Questions

Using the Sterling paradigm (http://www.corwinpress.com/dunklee.htm) as a model, and speaking from the perspective of a principal, evaluate the episode as follows:

What are the dominant behaviors exhibited by Sterling in this episode?

Is there consensus about this in the class? If not, explain the different viewpoints.

What were the primary actors' individual motives?

How effective was Sterling's behavior in this situation and why?

Can you identify other avenues or approaches that might lead to the same, or a better, conclusion?

If Sterling was a woman,

- As a female reader, can you identify methodology or behavior that you would change to bring the episode to the same, or similar, closure?

- As a male reader, what differences in methodology or behavior would you expect to see?

Specific Questions: Playing the Odds

Is the vice principalship a training position for a principalship? If not, what role should a vice principal plan in the administration of a school? If yes, what kinds of independent decisions would you want a vice principal to make? And are there any kinds of decisions you, as the principal, wouldn't want the VP to make?

What if . . . a vice principal in your building made a really bad decision? What actions might you take?

10 ⏵⏵

The Adams Years

Adams Elementary School was located in a predominately blue-collar neighborhood, but had a significant number of families on welfare. The school was built in the mid-sixties and had been meticulously maintained, mostly due to the continuing efforts of George Elliot, who'd been the principal at Adams for the past 14 years. He'd announced his retirement in January to be effective at the close of the school year. As Sterling pulled his car into the parking lot, he couldn't help noticing that the school stood out like a jewel in the middle of an older, somewhat rundown neighborhood.

"Hello, Grant Sterling!" Elliot was waiting at the door to greet Adams's new principal. "Come on in, partner . . . you can help me pack. I'm taking a lot of memories with me when I leave this old place. I'm leaving a few for you, however. Some of them have permeated the walls and will remain forever. Hope you'll let me come back and visit now and then! You're gonna love it here. Sit down, let's talk! The Supe brought me up-to-date on your 'need for a break.' Boy, you've got a winner here!"

"So, George . . . whatcha gonna do now? Where ya gonna go?" Sterling asked as he pulled up a chair in Elliot's office.

"We're not going anywhere, Grant. Our kids and grandkids are here. Millie and I are gonna play some golf—I'm gonna build some furniture in my shop at home, and I'm just generally gonna put my feet up and laugh every time I read about what's going on in the Greenwood schools. I'm leaving the politics, angry parents, and everything else to you young whippersnappers to maneuver around," he laughed. "Now, what can I do for you to make your transition easier?

"I can't think of anything I need to tell you about running a school, managing a staff, or getting along with kids and parents, with the kinds of experiences you've had. The master schedule is done; there are no faculty or staff vacancies—you've inherited a wonderful group of people, by the way—and the building is in tip-top shape except for a small leak in the boiler room down in the basement. You've got a great community

235

here that needs and supports the school. All in all, the biggest problem we have here is a continuous battle with . . . with . . . no, I'm gonna let you guess, Grant! This will be your first test! Betcha can't come up with the answer!"

"Well, uhh, free or reduced-cost breakfast and lunch—seeing that you have quite a few welfare recipients in the community?"

"Nope!"

"Uhh, nit-picking by the faculty, staff, or parents?"

"Nope! Close though!"

"Vandalism?"

"Nope! You're gettin' colder."

"Is the next game you're going to subject me to called hide and seek? Is this an elementary principal thing?" Sterling challenged with a laugh. "Am I going to have to relearn ring-toss, jacks, hopscotch, and all those things?"

"Wouldn't hurt, Grant," Elliot challenged back. "Head lice!" he snickered. "Head lice. We—actually a group of parent volunteers do it—spend a lot of time checking kids' heads for lice. Nit-picking, it's called. You've probably always wondered what that expression meant. We send home an average of 30 kids a day who are infested. Some of the same kids over and over again."

"You're kidding!"

"Welcome to Adams, Grant! It's like the book *The Little Engine That Could* . . . gotta get those lice, gotta get those lice . . ." They both laughed as Sterling joined in the chant, "gotta get those lice . . . gotta get . . ."

"Seriously, though, Grant." Elliot stopped abruptly. "The problems here, or at any elementary school, are basically the same as you've experienced at the secondary level. You'll be spending your days dealing with parent, teacher, staff, and kid problems. You'll experience your usual battles with the good folks in central office for budget, maintenance, and all that stuff. Somebody once told me that the elementary principalship is just one step from retirement compared to the secondary principalship. Hogwash! Everything's the same, except you don't have all those night and weekend activities. You'll be surprised when school starts and the stuff that happens looks awfully familiar."

"Head lice?" Sterling had begun to itch.

"Head lice, Grant! Oh, and you'll find it much easier on your back if you learn to squat or kneel down when you're talking to kids. Most of them, not all, however," he laughed, "are shorter than you."

"George, why is my scalp itching?"

"So, anyway, Grant . . . you're better prepared for this than you think. All the facts you'll need are in this folder. Take this home with you and study it. You're in for a treat. Trust me. Now, I've got a lunch date with Millie, and she wields a mighty powerful eight-iron when I'm late. Your secretaries will be back on duty August 1, and if you have any other questions, they . . . well . . . they really run the show, but don't ever admit that to anyone! And, as far as working with elementary kids goes . . . when you have your first faculty meeting before school starts . . . ask them, your teachers, to teach you! Be honest with them. They'll get a real kick out of showing you the ropes."

"I'll do just that, George. Thanks. Uhh . . . George . . . what do head lice look like?"

"You'll see, Grant. You'll see."

The Parade of the Ankle Biters

"So, now you know the facts about who I am and why I'm here," Sterling said to the faculty and staff of Adams, who had assembled in the multipurpose room for a "punch and cookies" reception to welcome him. "And I need your help. I want to learn everything, repeat everything, that you can teach me about elementary kids and their parents, elementary teachers and their needs, and anything else you feel I need to know to be as effective as George was for so many years. I can't fill his shoes, but I'm going to bust my butt to gain the same respect from you that you've shown him. I'm willing to learn, and to learn quickly. I'll take care of the office, the building, the grounds, and the budget. I know what to do with the kids you send to the office for discipline, and I know how to keep parents off your backs. But folks . . . I'm clueless about curriculum, the environment in your classrooms . . . especially primary, and I'm sure I'm just as clueless about some other things . . . so . . . teach me! I'd like to meet with the kindergarten faculty for a half day next Monday morning, primary folks Monday afternoon, and intermediate folks on Tuesday morning. They're your meetings . . . I'll have no agenda. I need to hear what you want from me that will make your jobs easier. And thanks for this wonderful reception today!"

For the next 2 weeks, just prior to the start of school, the faculty and staff at Adams kept Sterling jumping. Everyone took him seriously about the "teach me" request, and he was fast becoming more than a novice in elementary education. He would need to spend much time observing kids and teachers in their classrooms, but felt that he had the basics on which to build a better understanding of how kids this age are taught and how they learn. He still had some concerns about the "assertive discipline" program practiced at Adams. To Sterling, assertive discipline meant that when a kid is out of line, he would simply walk up to him and say, "Hey kid, if you don't get in line, I'm going to kick your butt!" As he understood the practice at Adams, he was supposed to approach the kid and say, "Kid, see how nicely everyone else is in line, don't you want to join them?" That wasn't assertive in his book; it was pretty passive behavior on the part of a principal. "But," he agreed, "if that's how the faculty wants me to play the game, then I'll learn to be assertively passive, and smile while I'm doing it!"

"So, I think I'm ready to go, thanks to all of you," Sterling hesitantly announced in the final faculty meeting before school started and kids arrived. "Well, at least, I feel much more comfortable than I did 2 weeks ago. School starts Monday . . . I'll be in the halls, meeting kids and parents before the first bell rings, and then I'll visit each of your classrooms sometime during the day to introduce myself to the kids. Again, thank you for your patience and understanding. I'm excited! See ya Monday morning!"

He wasn't being facetious when he told the faculty he was excited. Over the short period he had been in contact with the school and its staff, he had fallen in love with the whole elementary school concept. He looked forward to interaction with the soon-to-arrive children who would surely make Adams come alive.

"So, what do *you* think, Troll? Can I be a successful elementary principal? Are you going to help me or are you too scared of little folks to come out from under my desk? Some of them are about your size, I'd guess."

"Sterling, you've got about as much chance of success in this job as I would have as a center for the New York Knicks. Starting Monday, you're going to be surrounded by a herd of ankle-biting rug rats. And while they're working on your ankles, a hoard of parasites will be nibbling on your scalp. Then," he laughed, "you're going to have a nervous breakdown being nice . . . and passive . . . when you can't kick butt as usual. They're gonna lock you away somewhere, and I'll be watching you rock back and forth in a chair, reciting nursery rhymes and itching. This is gonna be fun for me, Sterling—watching you be devoured by snotty-nosed playground puppies. You owe me for all the crap you've given me over the years."

"Troll, you ain't seen nothin' yet! And . . . all I owe you is what you'll collect in my will. Remember, when I go, you'll go too," he warned as he scratched his head. "Good evening, Troll, I'm outta here 'til Monday!"

"Hey, Grant," the troll bellowed as Sterling started to close the door to his office. "You might want to stop by the drug store on your way home and pick up a case of delousing shampoo!"

"Oh, thanks, just what I needed to hear!" he said as he slammed the door behind him.

▬▬▬ For Discussion

General Questions

Using the Sterling paradigm (http://www.corwinpress.com/dunklee.htm) as a model, and speaking from the perspective of a principal, evaluate each episode as follows:

What are the dominant behaviors exhibited by Sterling in this episode?

Is there consensus about this in the class? If not, explain the different viewpoints.

What were the primary actors' individual motives?

How effective was Sterling's behavior in this situation and why?

Can you identify other avenues or approaches that might lead to the same, or a better, conclusion?

If Sterling was a woman,

- As a female reader, can you identify methodology or behavior that you would change to bring the episode to the same, or similar, closure?

- As a male reader, what differences in methodology or behavior would you expect to see?

Specific Questions for Each Episode

Itching to Get Started

1. Based on your experience, would you agree that there is basically no difference between the principalships at the elementary and secondary level, except for the extracurricular activities? Discuss.

The Parade of the Ankle Biters

2. What do you think of Sterling's approach in asking the Adams teachers to teach him about elementary education? List and discuss the pros and cons.

River Sharks and Baby Sterling

The faculty had forewarned Sterling about the Burroughs family. Both Mr. and Mrs. Burroughs were third-generation welfare and proud of it. They often introduced themselves to others in the predominately blue-collar neighborhood as "token white trash."

Mrs. Burroughs, all 250 pounds of her, often showed up in the main office to complain that her children, both students at Adams, weren't getting enough to eat. She typically wore the same outfit, a dress with a peasant blouse that gaped open, exposing a large tattoo on each breast. Sterling was usually called on to intercede because both faculty and staff found her to be somewhat intimidating. Sterling had slowly developed a rapport with the family by putting on a temporary persona that the adult Burroughs were comfortable with and could relate to.

"I'll bet the kids who pay for their lunch get more than mine do," was her normal complaint. Both Burroughs children received free lunches, as well as a free breakfast, each school day, due to their parents' welfare status.

"Mother Burroughs!" as Sterling called her. "I'm glad to see you again. I'll check with the cafeteria, but I'm sure that Kenny and Alice are eating well!" Kenny was a second-time-around sixth grader and Alice was a fifth grader in her sixth month of pregnancy.

Mrs. Burroughs would lean across the main office counter, exposing more of the surface areas of her tattoos, and pat Sterling on the arm. "I'm sure you will," she would say in what she thought was her sexiest voice.

"See you later," Sterling would respond, winking an eye at her as she giggled and waddled out the door.

"My kind of woman," he would often jokingly remark as soon as Mother Burroughs was safely out of earshot.

Social welfare was aware of Alice's pregnancy and was investigating, but Alice refused to tell anybody who the father might be. Sterling suspected that it could be Kenny.

Toward the end of the spring semester, Sterling found this note on his desk after returning from supervising lunch in the cafeteria:

FROM THE DESK OF:
Lillian Roberts, Counselor, Adams Elementary School

Date: April 17

Grant, we've got to retain Kenny Burroughs again . . . he's just not mature enough to be promoted to jr. high school. We, Bill Jones and I, feel that even though he's been held back before, he needs 1 more year in elementary school. The jr. high kids will eat him alive.
Please call me when you have time to visit about this.

He walked down to her office with the note in his hand.

"Lillian, you're suggesting that Kenny spend a third year as a sixth grader at Adams. What would we do with him? What kind of a program would we put him in?"

"The intermediate teachers and I have prepared this schedule for Kenny if we retain him. I think it looks good, and I feel that he can continue to achieve both academically and in terms of maturity. Please try to convince his folks that this would be in Kenny's best interest."

"Two questions, Lillian. What does Kenny think of this, and what is this 'you' crap? Do you see any certificate hanging on my wall that says counselor?"

"Kenny thinks it would be just fine. He really got scared when the sixth-grade classes visited the junior high school for preorientation last week. And, to tell you the truth, his parents scare me to death. If you tell me to talk to them, I will. I just think that you . . . you know . . . with your act that you do with them . . ."

"Lillian, we'll both talk to them. I'll set up a meeting. You provide the armor!"

The Burroughs family didn't have a phone, so he sent a note home with Kenny that afternoon inviting his parents to come in and visit with him the next morning, "if it's convenient."

"Good morning, Mother Burroughs, nice to see you again . . . and Mr. Burroughs, how are you today?" Mrs. Burroughs was wearing her favorite outfit accented with high-top tennis shoes, and Mr. Burroughs was sporting an almost-new pair of overalls with one side unbuttoned. His attire was highlighted by a pair of terrycloth bedroom slippers and an off-white undershirt.

"Today's fashion show provides me with my choice of mom's tattoos or dad's upper-left thigh. What a treat!" Sterling thought.

"Not good," Mr. Burroughs grunted in response to Sterling's greeting. "Somethin's been eatin' my chickins at night!"

Lillian entered quietly and took a seat in the corner.

"Whataya mean?" he consciously adopted Mr. Burroughs' speech mannerisms. "Somethin's comin' in your yard at night? Don't you have light out there in the yard?"

"Yep! An' I got a shotgun too! An' I'm gonna get whoever or whatever it is!"

"How many chickens didja lose?" he feigned extreme concern.

"Bout 25 or so . . . lost three good-uns last night!"

"Well, hell," a veneer of seriousness appeared on his face, "Did the river that runs by your place freeze over last winter?"

"Sure it did . . . what's that got to do with . . ."

"Didja walk along the river when it was frozen over? Didja see any holes in the ice?"

Lillian had a puzzled expression on her face. He could almost hear her mind asking "What are you doing? Where are you going with this?"

"Yeh, Sterling, there was some holes in the ice!"

"Well," he leaned toward Burroughs, "Was the ice along the edge of the hole broken in, and floatin' in the hole, or out, and lyin' on the ice? I'm bettin' the hole was broken out!"

"Ya know, I think you're right. You think whatever's gettin' my chickens come outta the river?"

"Yep! I've heard that them river sharks can do that. They use some kind of flippers to crawl on land . . . grab a chicken and drag it under water!"

"Ya know, I recollect somebody else talkin' 'bout them river sharks but I never seen one. I'll put some chicken wire fence between the river an' my back yard an see if that works." Burroughs nodded his head in agreement with himself.

"You know, it just might solve your problem . . . oh, and by the way, Mr. and Mrs. Burroughs, we need to keep Kenny here at Adams for another year. He's not quite ready to go on to junior high school. That's okay with you folks, isn't it?"

"Whatever you need to do with Kenny, you do it," Burroughs said forcefully as Mother Burroughs nodded in agreement. "Thanks for your idea 'bout my chickens."

He escorted Kenny's parents to the door, wishing them the best in their hunt for a solution to their chicken dilemma. He didn't forget to give Mother Burroughs a sly wink before he turned to go back to his office and finalize the "done deal" with Lillian, his reluctant counselor.

"You'll take care of the paperwork on Kenny?" he asked Lillian, as he reentered his office.

"You're crazy!" Lillian remarked as she left with a smirk on her face. "Did I witness directed or nondirected counseling in that encounter? And where did that river shark nonsense come from?"

He shrugged his shoulders. "I don't have the slightest idea, Lillian—remember, I don't have that piece of paper on my wall that says 'counselor.' Whatever I did . . . it worked, didn't it?"

Kenny happily returned to Adams in the fall, and Mr. and Mrs. Burroughs came in with their daughter Alice, who had been promoted to the sixth grade. Mother Burroughs was cuddling Alice's newborn baby girl as Alice hustled off to her classes.

"We named the baby after you!" Mr. Burroughs exclaimed, "Sterling Burroughs . . . after the man who solved our chicken problem!"

"You did? I did? . . . Wow, I'm impressed." He looked at the baby with amazement. "You're telling me that you haven't lost any more chickens since we talked in April?"

"Nary a one!" Burroughs proudly announced as he thrust the baby toward Sterling. "Here, hold the kid!"

Later that month, Sterling learned from a county welfare agent that the father of Alice's child, named after him, was Mr. Burroughs. The county attorney was bringing charges against him.

"Mr. Burroughs is an incontestable river shark!" he thought to himself, "among other things!"

The heretofore hypothetical "river shark" now became real, and the new baby, if nothing else, was worth an additional $600 per month from welfare to the Burroughs clan.

A Sterling Moment (You're Finished, Grant!)

"Grant Allen Sterling," the loudspeakers in the auditorium boomed as he walked up the stairs to the stage. "Ladies and gentlemen," State University's provost announced, "it is with profound pleasure that I confer the degree of doctor of philosophy in administration and foundations on Grant Sterling and warmly welcome him to the academy of scholars. Please join me in congratulating *Dr.* Sterling." As Sterling shook hands with the provost, his university adviser, Dr. Robert Sharp, placed the traditional doctoral hood over his head and carefully adjusted it on his shoulders. "It's been a long journey, Grant . . . Dr. Sterling. You've earned this!"

The first response that came to his mind was "Robert, you bet your sweet ass I have!" but good judgment won out. "Thanks, Dr. Sharp," he said, then turned, acknowledged the applause from his friends in the audience, and left the stage.

"Man, what a rush," he thought as he walked across the campus to his car. "Look at this robe . . . and the hood . . . and the fancy cap! Wow, did I really pull this off? Dr. Sterling? Me? Grant Sterling, PhD . . . finally!"

It was not the first time he'd been addressed by his new title. Two months earlier, after a grueling 2-hour session defending his dissertation in a required public forum, and after waiting outside the forum meeting room for 30 minutes while a doctoral committee secretly debated the acceptance or rejection of his dissertation, he had been relieved when Sharp opened the door and invited him in for the verdict. "Congratulations, Dr. Sterling," he had said, "you've successfully defended your dissertation. You're finished, Grant!"

The phrase "you're finished, Grant," kept repeating itself in his mind as he had driven back from the university that day. "My professional life has been a continuous start and finish, start and finish, over and over. Is that what it's all about? I finished my bachelor's degree. I finished as a teacher, as a supervisor. I finished my master's degree. I finished at Center, at Arthur, at Moundview, at City High. I finished my PhD. I'm *not* finished yet at Adams . . . I wonder what I'll be starting and finishing next, or . . . is Adams my swan song?"

Today, however, he was not thinking about finishing or starting anything. He had been momentarily swept up in the pomp and ceremony of his own graduation.

"Grant! Hold up a minute."

He glanced over his shoulder and saw Sharp hurrying down the hill from the auditorium toward him.

"Slow down, Grant. I can't move very fast with all this academic regalia flapping in the wind."

"You do slightly resemble Batman, Dr. Sharp!"

"Hey, look, Grant," Sharp was clearly out of breath. "Send me a copy of your resume, will ya? I wanna look it over and then I wanna talk to you about the possibilities of looking at higher education as a career move."

"Dr. Sharp," he laughed. "I don't have a resume. I haven't looked for a job in 20-some years."

"All right, I understand . . . but I'd like for you to sit down and put your career in resume form. With your background and experience in education leadership, with the fact that you've served in so many different assignments, and with your doctoral studies being in education law, I'm betting there're half-a-dozen or more universities that would like to have you on their faculty. Aren't you about ready for a change . . . a new challenge?"

"Dr. Sharp, I don't know diddle about how universities work . . . what they pay . . . what professors do. I don't know whether I want to even think about changing, about moving, about . . ."

"Well, think it over, Grant. Let's get together for lunch in a few weeks. Fair enough? And congratulations again. Drive home safely!"

"I'll call ya, Dr. Sharp," he said as he unlocked the door to his car. "You can buy me lunch and convince me that university professors are not overworked and underpaid, as I've so often heard you complain."

He glanced at his rear-view mirror as he drove out of the parking lot. He could see Sharp flapping his way back up the hill to the auditorium. "Professor Sterling? Professor-Doctor Sterling? Academic scholar? Pipe in corner of mouth, suede leather patches on the elbows of my sport jackets? Naw . . . that's not the Grant Sterling I know. Why did they have to announce my middle name during the ceremony today? Now people know my initials. Hey, GASman! Professor GASman, what's up? Hey Doc Sterling, I've got a bad case of GAS, can you prescribe something?"

▬▬▬ Do You Know How to Exorcise Gypsy Curses?

Two short rings of the school's main bell meant that Sterling was needed in the office. Knowing that his secretaries would use this method of locating him only in an emergency, he hurried back.

"Grant," Mary said, "one of our Gypsy mothers just came in the building and went upstairs. She didn't stop to get permission . . . thought you might want to know. I'm not sure, but I think it's Nadia Petru's mother . . . Nadia's in room 204 with Mrs. Hooper."

"I'm on my way," he said as he turned to leave the office. Just as he reached the door, it flew open, and Vickie Hooper rushed in. He could see Mrs. Petru behind her, yelling something then disappearing out the front door of the school as Hooper barreled into his office. Hooper ensconced herself in a chair and began sobbing loudly.

"Vickie, what's the deal?" he asked gently as he handed her a fistful of tissues.

Vickie, a first-year third-grade teacher, was very popular with her students and, as he would say, "one of my best recruitment efforts." She was 7 months pregnant with her first child.

"Grant," Hooper sobbed, "Mrs. Petru put some kind of a Gypsy curse on my baby! She's evidently upset with me because I had to scold her daughter yesterday for stealing crayons from another student. She barged into my room, loudly chanted some gibberish at me, then told me that my baby would be born deformed and a 'disciple of the devil.' What can I do, Grant . . . what about my baby?"

"Who's watching your students, Vickie?" he asked in a calm voice.

"I don't know," Vickie whimpered.

"I'll be right back, Vickie . . . you stay here, and we'll talk about this as soon as I get your class covered."

He quickly located one of the school's counselors and directed him to fill in for Hooper. He briefly explained the situation as best he could and returned to his office.

Hooper was still quietly sniffling, but was being comforted by the school nurse. He slowed his pace. "It will be easier to talk with Hooper," he thought, "after she settles down a bit."

"What do we know about the Petru family?" he asked Mary.

"They're part of that group of Gypsies that passes through this area about this time each year, Grant. They enroll their younger kids in our school for about 6 weeks, and the fathers and older kids do seasonal work at the train yard. Seems that there's some kind of shop down there where train companies send passenger cars for upholstery work. The mothers stay home with their babies. It's something like a commune. They all give their addresses as 14 Front Street. It's an old motel the train yard keeps for itinerant workers, and a pretty seedy place, according to some of our regular kids who play down there."

"So then, what do you know about Gypsy curses?" he chuckled.

"Well, I don't know anything about curses," Mary shook her head, "but I do know about the fragile emotional state of first-time expectant mothers! You've got some serious counseling to do, Grant. Good luck," Mary laughed inconspicuously as she reached to answer the phone.

"Another section missing from administration textbooks—'How to Exorcise Curses,' " he grinned as he returned to his office.

"All right, Vickie," he said firmly. "Let me work on this problem for a while and see what I can do. In the meantime, I think you ought to go back to your class as if nothing had happened and get your students back on track. Can you handle that okay?"

"I'll try, Grant." Vickie wiped her eyes as she left the office. "I'm worried about my baby!"

He sat and thought for a moment. He remembered a similar incident with a teacher at Moundview who was also pregnant with her first child. She had rushed into his office in a panic, sobbing that one of her eighth-grade students (who had just returned from a trip to Washington State) had put a pinch of volcanic ash in her coffee. Unknowingly, she'd taken a sip of the coffee, and now she was afraid that both she and her baby had been poisoned.

"What should I do?" she sobbed. "Should I go to the hospital, call a rescue squad? We've got to do something!"

Sterling had picked up the phone and called the regional poison control center. The center had been unable to answer his question, but had promised to call the geology department at State University and get back to him as soon as possible. He felt sure that volcanic ash was not poisonous; however, he and the school nurse had had to contend with the teacher's panic-stricken behavior when she'd gone to the clinic to try to self-induce vomiting.

It had taken 2 hours for the call to come back, but the news confirmed his amateur prognosis that neither the teacher nor her baby would suffer any ill effects. The student who "flavored" her coffee, however, had been suspended from school for 5 days.

Now, after telling Mary where he was going, he headed for his car. "14 Front Street," he grumbled to himself as he made a U-turn and headed toward the train yard.

Front Street looked like a war zone; burned-out buildings, boarded-up store fronts, and dilapidated houses. At number 14, he found the remains of an old one-story motel sporting chipped and dirty white stucco. "Flat roof, U-shaped courtyard . . . probably built in the '50s," he thought as he pulled his car into the littered courtyard. Straight ahead, he could see a group of women sitting on milk cartons cradling babies. He parked his car and walked toward the group. They didn't outwardly appear to notice him approaching, but he could sense that they were watching him cautiously. Suddenly, an elderly gentleman emerged from a doorway and confronted him.

"Whata ya want?" he demanded in a loud voice.

"I'm Grant Sterling, principal at Adams Elementary School," he responded in an equally loud voice. "I'd like to talk to Mrs. Petru . . . Nadia's mother. Is she here?"

"Whata ya want to talk to her about?" the man said as he positioned himself between Sterling and the group of women.

"Oh, just a little problem between her and Nadia's teacher." He smiled at the old gentleman. "Not a big thing. I just need to talk with her for a minute if she's here."

"Wait there," the man ordered.

He stopped immediately and waited as the man went to talk with the group of women, who had yet to acknowledge his presence. "Where are the brightly painted wagons . . . and the sashy red- and cream-colored clothes I've always seen in drawings of Gypsies?" he asked himself as he waited. Shortly, the old guardian returned with a woman at his side.

"This is Mrs. Petru," he announced. "You may speak your piece."

"Mrs. Petru." He extended his hand to the woman, whose stare was frozen. "And she's not even wearing a peasant blouse," he thought as she refused his hand. "I'm

Grant Sterling, Nadia's school principal. I understand that there's some kind of a problem between you and Mrs. Hooper, Nadia's teacher. What can I do to help?"

"You can tell her not to put any more blame on my daughter," Petru said in a monotone.

He didn't feel he was in a position to argue, much less to negotiate. He could handle Nadia himself if another problem arose. He just wanted some kind of resolution for Hooper.

"And if I promise that Nadia won't have any more problems with Mrs. Hooper, will you come back to school and remove the curse you put on her unborn child?" he asked innocently. A voice inside him was asking, "Am I really having this conversation . . . is this for real?" "She's terribly upset, Mrs. Petru, and she's really a wonderful teacher. I'd certainly appreciate it if you came back with me and made the curse go away."

Petru and the elderly gentleman turned aside and whispered.

"She will accept your promise, principal. She will come back to your school within the hour. You may leave now!"

"Thank you very much, sir and Mrs. Petru," he said as he returned to his car.

He waited near the school's front door, and as promised, Mrs. Petru arrived within the hour. He had made arrangements for Hooper's class to be covered so that Hooper and Petru could meet in the first-floor hall, away from students. As Hooper came down the stairs from her room, he gently took her arm and led her toward Mrs. Petru. He could feel Hooper trembling. Petru said a few chantlike words in some language he couldn't recognize and turned to leave the building.

"Your child will be okay now, teacher. It will be a girl with blond hair like yours and blue eyes like your husband's. She will have mole on the inside of her upper-left arm."

Sterling could feel the tension in Hooper's body disappear as Petru left the building. "Anything else I can do for you today, Vickie?" He laughed as he headed back toward his office.

"Another chapter written in school-community relations, today," he announced to his secretaries as he walked by their desks.

Two months later, Richard Allen Hooper was born. He was a healthy baby with dark brown hair, glistening brown eyes, and . . . no mole under his upper-left arm.

The Inevitable To-Do List

- Meet with PTA president/vice president to compare/develop goals and objectives for the school year. Long range-short range.
- Schedule follow-up meeting with Ms. Johnson re her response to her formal evaluation—her comments—"a caring person"—vs. my comments—"technically competent in teaching."

- ~~Originate request for transfer of money. General fund—$200.00 from supplies to inservice.~~
- Set up meeting with the middle school principals. Need to initiate some kind of orientation program for rising sixth graders.
- ~~Locate and contract full-time substitute for Claire Osborn. Baby expected in Feb. Will take 6 weeks maternity leave.~~
- Set up a committee to handle the retirement party for Larry Tillison.
- ~~Call personnel and set up interviews for replacement of Larry Tillison.~~
- Need new screens installed in food service preparation area. Call shop to see what kind of work order they need.
- ~~Meet with Mr. Goodrich re field trip discipline problem last week.~~
- Work orders needed:

    Replace broken glass in window   rm. 109

    ~~Switch plate cover missing in hall outside rm. 233~~

    ~~Replace ballast in hall light outside rm. 100~~

    Repair or replace jumping board in long-jump pit.

    Repair leak in boiler room outside north wall

- Meet with sixth-grade sponsor (Elliot) and representative of the sixth-grade class to discuss end-of-school-year activities.
- ~~Pick up shirts at the dry cleaners.~~
- Draft a letter in response to the superintendent's request for info about starting the school year earlier next year.
- Talk to Mr. Jefferson again about the black snake in his room getting loose at night!!
- Need something for the newspaper. Check classrooms for current newsworthy projects.
- Call Mrs. Hughes (daughter: Susan Pile). Ex-husband has been picking Susan up after school. Does she approve?
- ~~Meet with student teachers. Go over policy matters.~~
- Look for alternatives to usual money raising activities. Most earned in a year: $5,000. Make some phone calls and see if local business will set up a foundation guaranteeing that amount. Eliminate kids selling items in the community at night.
- Need an "honor code" re cheating. Faculty meeting agenda item.

- ~~Call exterminator re cricket control.~~
- Re accident involving fourth grader Kevin Martin. Was parent notified in an appropriate manner about what happened? See Mrs. Williams.
- Talk to Ms. Edwards re number of phone calls and messages we receive in the main office from her boyfriend.
- ~~Fire drill this week!~~ Tornado drill next week!
- Need some kind of fun, educational assembly for primary grades. Call some other elementary principals re suggestions.
- Haircut!
- Draft letter to personnel re demographics show new apartment complex in neighborhood will yield about 15 K-1 kids. May need to open additional kindergarten or first grade next school year. Start sales pitch now!
- Classroom visitations:

    ~~Scully~~

    ~~Romero~~

    ~~Gladstone~~

    ~~Albert~~

    Finley

- Call City High and see if they will loan us a harp for a week. (Ms. Jasonette)
- Call Mr. Greenwald about his daughter's propensity to lose her belongings at school. Continuously brings gadgets from home.
- ~~Meet with auditor to discuss change-over in activity account ledger and reporting.~~
- Faculty meeting agenda item: discuss with faculty different way to notify them of outside vs. inside recess . . . re weather.
- Walk over and visit with Mr. and Mrs. Bell across the street about the soccer ball incident. Offer to replace the rose bush if necessary. ~~Call the shop and see if they will handle this if the bush needs replacing. What budget would this come from?~~ If needed, shop will pay (confirmed by GS).
- Arrange transportation (school district buses) for fifth-grade trip to Colonial Reenactment Exhibit.
- ~~Need more recycling containers.~~ On order.
- Send birthday card to Dad!!!
- ~~Check library budget. Mr. Hogan needs more videotapes for his classroom project.~~

- Librarian agreed to provide tapes out of her budget. Notify Mr. Hogan.
- Talk to head custodian. I want main halls dry mopped at least three times during the day. Wet mopped with water-wax each night. We need to talk "team effort."

Soliloquy—Redux

The school was quiet now, except for the occasional sound of the night custodians' brooms banging against student desks somewhere in the building. Sterling was working late. He had fallen behind on his paperwork and was pushing hard to meet a number of different deadlines. It was well past 11 o'clock when he put his final report in the interschool mail. As he cleared his desk, he rediscovered a note he had received from a parent earlier in the week. The parent had closed the note with, "Thanks for your leadership . . . you are an original."

"An original what?" he laughed. "What leadership? I spend most of my time managing. I'm not a leader; I'm a manager . . . a survivor. If I manage things well—if I resolve a multitude of diverse challenges everyday—if I make decisions that work—if I keep extinguishing brush fires, then . . .," he laughed again, "people think I must be a leader.

"Many days, after watching me deal with kids who think they're adults, teachers who act like kids, parents who send us their best, and secretaries who are always tangled up in phone and computer cords, people might see me more as a zookeeper!

"SOR-ry, folks," he looked out his window, "sorry, but I administer . . . a leader innovates. I maintain . . . a leader develops. I accept reality; I don't have time to investigate it. I keep the boiler running, the building clean, and build and implement schedules. I don't have time to focus on people. I keep the lid on this place each and every day. I worry about today, tomorrow, and the bottom line. The phrases 'long-range perspective' and 'eye on the horizon' are not in my vocabulary. I am the classic soldier . . . yes sir! yes ma'am! I can be my own person only outside of my job—limited, of course, by your ever-watching, ever-critical eyes. All of you who see me as a leader see me doing things right! If I was a true leader, I would be doing the *right thing*!"

Suddenly, he felt a sharp pain in his ankle. "What was that for, you little troll? I wasn't talking to you!"

"Shut up, Sterling, or I'll kick you again. Your frustration venting is keeping me awake. If it makes you feel better, I live under your desk 24 hours a day and, at least most of the time, I see you just the opposite of how you describe yourself. Go home . . . now! And don't even think about starting another diatribe on how lonely it is at the top, or how each phone call introduces a new problem, or how each person who comes into your office brings a new personal crisis for you to resolve. I've heard all those before in other late-night gripe sessions. Give me a break from your whimpering and whining, and let me get some sleep!"

"Good night, you evil little troll," Sterling thought as he turned off the lights and headed out the door. "May a dust bunny poop on your head!"

"Yeah, Sterling," the troll shot back, "and guess who'd have to clean up the mess in the morning!"

For Discussion

General Questions

Using the Sterling paradigm (http://www.corwinpress.com/dunklee.htm) as a model, and speaking from the perspective of a principal, evaluate each episode as follows:

What are the dominant behaviors exhibited by Sterling in this episode?

Is there consensus about this in the class? If not, explain the different viewpoints.

What were the primary actors' individual motives?

How effective was Sterling's behavior in this situation and why?

Can you identify other avenues or approaches that might lead to the same, or a better, conclusion?

If Sterling was a woman,

■ As a female reader, can you identify methodology or behavior that you would change to bring the episode to the same, or similar, closure?

■ As a male reader, what differences in methodology or behavior would you expect to see?

Specific Questions for Each Episode

River Sharks and Baby Sterling

1. This episode illustrates an extreme example of a principal adapting verbal communication to a distinct audience (in this specific case, parents). Do you think that this is an appropriate communication strategy? Why?

A Sterling Moment (You're Finished, Grant!)

(No specific questions)

Do You Know How to Exorcise Gypsy Curses?

2. How would you define the role of the principal in mediating problems between parents and teachers?

The Inevitable To-Do List

(No specific questions)

Soliloquy—Redux

3. What, in your opinion, is the most important difference between management and leadership?
4. Recalling the statement regarding linear behavior in the Introduction to this book, how important is it for a leader to vent his or her frustrations?

If a leader chooses to vent his or her frustrations to a second party, what potential problems can you foresee?

Turning Point

"Why Chicago? Why Chicago at this time of the year?" Sterling complained as he maneuvered around busy sidewalk traffic that morning. "Tucson! San Diego! Florida! I love Chicago . . . but in January? Damn, this wind is cold . . . and the sleet . . ."

"Hurry up, Sterling . . . we're gonna be late," Dave Ealey yelled over his shoulder.

"Slow down, you overstuffed ex-jock," Sterling huffed back at him. "I'm vertically handicapped!"

"Right! And, after what you had for breakfast this morning, you're horizontally handicapped as well. You devoured enough biscuits and gravy to feed a battalion, Grant!"

"It's the cold weather, I need the calories!" he explained as he and Ealey pirouetted through the revolving doors of the hotel. "I just couldn't stomach another morning of that hotel dining room gourmet crap!"

"Well, we'll see if you can stomach the meeting we've selected to attend this morning. Let's see . . . my conference program says it's in the Green Room . . . second floor east. Escalator or stairs?"

"Escalator, of course!"

"Somehow I knew that would be your choice . . . you know, you really need to . . ."

"Enough, Dave, I'll have Melba toast and water for lunch, okay?"

"Ladies and gentlemen, welcome to this morning's session. Just a little housekeeping before I introduce this morning's guest speaker. First: Remember, checkout time is 2:00 tomorrow. Limos to the airport depart from the main entrance to the hotel each hour, on the hour. Be sure to pick up registration material for next year's conference, to be held in Detroit."

"Damn!"

"Shhh!"

"Our speaker for this morning's session is Dr. Filbert Graham, professor of education leadership at Century University. Dr. Graham is an experienced educator, having spent his early years as a social studies teacher and the past 20 years as a professor. His topic this morning is 'The Mystery of the Principalship.'"

"Did she say *misery?*"

"Mystery!"

"Ministry?"

"M-y-s-t-e-r-y."

"Thank you, Dave."

"The school principalship is, by all accounts, a critical position in American education," Graham declared to the microphone. "In recent years, a number of studies have confirmed the prevailing wisdom, which holds that the climate and effectiveness of a particular school are inspired by the leadership, which, of course, the principal provides."

"Well, duh!"

"Shh!"

"For a long time, we have known teachers, students, central office, and others often differ in their expectations for principals, and that these differences render the principalship a very arduous position. The nature and implications of these differences have been the subject of considerable conjecture, as have the ways that principals can and should deal with them."

"Tell me about it!"

"Shhhh!!"

"Did he say *render?*"

"Among scholars of school administration, the school principalship has remained an enigma. The job is still quite unlike its textbook portrayal, and the lack of symmetry between theory and practice continues to puzzle us."

"Yeah, that's a mystery, all right!"

"Shh!"

"Did he call me an *enigma?*"

"Much of any administrator's decision making is by the book, but we discovered that a dominant segment of the principal's time is devoted to behavior that is ad hoc and situation specific. Principals must often work without 'the book'; they must make up rules and precedents as they go along. How does an effective principal behave when the guidelines for action or inaction are missing or are so ambiguous they offer no guidance?"

"Well, for starters . . . they often . . ."

"Shhhh!!"

"Ad hoc is what I feel like doing after eating one of the hotel's gourmet breakfasts."

"Shh!"

Giggle.

"Shhh!!"

"And what about these different hats that a school principal is forced to wear? One moment, the principal is an advocate for teachers; then students, parents, patrons, bosses, his or her own career promotion . . ."

"The mad hatter attacks!"

"Grant!"

"What about the hat to cover male pattern baldness?"

"Grant. I don't think . . ."

"See ya later, Dave. I can't deal with this nonsense this morning!"

"Hold on . . . I'll come with you . . . I have a couple of nagging problems at school I want to pick your brain about."

Dave was in his second year as an elementary principal, and Sterling had taken him under his wing. "I like what you've accomplished at your school, Dave. You've got the common sense that's needed to succeed in our business," he said as they approached the coffee shop. "And, I'm sorry, Dave. You might have enjoyed that presentation. But I gotta tell ya, I've about had it with these university types, who have never served in a principalship, telling us what's right, what's wrong, and all the theory in between. I'm about ready to shuck the principalship and move to higher education and clear out some of that ivy-covered nonsense. Somebody needs to start dealing with reality. There's no enigma, no mystery. Just plain endurance and street smarts. The good professor should be talking about how we can get better at practice; not stuff like the job lacks symmetry or whatever. Oh, well . . ."

"So, Grant . . . why don't you move to higher education? I've heard rumors that you might jump ship. I bet you'd enjoy being a professor type! Then you could give presentations like old Filbert up there in the Green Room, and I could sit in the audience and make snide remarks!"

"To be honest with you," Sterling laughed, "I'm seriously thinking about it, and I've had a couple of good offers. I'll finish 25 years this year—17 of those as a school administrator. The job is getting a little boring. And although I've enjoyed the past year and a half at Adams, I can't seem to get myself motivated . . . I don't see new challenges in the future for me. The professor who served as my adviser during my doctoral studies has suggested that I 'see what's out there.' I really think I'd miss the kid interaction though."

"Grant, look at me," Ealey leaned across the table. "You've taught me more in the past couple of years about leadership, management, and effective practice than . . . well . . . much more than I learned in graduate school. Come on, think of us neophytes, those of us who want to enter the principalship or are new at it, as your 'kids.' We're just a few years older, that's all. Besides, you can go and visit a school anytime if you need a 'kid-fix,' " he laughed.

After attending an afternoon workshop on visionary leadership, Sterling went to his hotel room, ordered a club sandwich from room service, and spent much of the rest of the evening staring out his window at the Chicago skyline.

"Professor Sterling, huh? Why not," he said aloud as he pulled a couple of blank sheets of stationery from the bedside table and started scribbling some notes . . .

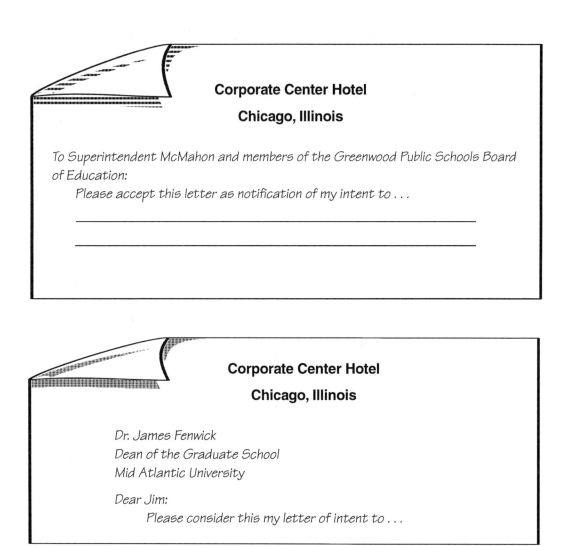

Corporate Center Hotel

Chicago, Illinois

To Superintendent McMahon and members of the Greenwood Public Schools Board of Education:
    Please accept this letter as notification of my intent to . . .

_____

_____

Corporate Center Hotel

Chicago, Illinois

Dr. James Fenwick
Dean of the Graduate School
Mid Atlantic University

Dear Jim:
    Please consider this my letter of intent to . . .

For Discussion

General Questions

Using the Sterling paradigm (http://www.corwinpress.com/dunklee.htm) as a model, and speaking from the perspective of a principal, evaluate the episode as follows:

What are the dominant behaviors exhibited by Sterling in this episode?

Is there consensus about this in the class? If not, explain the different viewpoints.

What were the primary actors' individual motives?

How effective was Sterling's behavior in this situation and why?

Can you identify other avenues or approaches that might lead to the same, or a better, conclusion?

If Sterling was a woman,

▪ As a female reader, can you identify methodology or behavior that you would change to bring the episode to the same, or similar, closure?

▪ As a male reader, what differences in methodology or behavior would you expect to see?

Specific Questions

(No specific questions)

11 ◉))

Epilogue

"Are you sure this is what you want to do?"

"You've got 25 years of sweat invested in this school district."

"Are you unhappy? Do you want a different assignment? Tell us what it would take to change your mind."

"You're not gonna like it very long at a university!"

"Damn it, Grant! You don't really want to resign!"

This, and more, was what Sterling had been hearing right up to the minute the board of education accepted his resignation. The president of the board had even called him the afternoon of the board meeting to convince him to change his mind and stay. "It wasn't an easy decision," he had responded, "but I need a new challenge, and the invitation to teach and do research at the university level is just too attractive."

The tirade of objections continued for a few days after the board accepted his resignation—then silence. The deed was done. He was about to embark on another phase of his career. Soon, however, the silence concerning his resignation evolved into reminiscence, and "Remember when . . ." became a common conversation starter.

About 3 weeks before Sterling's last day, a group of his administrative colleagues sponsored a going-away party that turned into a "roast." Associates took the microphone, one after another, telling humorous tales about some of his escapades in the school district.

"Finally, Grant," said Sonny Hilton, president of the administrators association, "as we send you on your way with our best wishes and, in many cases, envy, we want to present you with this cap. Please note that we have emblazoned it with the words 'WHAT IS IT?' We know you'll wear it proudly, but we also know that most of the younger administrators in the room don't know the meaning behind the message. So, you must, as your final act, recount the notorious 'tool story' before you can claim this memento."

"What if I don't want the hat?" Sterling laughed.

"Clean out your office, hand in your keys, tell the story, and claim the cap, Sterling . . . that's an order," recently appointed Superintendent Tony McMahon hollered from a corner of the room.

"Many years ago," Sterling started, "when I was a very young and innocent supervisor, my office was at the instructional resource center. About once a month, we supervisors took a trip to a government surplus warehouse, where, on occasion, I could find old musical instruments. Most were marked with the name of some military base or government hospital. Some, with minimum expense, could be fixed and returned to playing condition and added to the district's inventory of loaners.

"On one particular day, I was looking for tools I could use to make repairs or adjustments on instruments that various schools sent me for repairs. I could save the district some money if some of the minor work could be performed at the IRC. Past visits had shown me that some of the best tools for this type of delicate work could be found in the medical surplus bins.

" 'Wow, look at this tool!' I remarked to a couple of supervisors who had made the trip with me this particular day. I showed them something that looked like a pair of pliers with a side-facing, duck-nosed, grabber sort of thing. I was amazed as I demonstrated how the gadget worked. 'Look!' I exclaimed. 'When I squeeze the handles, the grabbers open . . . and when I release them they close, just the opposite of a normal pair of pliers . . . these will be perfect to hold woodwind pads in place while I melt the glue to cement them to keys!'

" 'Interesting tool,' they both remarked with noticeable disinterest.

"On the way back to the IRC, I sat in the back seat and studied the unusual tool. I guessed that because I found it in a medical surplus bin, the tool was used for surgery to perhaps hold things apart—like muscle tissue or something—while the doctor reset a broken bone.

"When we got back to the IRC, the secretaries were all on break and sitting around a table in the staff work room. Someone always brought donuts to work, and this day was no exception. I glanced at my watch and noted that it would still be a while until lunch, so I decided to take a donut back to my office.

"I was strangely proud of my new toy, and eager to show it off as I foolishly reached across the table and picked up a donut with the duck-nosed tool.

" 'I'm sorry,' I remember saying, 'would any of you ladies like a donut? I have a new serving doodad here,' I bragged as I flashed my new-found instrument repair tool around the table.

" 'No thanks,' was the rather cold and brittle response of the assembled ladies.

"Later that day, Janice Starkey, one of the secretaries, walked into my office and sat down. I guessed later that it must have been Janice who drew the short straw.

" 'Grant,' she said quietly, 'I don't think you know what that instrument you got out at surplus property really is . . . you know, the one that you showed us at break this morning?'

" 'You mean this one?' I said as I reached down and pulled the gadget from a drawer.

" 'Grant,' she said in a calm teacherlike voice, and then she whispered in my ear.

" 'What's that?' I remember asking her. I had no clue what she was talking about.

" 'Grant, listen to me carefully.' She whispered again.

"The light suddenly came on! 'Oh, my God,' I exclaimed, 'I'm really embarrassed . . . I honestly didn't know!'

" 'Well,' Janice laughed with a sigh of relief, 'we all thought so . . . I suggest you get rid of that thing so that you're not embarrassed again, and more important, we're not embarrassed again!'

" 'Oh, right. Consider it done, Janice,' I responded gratefully. I thanked her for telling me about my blunder!

"Janice just smiled and shook her head as she left my office. Later that day, and very secretively, I took a quick survey of the other men in the building . . . they didn't recognize the gadget either.

"I remember trying to explain my stupidity and embarrassment away, at least in my own mind, by thinking, 'we guys would never have an occasion to see one of those things!' I felt better about the situation for a while. The story of my screw-up quickly found its way from secretary to secretary, throughout the school district.

" 'How is your donut server today, Grant?' became a standard greeting as I visited schools over the next few months.

"I don't think I've ever been so embarrassed, and for you folks who haven't figured out what the infamous 'tool' was . . . it was a . . ." A sharp rap at his office door jerked Sterling abruptly from his reminiscing and back to reality.

For Discussion ▬▬▬

General Questions

Using the Sterling paradigm (http://www.corwinpress.com/dunklee.htm) as a model, and speaking from the perspective of a principal, evaluate the episode as follows:

What are the dominant behaviors exhibited by Sterling in this episode?

Is there consensus about this in the class? If not, explain the different viewpoints.

What were the primary actors' individual motives?

How effective was Sterling's behavior in this situation and why?

Can you identify other avenues or approaches that might lead to the same, or a better, conclusion?

If Sterling was a woman,

■ As a female reader, can you identify methodology or behavior that you would change to bring the episode to the same, or similar, closure?

■ As a male reader, what differences in methodology or behavior would you expect to see?

Specific Questions

(No specific questions)

12

The Contemporary Years

"Hey, Grant! Sorry to interrupt your concentration, but we're going to be late for the faculty senate meeting . . . you'd better move it!" Bob Rowen, one of Sterling's university colleagues, barked. "What in heaven's name is so intriguing outside your window anyway? I've walked by your office a dozen times today, and you've been staring out that window for hours. We're gonna have to find something more to keep you busy," he laughed. "People will start to believe that you're underemployed if you keep that up!"

Sterling looked at his watch. "Geez, sorry, Bob . . . let's go. I was engaged in a pastime notably characteristic of people of my senior status. I was reminiscing . . . no, actually reliving a few of my past experiences as a school principal. Don't ask me why!"

"So, you've decided," Rowen laughed as Sterling closed his office door behind them, "that you're ready to start all over again?"

"You know, Bob . . . sometimes I wish I could. I miss the frenzy. I miss the passion. But, I gotta tell ya, I really enjoy what I'm doing now. I get to 'go back,' albeit vicariously, each time one of my students gets promoted or calls with a question. I think I'm doing what I should be doing at this stage in my career . . . helping future school leaders."

"I feel exactly the same way, Grant. I spent 20 years as a school administrator and I consider my university work as 'payback.' . . . I owe it to my profession to pass on as much of my practitioner knowledge as possible to the next generation of leaders. I wish, however, that I could figure out a way to instill a greater level of practical knowledge and professional maturity to my students. But, you know, you can't teach the reality of practice in a university classroom. You've got to learn the basics on the job and learn them rapidly."

"I couldn't agree more. Speaking of 'rapidly,' we're not going to make it on time if we don't hurry. What do you mean by 'professional maturity'?"

"Oh, I don't know . . . maybe the ability to see rationality in irrational situations. Maybe the ability to think linear when all the events around you seem to be nonlinear. Does this make sense?"

"Yeah, it does, Bob. I think I might add another ability . . . the ability to develop, early on in your career, a very powerful self-image. The kind of self-image that blocks out self-doubt and the fear of competition. In my own case, I matured quickly. I had no choice, and I loved it. I was continually being cast as the 'clean-up' guy, the pinch hitter whose responsibility was to 'get this mess cleaned up ASAP' and move on to the next challenge. And you know . . . if I had competition for that role, no one ever leaped forward and claimed that he or she could do it better. As a result, I was able to shed the youthful need to look at myself—check out my image in the mirror—worrying about how others viewed my performance, early in my career. It's one of the continuing problems I have with my students."

"I know what you're saying, Grant. Students are so concerned about their image and what the competition is doing that they're afraid to take risks."

"And you know, Bob . . . being hypnotized by one's own image, along with uncontrolled competitive zeal, can really be a career stopper. Calculated risk taking is an important part of effective leadership. My biggest competition was always myself. I used to study other school leaders to figure out what they did to be considered effective. I admired their insights and accomplishments and, being able to lay youthful competitiveness aside, I had the freedom to wonder how someone else did something well so that I could imitate it—steal it, to be blunt."

"You're not suggesting that competition is a negative leadership trait?" Rowen asked in a challenging voice. "I have a hard time believing that, Grant!"

"Mature, carefully orchestrated and controlled competitiveness is necessary to succeed as a leader. Youthful competitiveness ages you, however; it wears you down. Except in sports, love, and a couple of professions, unmanaged competitiveness can be a killer. It's cheapening and corrosive in itself, and it denies access to self-scrutiny, self- improvement, and, most critical, self-respect.

"One of the important lessons I learned from my early days as a musician and music educator is that musicians do not compete with each other—at least not while they're performing—because each individual's efforts lift the entire enterprise. Just as a stage play is lost if actors hog the lights and upstage one another, or a game is lost if individual players hot dog at the expense of a team victory."

"So," Rowen laughed as he opened the door to the meeting room, "as president of the university's faculty senate, you're now trying to get 120 egocentric professors to forget individual competitiveness and turf protection and work together as a team?"

"Of course."

"And you didn't consider the other professors who ran against you for the presidency of this sagacious body as competition?"

Sterling looked back over his shoulder as he walked toward the front of the room, "They weren't the ones I was running against," he laughed. "I rest my case!"

Author's Note

As the reader undoubtedly recognizes, Sterling has always been enormously amused by the passing parade of life. His curiosity is as insatiable as his need to see the humorous side of a very challenging profession.

Searching for new ideas in Sterling's life work might yield few. Searching for and implementing new or innovative ways to solve old recurring problems might be the key to Sterling's success in school leadership . . . or maybe he simply practiced a common-sense blend of aggregate leadership, situational management, and smart guessing.

In a profession where irrational events are often the operative expectation, Sterling attempted to make the irrational rational. Irrational events often have to be interpreted and resolved by unreasonable methods, however. George Bernard Shaw observes that "The reasonable man adapts himself to the world; the unreasonable one persists in trying to adapt the world to himself. Therefore all progress depends on the unreasonable man" (1980, p. 161).

For Discussion

General Questions

Using the Sterling paradigm (http://www.corwinpress.com/dunklee.htm) as a model, and speaking from the perspective of a principal, evaluate the episode as follows:

What are the dominant behaviors exhibited by Sterling in this episode?

Is there consensus about this in the class? If not, explain the different viewpoints.

What were the primary actors' individual motives?

How effective was Sterling's behavior in this situation and why?

Can you identify other avenues or approaches that might lead to the same, or a better, conclusion?

If Sterling was a woman,

▪ As a female reader, can you identify methodology or behavior that you would change to bring the episode to the same, or similar, closure?

▪ As a male reader, what differences in methodology or behavior would you expect to see?

Specific Questions

1. How important is positive self-image to an effective leader? Is there a difference between a positive self-image and an overinflated ego? How do you keep a positive self-image from becoming an overinflated ego?

2. What's the difference, if any, between "youthful" and "mature" competitiveness?

3. The Author's Note states that "irrational events often have to be interpreted and resolved by unreasonable methods." Explain this statement in light of school district policies, procedures, societal expectations, and the like.

Reference

Shaw, G. B. (1980). The revolutionist's handbook. In *Man and superman*. Mattiuck, NY: Amereon.

CORWIN
PRESS

The **Corwin Press logo**—a raven striding across an open book—represents the happy union of courage and learning. We are a professional-level publisher of books and journals for K–12 educators, and we are committed to creating and providing resources that embody these qualities. Corwin's motto is "Success for All Learners."